Bill and Alice in Africa

1952 – 1959

W. C. and A. H. Latimer

Edited by: Dr Lorraine R Latimer

Published 2026

Photos by: George Hardgrave, Estelle Yeaman, Bill Latimer and Alice Latimer.

Dear Reader,

My parents were prolific letter writers and it was their letters to each other which persuaded them it was not a risky undertaking to marry after only five days in each other's company! As children our parent's life in outback Australia and Africa in the 1950s was the stuff of family legend. Periodically throughout the 1960s and 1970s dad would hold slide nights for friends and family and out would come the projector, slides and screen. We kids would lie on the floor with the adults on chairs and we would watch the projected pictures while mum and dad told amusing and animated stories about each.

For the first time, in 2024, I read the more than four hundred and forty letters Bill and Alice wrote to one another. I realised that here was a valuable record of 1950s life in Australia, the United Kingdom, South Africa and Northern Rhodesia. The letters were worth sharing and so I began the task of turning them into typed text and arranging them into four stand alone, interrelated books. This book is the third in the Bill and Alice series. I do hope you enjoy reading *Bill and Alice in Africa 1952 - 1959.*

Lorraine R Latimer

Titles in the Bill and Alice Series

Bill and Alice in Australia and Britain 1949 -1959

Bill and Alice in a Courtship without Kisses

Bill and Alice in Africa 1952 – 1959

Bill and Alice at Home in Northern Rhodesia 1954 - 1959

Contents

PROLOGUE

In 1951 New Zealand adventurers Bill Latimer and George Hardgrave felt the call of Africa. Being in London they were advised to apply to the Union Corporation for mining jobs which they did, resulting in a passage to Johannesburg and work on the Grooty mine. Bill and George worked in various jobs across South Africa and Northern Rhodesia with Bill writing about his adventures and experiences to his Australian pen pal Alice White. This book contains those letters.

In 1953 Bill asked Alice to marry him and in 1954 they set up home together in Lusaka, capital city of Northern Rhodesia (now Zambia). After recovering from culture shock at her living conditions, minority status and the imported British class system Alice began to settle down and enjoy her life in Northern Rhodesia. Knowing she was missed at home Alice wrote detailed weekly letters to her parents all about her domestic life and about Bill's work with the Public Works Department.

When Alice first arrived in Lusaka she described it as a boom town. It was undergoing major road, housing and public building construction and further out there was the construction of the Kariba dam and the Hydro Electric Scheme on the Zambezi River, various small airports, a myriad of small remote towns, fishing enterprises, training centres and so on all of which required repair and maintenance by the men of the Public Works Department.

Unbeknown to Bill and Alice they were recording the last decade of the British Colonial Service in Northern Rhodesia and the passing forever of the life that had been lived there. The detailed descriptions of their lives while in Africa provide a fascinating window into life in 1950s Africa.

PART 1: BACHELOR BILL

A grand plan

24 October 1951 c/o Petershill Road, Glasgow Dear Alice, You are pretty good at getting off the mark alright with that last letter that just dropped in on me and I'm not so slow at starting one on the return journey either am I? Things are much the same with us as I last wrote but we have a great plan on hand that is about to change our immediate future.

If we have the guts to go through with it gone will be the routine of getting up, starting work, coming home, having tea and going to bed along with millions in the crowded warrens of a big city. Our idea is to go overland to South Africa travelling light by hitchhiking, trains or anything that will pick us up and advance us a few miles, walking included. Pretty ambitious I agree. Mum and dad might say crazy but if George and I get through it will be something we can feel we've achieved, something with the thrill of living in it and an adventure which I don't doubt we'll have our fair share of. George put the thought forward and now I'm as keen as he is on it. If we get offers along the way we will bide a while and work, then be off.

We want to reach either Rhodesia or South Africa and find a decent job on a mine or plantation - somewhere that lets a fellow use his own initiative and his own head to work things out for himself. A place that has eternal sunshine and wide open country where you can maybe do some hunting or fishing along a lonely river. I have in mind the Northern Territory of old Aussie and I think Africa can offer young blokes the same life and maybe a lot more.

Anyway we will pull out of Glasgow in about ten days time for London and go through the necessary red tape for visas and permissions etc. From London we intend to cross to France and through Paris, Bordeaux to Spain, Madrid to Gibraltar, then a ferry to Morocco and into Algeria, across the Sahara for Nigeria, then east through equatorial Africa and Northern Congo to Tanzanika and Uganda. South through Rhodesia and we are in South Africa. Most of the travelling will be through French territory in north and central so we are counting on help from their colonial administration. We've got something to work for now. I've given up the idea of going to sea although I have three applications in with companies and am liable to hear any time. We will see a lot more of the old world. At sea you only see the sea or the engine room and if you are working on the engine in port only the waterfront in the main street before it's time to sail again.

15 November 1951 Esmond Road, Beaufort Park, Cheswyck, London, W4. Dear Alice, Here I am once more this time in the role of the British working man sitting in an armchair in a top floor room of a house on the outskirts of London town. The gas fire is hissing noisily and its heat is cut off by reason of George's clothes hanging in front to dry. He is making a nuisance of himself as usual by trying to talk to me.

18 November 1951 *Sunday.* I opened another letter from you when I went over to Mosley to see my 'little' brother Ed. You are pretty well on the mark saying we would be held up by red tape which we realise now is more or less for our own good. We spent the week after we arrived here going about London from one office to another. The French consulate really disheartened us a bit when we found that a pretty hefty bond has to be put up to cross their territory in North Africa. It is under military control and though there is transport crossing the desert they don't want stray wanderers left on their hands. The officers for Nigeria said similar and that white men just don't wander about there unless they have a good deal of money as living is expensive.

One thing led to another and we were advised to see the *Union Corporation* who run several gold mines and timber concessions in South Africa and Rhodesia. The outcome was that we were offered engineering jobs at their mine out of Johannesburg, our entry being guaranteed into South Africa as otherwise a bond is required for entry. Africa is a bit different from Australia where anyone can go in.

The firm sent us to a doctor in Harley Street who went over us from head to toe. Medically we were told we were pretty good specimens of humanity which made us feel quite smart. We had X-rays taken and ordinary photos taken - must have spent half a day dressing and undressing. Our immigration papers are filled in and we can get a reduced airfare out which we are taking. We could leave before Christmas but would like to have that here all together so it will be early in January. Only skilled tradesmen can enter South Africa. Nearly all the manual work is done by blacks, which a white man cannot compete with of course. The government policy and set up cannot be compared with Australia where there is no colour problem to speak of. It will be very interesting.

I can't complain about you Alice, you're pretty good at this writing business. I can think plenty but I can't put them down on paper often. *The Place Where I Worship is the Wide Open*

Spaces - that song, it is about my sentiment and I'm just marking time in this old England from where my ancestors came. My future is in the new countries, maybe on the edge of the populated places I don't know. We should live today fully for yesterday is dead and tomorrow isn't born.

England is grand for those who have everything here and for us visitors but to live and die here in a one street existence that would be impossible for such as George and I. We are quite ready to leave now and though it is a gamble and we will arrive pretty poor, there will be an adventure and we shall see the land that stretches into the blue as it does in Australia.

*12 December*1951 *Esmond Road, Beaufort Park, Cheswyck, London, W4.* Dear Alice, We definitely leave on 8 January now taking four days on the journey. First stop Amsterdam then Nice and Malta where we stop overnight, next day Tobruk (famous place of the desert war ten years ago), then across Egypt to Wadi Halfa for the night. The third day is to Khartoum stopping at Entebbe in Uganda for the night. Next Ndola in Northern Rhodesia and to our destination Johannesburg where we will be met on arrival and our destiny for the next year will have started.

Flight to Africa

19 January 1952 c/o Springs Hotel, 1st Avenue, Springs, Transvaal, South Africa. Last year is just a very pleasant memory now. Nothing to show for it I'll admit but it was damn good fun living. This year will be equally so I'm sure and for you too Alice. We got jobs in the *Grooty Gold Mine* in the Transvaal and were transported there by a chartered *Tropical Airways* plane. After a round of farewells in old England we left on 9 January - parting is such a sad affair.

We were both relieved when we left the ground and came down for breakfast in Amsterdam. As the coast of England appeared under us a host of memories and remembrances passed me but when the Channel was beneath us and we set foot on foreign land I felt reborn again. We were supposed to pick up eight people in Amsterdam but they were left owing to visa trouble for which we were grateful as it made a lot of extra room to stretch out. Flying along the Alps, glistening white in the sun with Mont Blanc being outstanding. Next stop was Nice in South France for lunch. Lovely place built around the hills and bays. Oh to own a gold mine!

Our night stop at Malta was quite hectic. A group of us, the pilot and engineers included got together and turned in at 2:00am. Everything was very informal and everyone friendly being a charter plane and not a big stuck-up airline. We had represented on board: England, Scotland, Ireland, a big talking American, South Africa, Germany, Denmark, Switzerland and Holland, not forgetting New Zealand. Australia was not present so was represented by us.

Tropic Airways – January 1952

George Hardgrave & Bill Latimer on 3 day trip at 8,000 feet, London to Johannesburg via Amsterdam, Nice, Malta, Tobruk, WadiHalfa, Khartoum, Entebe and Lusaka

(The next flight of Tropic Airways ditched into the Mediterranean)

Bill & George en-route to Africa 1952

We had lunch next day at Aden near Tobruk and were delayed some time there while a doctor examined a South African girl who had taken very ill. She was the colour of paper due to a haemorrhage. The previous morning she was drinking champagne while travelling by bus to the airport with her sister, also with us. A scatty a pair I never remember seeing. The 'I-know-what-I'm-doing' type who look on sleep as a nuisance. We dropped her off at a hospital in Entebbe, Uganda.

Over Tobruk the old slit trenches from World War II are still there well into the desert and bomb craters, trucks and gun relics of that nearly forgotten war where things came suddenly to a lot of fellows down there. It makes a bloke think you know to look down at that country, even though he didn't see the show himself. The land is indescribably barren, hard brown near the coast turning into sand with hundreds of miles of dunes and ridge on ridge across Egypt 'till the Nile cuts through it. We came into Wadi Halfa, Sudan at dusk and stayed at a luxurious hotel overlooking the river, surrounded by gardens with silent-footed natives flitting about giving the last word in service.

We followed the Nile all next morning - a ribbon of life in the midst of deep desert sand. Lunch was at Wadi Seidna near Khartoum, then on again into Uganda and jungle beneath. Slept that night at Entebbe Hotel on the shores of Lake Victoria, a beautiful hotel but with an air of snobbishness about it caused by the superior colonial officers and wives inhabiting it - it was great fun. Next day we were in storms all morning getting tossed about a bit, lightning flashed and black clouds. It was a change from the smooth going, though unwelcome by many.

We arrived at Johannesburg in the afternoon last Friday after a rigorous time with the customs and immigration people. We stayed in town until Saturday then on to here at Springs, forty miles away. I started work at the Grooty gold mine last Tuesday, so far so good. Work here is much the same as anywhere except for the surroundings - about 8,000 blacks on the job and four to five hundred whites. Just lift a finger and a boy is on the spot though it's hard making him understand when he can't talk English. I will learn some of the universal language spoken here. The boys are from all over Africa.

Well, Alice the parcel of yours with the pullover you knitted will be sent down okay. You're a beaut no doubt about it. Until next time when I'll be on my feet more for this writing game cheerio. God bless you Alice. XXX etc. etc.

Springs and the Grooty Mine

30 January 1952 c/o *Springs Hotel, First Street, Springs, Transvaal, South Africa*. We are liking it fine here though the people seem a little different at first, the great majority being bilingual, but once you gain their confidence they see you are similar to them and they welcome you. The main thing to avoid trouble here is to have no discussion on politics or the native problem. Being from New Zealand the *Springboks* regard us as an object of interest and we have respect and a healthy rivalry for each other on the rugby field. The New Zealand *All Blacks* have a good name here for which we are thankful.

Here work is just the same as anywhere in the world - engineering and oh, we have been congratulated on our ability. We don't see eye to eye with the chief though. The foreman and all the lads in the workshop are fine. I must say it was strange at first to be so outnumbered by natives, about 7,000 in the compound and three hundred of us. There are many tribes: Zulus, Basutos, Wyasas all mixed up and recruited from all over South Africa.

Labour is cheap, about two shillings sixpence a day but some of the labour is pretty inexperienced. I am picking up a few words of a sort of universal language among them. Most of the boys from the bush are very quiet and from remote places. The weather after Britain is a dream - beautiful days and nights which are just a bit too warm. Actually there is a drought on but it broke a bit with a wild storm yesterday, rain in sheets and lightning, hail too.

31 January. Today has been very warm. We feel the heat of the iron workshop roof and it is okay to have a boy run off for a cool drink. I see in the papers here that the heat has been well over the hundred degree mark around your way. I guess that you have all been panting a bit. We work a forty hour week here and I was at it last Sunday too.

On arrival we intended to live at the mine quarters which we understood to be furnished but we found we had to buy our own furniture which would be a burden. We weren't having any as we are liable to go walkabout any time so we are at this first class hotel at £14 each a month. For the same in Australia it would be nearer £40 a month. It is a good living. The food is extra. After England it is a lot of food but we are getting used to it now. Five or six courses for dinner and no sooner finished than a servant is at your elbow. The manager is very friendly and the place is comfortably furnished. George and I are in one room and an English chap called Gordon who we met on the plane is next door. There is a balcony outside to sit on overlooking the street and facing the railway station.

All servants are native here and labourers too. There is absolutely no room for unskilled white men in South Africa. Life for Europeans is easy, especially for women who can have a native doing the house work from dawn 'till dark for £2 or £3 a month.

Bill outside the Springs Hotel

In the town of Springs there are about 10,000 to 12,000 whites and more like 70,000 to 80,000 blacks because of the gold mines. There is amazingly little trouble, only occasionally an assault or robbery against Europeans. They fight among themselves though with tribe against tribe and a lot of them carry clubs and small picks. We saw a mob of a hundred or so the other night going armed and trotting along the road. Nearly all killings are amongst themselves and to prevent that and other crimes there is a curfew on. No native without a pass must be out of his location between 10:00pm and dawn under heavy penalties.

Springs is a modern town, or city they call it, built American style as seen in Hollywood. Even the streets are numbered. There are four cinemas, maybe six hotels or so and lots of flash shops. No dances, except the ultra modern town hall where they have Dutch style square dancing. Last Saturday some miners we are friendly with took us along to a beer garden. It turned out quite novel for us. There is an overwhelming ratio of men to women but what single girls there are seem to go along to this place - maybe for free drinks. I nearly got into a fight with a fellow but everything turned out fine and a good time was had by all. Life is a bit different here.

26 February 1952 c/o *Springs Hotel, PO Box 6, Springs, Transvaal.* We've heard a lot about Rhodesia recently so are keen to get moving up there and see for ourselves. I'm writing a little at a time but as long as I post it Friday, the earliest it will leave here anyway. The mail goes on a roundabout route from here to Australia.

Last week we made a trip down the mine, the longest lift ride we ever made. It was 6,000 feet into the ground going down 1,000 feet a minute. The thought of being held by just a cable from death is a little thing to think about but there is actually nothing in it except for slight deafness at the speed of descent. At the bottom we climbed out of the cage and into a pokey little electric train which took us and the miners going on shift, amidst much shouting of orders to natives who do all the actual labour of mining: drilling, propping, loading trucks etc. One European oversees a gang of twelve or so boys.

We hopped off the train at last and walked up after rattling along for a couple of miles. There was plenty of headroom, well propped and electric light but every twenty-five yards or so dark tunnels went off only three feet high. More or less just room enough for a man to use a jackhammer. The rock the gold reef is in is only a few inches thick so only just enough rock to give a work space to be taken out. This is dumped on top and the mine dumps grow into huge white heaps which are the only thing noticeable on the Rand wherever you look around the flat landscape of Johannesburg. They are inescapable. So the natives crouch in the side drives or stopes sweating over the bucking drills following the reef.

The temperature down there is pretty humid though air is supplied by giant vents on the surface and everyone sweats plenty. The ore is brought to the surface in bins on the same cable that lowered the cage and goes through the works to be crushed and treated with cyanide to extract pure gold. The waste rock is brought up by another cable and taken by trucks to the summit of the dump where they tip out endlessly.

So much for gold mining they can keep it. A little parcel of gold about sixty pounds in weight would make our outlook change though. No harm in meditating. George and I saw a film last night called *Vultures Fly* about game conservation in Kenya. The animal filming is great. I wish I were up there and will be one day. That's why we want to push north, first Rhodesia then Tanzania, Uganda and Kenya. We will be satisfied out under the stars, herds out on the plains or at waterholes, drums in the distance and the noises of the night. When we hear that we will know what a terrific country Africa is. We are so near to this primitive part of it now, only a thousand miles or so that it would be a crime to leave before experiencing it.

27 February. I had a letter from mum yesterday in which they say I am a bit behind in writing only having one letter since our arrival here. I have written at least three so there's something wrong somewhere. The mail is bad from here going roundabout north to Aden in Yemen, across to Karachi and Calcutta, then to Singapore and Australia. Our luggage has arrived from England after six weeks which isn't bad. The bill of £20 is pretty bad. We haven't collected our gear yet but will. The tools are what we want. The clothes are not so important.

We are still in the mine workshops repairing and making new parts out of old but will be going to underground workshops soon at our own request to see what it is like being a human rat. George is in the diesel loco shop this week picking up a few clues and next week will relieve a fellow below whose job it is to keep the underground trains running.

The natives have become commonplace to us now, no longer strange. They are at hand all the time for any lifting or messages and cleaning the floor and machines continuously. The result is a very tidy workshop. It is good to see and hear them lifting or pushing something heavy led by the head man who chants and the rest going in and pushing as one man on the right word. They don't seem to put much effort into it but they certainly shift things with music, otherwise they are hopeless as a team.

You don't wander around just anywhere here at night as it is quite likely to end in disaster. There are quite a few cases every day of robberies and even murder, especially in the native quarter. Out here it is not so bad. One of our apprentices had a narrow escape last week going home from overtime. He was attacked and hit with sticks but a car came along and they made off. He got a scare. A native will count it worthwhile if he takes a few shillings that you may have, regardless of half killing you.

29 February .Well Alice I was sorry I could not finish this last night but was called away by some rather wild Afrikaans. What's all this about you hopping round with a crook leg through over doing things? Let's hope the doctor has put it right by now and mind what he says about over exertion. Do not do a man's work - remember you're not six feet high or weigh a hundred and eighty pounds or so - I wouldn't like to see you in a wheelchair next time.

George and I have booked our passages home leaving November next year 1953. We haven't told them at home yet but will soon. Our people are expecting us back for this Christmas so they will be a bit downhearted at first 'till everyone gets used to the idea. We will be three and a half years out from home, quite a decent trip and our education should be about complete by then, though it is a foolish fellow who thinks he knows all. In a letter from mum she says she has everything ready for us when we come back home with the bedrooms reconditioned throughout.

It'll be great to hit the old place again and carry on the old life for awhile but it will flag after six months or so. I know it will. I can see it all in my mind now as it happened last time. I came back the first time and everything was beautiful and fresh again, and then gradually that feeling increases month by month of terrible restlessness. I just had to go walkabout again.

That is the past, of the future who can say. He keeps our destiny secret from us. To return home will be a supremely happy moment. The event that makes the sadness of leaving worthwhile whether it is next month or next year it will come and we want to have something to show for it.

Having set our minds on a car each we must fulfil that promise to ourselves as we are a little independent, sometimes also wishing to have something to move about in when and where we like on our return. So we are now doomed to volunteer for another twenty months, though it isn't bad out here. The climate is lovely Alice really no kidding. It will be hotter north of course but the human being is made to take punishment. Darwin for example has a bad name but to us boys it is ideal for outdoor life. There are disadvantages of course but in my mind the advantages outweigh them.

I had a letter from the three Melbourne boys you remember who we teamed up with on the Blitz truck, fair dinkum blokes. Well they are still there and leaving in July making toward the home stretch. They are coming to New Zealand next January and we of course are meeting them but now our plans have changed so have asked them to postpone it 'till January 1954. I reckon they will and we will show them a slap up time and what really breathtaking scenery is like. It'll be heavenly to camp around the islands again – 'the land of the long white cloud I do love you honestly, your snowy and bush clad mountains, bubbling creeks and blue lakes with the roar of the Pacific not far from anywhere'. I can see it all as I lay here Alice, though I have temporarily deserted the shaky isles. It seems so unreal now when in the street outside I can hear the babble of natives.

To Northern Rhodesia

9 April 1952 c/o PO Box 109, Lusaka, Northern Rhodesia. The last week has seen us on the move again upsetting the quiet routine we had got into at Springs. So here's hoping you pardon the delay in writing and replying to your chatty letter -

almost a full length novel. This effort of mine is poor by comparison, but I will get some paper and stamps when we go into town. Our roost here is over a thousand miles from the Transvaal which we left last Friday morning and only fifteen degrees south of the equator.

We went by train out to Mafeking from Johannesburg through interesting country, then north into Bechuanaland, a pretty average country resembling Central Australia with its red earth. Stopped at lots of little places where natives gather together and sell curios of carved wood or just staring at us, children begging. At Bulawayo in Southern Rhodesia we stopped for three hours, time enough to see the main street and have tea before pushing on again. The trains are quite comfortable all being sleeping berths. The seats are made to become bunks one above the other, as on a ship. It would be a bit grim sitting up for sixty hours as we did on the journey up into Queensland. Remember that Alice? Must be just on two years ago now.

The sight of the Victoria Falls at Livingstone on the Zambezi River was worth the trip alone. It was a terrific sight as the train pulled slowly over the bridge, seeing the water thundering over and roaring through the gorge far below us and to feel the spray on us like rain as we stood on the carriage platform. You can see the white geysers of spray in the air quite a long away from the actual falls and the bush about it is extraordinarily green from the continued watering - one of the mightiest works of nature in the whole wide world. After a full day chugging through thick bush country little inhabited except for native villages here and there we arrived in Lusaka late on Sunday. We didn't see a single wild animal all the way. I don't blame them for keeping away from the railway.

19 April 1952 c/o *PO Box 109, Lusaka, Northern Rhodesia.* Dear Alice, you're very welcome letter arrived the other day a bit late being dated 5 February but still very acceptable. You might identify it if I say that in it you write of Margaret's brother being caught when unloading logs which is a very nasty sort of accident that can easily be fatal. It happened at the logging camp I was at once, the man being killed leaving a wife and large family behind. I enjoyed the maps and the magazines they are beaut fair dinkum Australian - especially *Saltbush* which reminds me of my roaming in the Mulga west of the black stump.

Well Alice, George and I are settled in here now in our new home in Lusaka though for how long is anyone's guess. We have got an open air job which is grand after being perpetually under a roof. We are left alone and are not being tampered with too much so if we can use our own initiative it will be alright for everyone. If not, we will push on as we are in a state of mind not to be pushed around by anyone. It is grand to be out of a workshop for a spell operating on machines I am very familiar with. Now I'm fixing up broken down bulldozers and am very dirty, but happy. There is not much in engineering that we can't turn our hands to including bush carpentry if necessary.

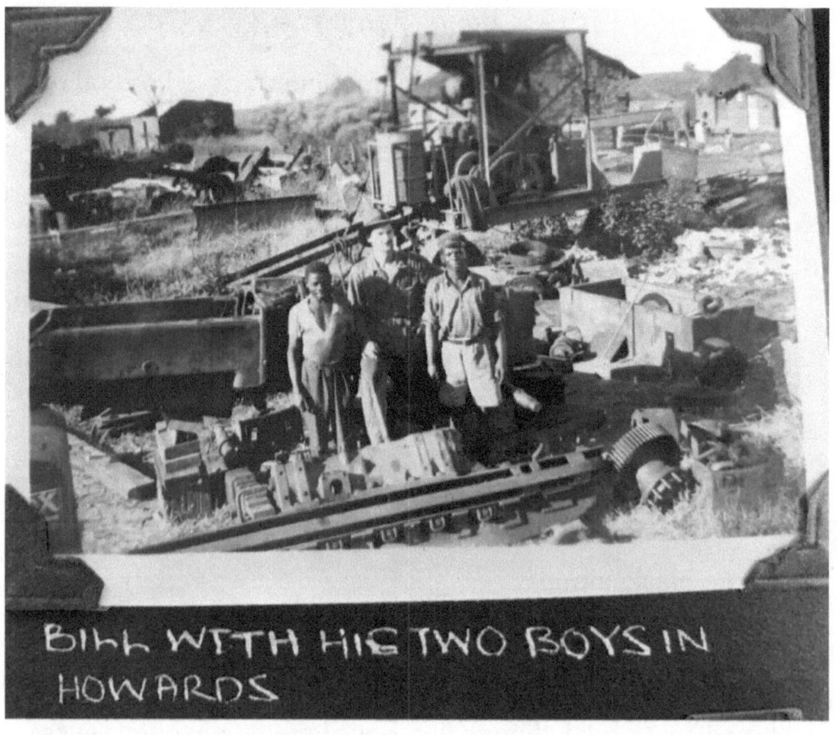

Fixing bulldozers at Howards, Lusaka

The sun is powerful as I think I said before. Now I can vouch for it as I had it on my neck last week and was quite a sick boy. Now instead of a beret I wear a broad brimmed hat, learn by experience.

20 April. Well Alice to continue: our food and quarters are extra and pretty quiet considering the single men here. There is a *Worker's Club* just near which is very pleasant for a change. They have table tennis, darts and a radiogram, also a bar, very English-like. George and I are getting pretty steady most of the time but will be ever more so in the immediate future as we intend to get some sort of wagon to continue our travels north. The railways finish in the Congo a hundred and seventy miles from here and the only way to go to Tanzanika, Uganda and Kenya from there is by road.

The interesting part starts from now on and we intend to get off the beaten track and see some of it. The Kafue River is only thirty miles from here and joins the mighty Zambezi a little further down seventy miles. There are all sorts of animals only a day's car ride from here lion, leopard, elephant, rhino, hippo and crocodiles in the rivers. In fact nearly everything you could see at the zoo from monkeys upwards, also pretty primitive though harmless natives. You can be certain we will venture very cautiously at first until we get the feel of the country. Africa as the old ones say is still Africa back into the dim past, a country where risks can be fatal, where death is as necessary as life to each human and animal inhabitant.

The natives around here are quite interesting and colourful to our new chum eyes, more backward than in South Africa and because of this easier to get on with. It is safe to go anywhere at night here without fear of a gang attack which is quite common in South Africa. There is no segregation law though Africans don't live around European houses. They have their own villages with traditional mud and thatched huts, living communally as they have always done. The women carry everything on their heads from bundles of wood, tins of water, to packets of tea with the child youngest at the time carried on their back. A piece of cloth over one shoulder and under the other arm tied in front supports it. They do all the work of course for the 'superior' male's comfort.

It is hotter altogether around your place than it is here. We get it evenly around eighty degrees and not much difference between night and day really. I laughed in your letter about explaining how you knew I had long arms. You certainly get out of a leading question very neatly and diplomatically. We are leaving here next year in November as I write but the sailing day isn't out yet, being a long way off. It'll be good to see the old hills of New Zealand again by then. Before I close Alice, now please what does H. stand for in your initials A.H.W? You've got me guessing you know. Well I'll close down for now. Sending my thoughts over the sea to you Bill XXX

Back to South Africa in a Ford Prefect

12 May 1952 c/o GPO Poste Restante, Durban, South Africa. Dear Alice, just a small note letting you know we are on the hoof again this time down to Durban about 2,000 miles by road from Lusaka. George and I leave early in the morning by car and should be there in about ten days. It will be good to see the sea again and the Indian Ocean right across to Australia. Anyway we finished work here on Friday, not that we are surprised. We are pretty popular here except with the two in the right place who make it too tough for independent types like us to do a job, so we were on the market for employment. Then something quite unexpected turned up with a man in the mess here asking us if we would like to drive his Ford Prefect down to Durban where his family lives. We said yes in about a minute, so our life has altered again

We have let ourselves on a great tour by way of Salisbury in Southern Rhodesia, Beit Bridge on the Limpopo River,

Kruger National Park - world famous place where we hope to see animals - Johannesburg then out to Durban on the coast. There we have an idea to work with the *Union Whaling Company* on their ships outfitting for the whaling season which begins in December. We are hopeful of making a trip to the Antarctic with them as this chap whose car we are delivering did last year, but that is in the lap of fate as anything can happen between now and then and probably will too. Anyway, we would both love to make a trip away whaling in the south. We intend to camp and cook on the way down to save expenses, except for a stray hotel here and there. I'm expecting a letter in a day Alice but it will probably be a little while reaching me now. Regards to family Yours Bill XXXX

23 May 1952 *c/o GPO Poste Restante, Durban, South Africa.* Quite a lot has happened since we set sail from Lusaka nearly two weeks ago so I will start now to let you know a little of what we have been up to since. Then when your letter comes that I'm expecting, I will answer and then pop this in the box, so hurry on aeroplane. Well we left Lusaka on a bright sunny Tuesday morning and headed the little car south. I don't know if I said last time but it was a Ford 10 Prefect 1949. Not exactly the car for rough roads and we had her laden down with suitcases, two toolboxes, two bicycles not forgetting two frame packs.

We bowled along merrily, joyful to have the open road ahead and prospects though uncertain ahead. Just the African bush and the hills about us with the road winding ever on, sometimes just rough detours where the road making gangs worked giving us a cheery wave as we bounce slowly by. Coming around the corner we slowed down to watch several baboons cross the road and climb a big tree. Honestly we felt like kids just let out of school for the holidays. Climbing to the top of the range we pulled up to gaze on the mighty Zambezi River winding like a silvery snake into the distance. In a little while, after zigzagging down through the bush, we stood on its banks where a big steel bridge crosses.

25 May. The ground was hard for the first night, even with fresh cut grass beneath us. Up at first light in the morning we were back on the road after breakfast. A petrol blockage held us up for an hour but we soon fixed that and driving down through flat country dotted with tobacco farms arrived at Salisbury the capital city, late afternoon. That night we spent indoors at the house of some people we met on the train coming up. George had written to the daughter and we were invited to stay whenever passing through. A very nice place too.

On the way to Durban from Lusaka

Away again about 8:00am the next day intent on camping at the Zimbabwe Ruins. It came as a shock while boiling the billy midday to hear George call out that we had a broken front spring. The undercarriage had been knocking loudly all morning over quite small bumps. Nothing much to do except potter along to the next town about sixty miles down. A sleepy place called Fort Victoria. We had some luck there as the garage came to light with a front assembly fitted. We stacked it in the back and headed out to the Zimbabwe Ruins eighteen miles from town just as darkness fell. We piled into a rest hut for travellers while a native boy chopped wood and got a fire going for us to cook on. We slept the sleep of the dead that night with the thought of the spring to replace and a little exploration of this remarkable place and the natives chanting, drumming and singing didn't worry us for long

27 May. We saw the ruins of the fortress on a high hill and temple below with the valley scattered its length with other remains -a truly remarkable sight all that is left of a lost people. George and I had a good old climb around with the warden telling us about the time he was in Australia when we spoke to him. He also told us about this lost city and showed us relics, some of them gold. An elephant hunter seventy or eighty years ago discovered the place (overgrown with bush then) through stories told by local natives who shunned the place. Between when he found it and when it was made a national monument, treasure hunters took many gold ornaments away and wrecked some of it in the process. Chinese and Indian crockery have been found, proving some connection with the East, though Zimbabwe is a long way from the coast.

The buildings are of stone blocks not an ounce of cement used to put them up and as the local natives, like all through central Africa don't aspire to anything more than mud and thatch, it has given archaeologist something to argue and speculate on. It was quite awe inspiring to stand and wonder, imagining what dark deeds this site had seen and how we would've been received if the clock could be turned back to those centuries.

Contemplating the Zimbabwe Ruins

We jacked the car up using a lot of stone (nearly all ruins George said) to give us some height and after some struggle and helpful curses removed the offending spring and replaced it with the new one. Mobile again the silent valley of ruins was soon left behind and we settled down to a long day's drive intent on crossing the border into South Africa before sundown, when the bridge gates over the Limpopo are closed.

The scenery now was not very interesting though we passed over one low range of hills. Just on and on passing many native villages and sometimes a European town where we stopped for petrol and an oil and water check up. In the afternoon we came into country not unlike the Barkley Tablelands west of Camooweal in Australia - flat, light scrub country where water is not thrown away and the road a straight black ribbon across it. After wearying hours the welcome Union Jack came into sight flying high over the Customs House. The Rhodesian people just stamped our passports and we rolled across into South Africa the great land of two languages and two people at loggerheads.

The South African Customs wouldn't take our word that we had nothing dutiable - no guns, drugs or gold dust. Oh no, they had to take everything out and look in a couple of our cases and the car! The same welcome as at Johannesburg. This ordeal over it was now nearly dark so we went a little along the road and camped near the town of Messina. By the light of the car we rolled out our kit and after a meal were soon in slumber land.

Up bright and early next day and on the road before seven on the beautiful new national road, the length of the Union. The northern Transvaal is very open and dry country nothing but rolling country (veldt). About midday we crossed the high hills and dropped down to Pietersburg the main town of the north and just in time to do the weekend shopping. We kept on all afternoon driving in turns, stopping to stretch our legs now and then from the car designed for midgets. That night Saturday, we got within twenty miles of Pretoria and camped on a spot two miles off the road. It took some finding as now there were fences around the farms. The natives on the farm some way off kept up a din well into the night - the usual Saturday night recreation of drinking homebrew and letting off steam. It must have lulled us off in the end however.

Pretoria is the actual administrative city of South Africa, like Canberra is to Australia and similar in build. It was peaceful on Sunday morning as we drove through, many people walking with books in their hands to church along lovely quiet tree lined streets. Made us feel our position as wanderers with no home to sit in as these people had. We stopped at the town of Springs, our home of five weeks before, and had lunch with a chap we worked alongside at the mine and his wife. We had a nice wash and brush up at the hotel before moving on again. Now it was just a straight run to

Durban four hundred miles away with the coast in front of us. Black clouds were gathering on the horizon and before long lightning flickered in the hills. Not being too keen on camping in the rain or the car, being highly uncomfortable to sleep in we decided to drive on through the night. So through the darkness we drove with the rain pelting down and at intervals the sky zigzagging into brightness. It felt cosy and comfortable inside with the engine humming and the rain drumming on the roof. Also glad of the blanket across us as it turned cold.

31 May. Well Alice another few days gone forever as we mark time in Durban. Driving through the night from Springs and in and out of Ladysmith, Pietermaritzburg and many small places we came to the outskirts of Durban at 4:00am. The weather cleared after we left the Drakensburg Mountains behind and was beautiful, clear and moonlit as we climbed out and lay down to sleep before the dawn came.

I woke about 8:00am from a dead sleep to broad daylight and was amused to see a native with a loaf of bread in one hand and an open mouthed stare in his face just standing gazing at us. Evidently not used to seeing Europeans sleeping out. A few short miles and Durban lay before us and the blue Indian Ocean beyond. George and I went straight to the centre of town and got ourselves a good feed before doing anything further, then to the train station where we put most of our gear in so that Mrs Kenny, the wife of the friend who we work with, wouldn't be shocked by the cargo being carried. We went up to their house where we have been staying since.

8 June. Received your letter today Alice. I will get cracking and finish this news sheet. So your dad has a weak spot for Durban visiting during the first world war. Well I must admit it is a nice place for a holiday only though as it is concerns us now. The city is much the same as cities anywhere, big buildings and streets full of all coloured people from pasty white to jet black. The main attraction is the Marine Parade. It's quite outstanding as a beach resort. Between the wide road and the sea green lawns, cafes, swimming pool, snake pit and amusement park, where people see how much revolving they can stand, and a boating pool. Flanking the road on the other side is a continuous string of hotels and flats all very modern and semi skyscrapers. I don't think they would have been there in your dad's day.

On south beach a large portion of the population are Indian. They are everywhere and have their own district to live in. Similarly the native African, who hates the Indians for the stranglehold they have on shops and businesses. You will remember reading about the riots here in 1949 or 1950 when many were killed, mostly Indians by Zulus.

Work on ships in Durban

George and I tried our best but we just couldn't get on with the whaling people. The engineer was sympathetic but he explained that though we would suit he had been putting off men lately. So another castle in the air came down. In fact we found it very hard to get started with any decent firm at all. The Union had nothing on its books so we just cruised around on our own account getting a job with the *Lion Match Factory* workshop in the end. It is just a job, that's about all you could say. Just something until we can get up bush again. You see Alice, George and I decided as soon as the Union Whaling said no to get out and back to Rhodesia and beyond. This business of living in a city however nice, it's just not our idea of enjoyment. After two weeks or so the novelty has completely worn off.

5 June. Our need now is for a car of some sort. We don't feel like moving again 'till we get one. You can't get where you want and our luggage is a great trouble. Trouble with us is financial more than anything. It certainly goes when on the move but we've a plan in mind.

It's just come to me that two years almost exactly have gone by since we climbed on that old train bound for Queensland. A lot of things have happened since then, maybe not so much to you but I've covered a few miles and seen a few things - sound a bit worldly wise now don't I Alice. But you've certainly got to leave home to see that the world doesn't just end in your own town or even country. This Africa is as different from Australia as I imagine China is and this country is in one big political mess right now, so far only verbally, though people have been injured at meetings. On one side are the present South African government - anti-British and pledged to break from the Commonwealth to form a Republic, and on the other are pro-British who want their rights. The situation could eventually lead to civil war. Tomorrow night there is a huge meeting in town, the *United Front* and *Torch Commando* protesting and Natal threatening to secede from the Union. Things will go with a bang here if that happens but I guess you will be reading all about it in your papers at home.

24 June 1952 c/o *Avondale Road, Greyville, Durban.* We were in the city this morning so called in to the post office not really expecting any letters, so was very pleased when your extra letter as you call it was slid across to me. Actually I intended getting down and writing again tonight so when I last wrote I think I gave an address as GPO Lusaka, Northern Rhodesia but we are not leaving Durban as soon as we thought. You see George and I now have a car, bought last week with some financial assistance from home. Even so we are near enough to being broke as usual and have to stay here a little longer to get a little money together for petrol, food and any emergency that might crop up with the car. You will see what it's like in the photo, a 1939 Chevrolet Coupe - a popular model that will take us just about anywhere.

Well Alice that's us now, mobile and independent of buses and trains at last. We finished at the match factory thank goodness. It felt like being let out of prison, whatever that is like. Unemployed again but not for long as this morning we were signed on by *James Brown Ltd*, the big ship repairer here in Durban. They have two oil tankers in for overhaul both Yankee but flying the flag of Panama.

Our own transport, Durban

Before when we applied on arrival in Durban they had no work, but now have plenty. That's typical of the shipping business – in port one day and out the next. Anyway these tankers couldn't be in at a more opportune moment for us and we are told four hours extra a day and Saturday and Sunday are being worked as well to get them away. Tomorrow morning at 7:15am we go aboard. This is more our element for the next couple of weeks and they can keep their old match factory.

It is noon now and we are parked on the grassy slope overlooking the silvery sea. George just below on the sand lying in the sun reading and I have this pad propped against the steering wheel writing. The day is perfect and the sun very warm. So much so it is becoming uncomfortable in here under the steel roof. Therefore I will adjourn 'till we get back in the house this evening. We are just spending a lazy day today now secure in the thought of starting work tomorrow.

25 June. I didn't write at all last night after all but went to bed around 7:30pm with quite a headache. Maybe a bit too much sun. Anyway we were up bright and early this morning and down to our new job from the workshops. We didn't go on board 'till about nine and sat around with the gang waiting for work to be allocated. George and I struck it lucky getting a nice job on deck dismantling electric motor fans for supplying air to the engine room. It has been a lovely day and we saw part of the fleet that is exercising here come in, also a submarine.

Most of the afternoon we just hung over the side watching the natives chipping and painting another tanker astern of us, or a Norwegian and Portuguese freighter loading just across from us. Much better than being cooped up in a factory I think you'll agree. The other boys were below some in the boiler room which we visited were stifling hot as she has just been shut down.

Working on a ship in Durban Port

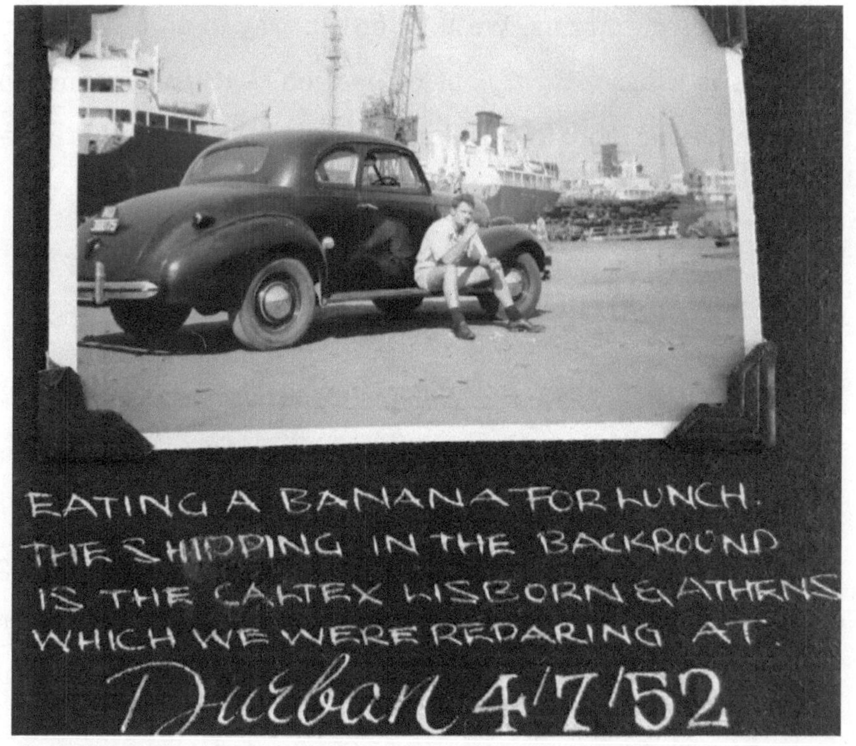

George Hardgrave on his lunch break

The engine room is very clean, painted white and cream. They are not mean with the paint. The crew are all Chinese with American officers and the ship is an all welded 10,000 tons. It was registered in Panama because Britain and the US steer clear of these ships now due to several just disappearing with all hands, presumably with a broken back. There is a sailing date set so there is a good bit of overtime going to be worked which suits us down to the ground for the next couple of weeks. Everyone gets fired then if no other ship turns up but that won't worry us. We'll be on our way to a far destination. This is a lucky break, out of one job, a day's rest, and into another one more to our liking financially too for outfitting our next expedition.

A grand trip back

4 August 1952 c/o Public Works Department, Lusaka, Northern Rhodesia. Well we had a grand trip up here again though a bit trying at the start. We didn't get away until last Wednesday 23 July at 7:00pm. We were both keen on seeing a bullfight at Lourenco Márques in Portuguese East Africa the following day so set our minds on going right through the night. The roads are poorly marked especially at night and taking a wrong turn to Eshowe the capital of Zululand, set us back somewhat. But taking another wrong road spelled the finish for the bullfight completely. Not that we missed much but it would have been something new.

Anyway we landed dead centre in the *Hluhluwe Game Reserve* climbing a track over a range of hills. George was driving and I had just woken from a snooze at the first light of day when we saw a big herd of bush buck grazing on a distant hill. This seemed strange so near a main road so we had just been remarking that the track seemed unusually rough for a highway and our fears were confirmed. When rounding the corner we ran bang into the centre of a rest camp. However, nothing daunted and making the most of our mistake we went on slowly in order not to miss any game that might cross our path. We saw buffalo, zebra, pigs, baboons and many varieties of buck along the way.

Bill cooking up at a rest camp

Leaving the reservation we had entered by accident and finding the right road again, night-fall found us out of Zululand into the heart of Swaziland. After cooking up a welcome hot meal to lie out on the old earth and sleep seemed the height of luxury. Not even the persistent drumming from a nearby village kept us awake long, up at daylight before the sun and on to Stegi. After breakfast we bought stores and petrol.

Crossing the border was not without incident into Portuguese East. At the South African border they just stamped our passports but not so our dear Latin friends. They read our passports from cover to cover and back again then started a gesturing conversation among themselves. It appears that though we had a visa our passports were not endorsed for Portuguese colonies. They rang the South African border who explained that we have no Consular representative at all in Africa who could endorse them. That seemed to reluctantly satisfy them and they banged their stamp down.

Next they looked the car over and seeing we were carrying petrol in tins made out an order that we were to leave the country with as much petrol as we entered with the idea being to make us pay for Portuguese petrol at six shillings a gallon. However they missed a five gallon drum in front so we had the satisfaction of not buying any of theirs. Borders can be wearing places and what we said about all Portuguese for ten minutes or so will not bear repeating now.

Lourenco Marques looks quite continental. Though a very native city it's hard to pick white from black, everyone is so mixed up. There are no colour barriers here and it was quite interesting compared with the South Africa we had just left. After a rough first look in the quiet of early afternoon we drove out to the beach and had a lovely swim, and a shower made us feel new again which is only natural considering this was our first contact with water since leaving Durban.

Feeling on top of the world we made our way back to the city as dusk was falling. How everything had woken up from earlier, as the people have the custom of the motherland taking a siesta all early afternoon. Now as we entered in the evening with the fiery sun gone, life was beginning to emerge, some of it extremely eye-catching to say the least. Groups of well-dressed dons laughing and talking on street corners, old couples and young couples, taking the evening breeze and chattering, knots of laughing, languid, dark senoritas mixing through all the Indians and natives. Their talk meant nothing to us but we enjoyed every moment of it. Sitting in a cafe sipping cool ale and nibbling fish patties we watched the little part of the world before us - just two unknown foreigners from a far away land, they not knowing our ways and we just watching.

That night after mending a puncture (the only trouble we had throughout) we camped near the beach with the murmur of the Indian Ocean in our ears - the ocean we won't hear again for awhile. Next morning after a hectic few minutes churning out of sand onto the road we spent our remaining escudos at the market before heading for Ressano Garcia on the border and the famous National Park full of new sights. We crossed the border again with no bother except for the usual form filling on the South African side and entering the *Kruger National Park* late afternoon, we drove slowly along to the *Sabie Rest Camp.*

We saw quite a few buck (I can't tell the different names), baboons and a few graceful giraffe that crossed the road. We arrived at the camp just in time and set to with the evening meal. No one is allowed to camp out in the reserve but must be in a camp by night fall and remain 'till daylight. The camps are well set out having thatched huts, tents, cooking places and good washing facilities and the bigger ones have a store and cafe for those who wish to eat there. The whole lot is surrounded by an ordinary six or eight strand fence which must be quite sufficient or you would read in the papers of people being carried off.

The next day Sunday we were up long before daylight, being first in the queue when the gate opened shortly after 6:00am. During the day we saw a herd of more than sixty buffalo and many small groups of all sorts of buck and antelope in their hundreds grazing or bounding majestically away. The country was well wooded with little undergrowth and having more the appearance of an English Park. Herds of zebra passed us, wild pigs and ostrich too. We got very close to a giraffe and will have what we hope will be some good photos. I climbed out of the car once to try and get a closer shot of a baboon not noticing a tree full of them close by. They came jumping and crashing down on my approach by the dozen in all directions. I was surprised, needless to say George thought it very funny.

At 1:00pm we arrived at *Letaba Rest Camp* deciding to stay the remainder of the day on being told elephants were in the vicinity that we dearly wished to see. We had good luck that afternoon seeing eight of them, some feeding, others playing about squealing and trumpeting. Not a noise to forget easily. Two we photographed were only twenty-five yards or so away, quite close enough as these are not prisoners in a zoo. The big African elephant is considered untameable, different from his Indian cousin.

Early next morning about 4:00am we were awakened by lions roaring and coughing not far off. A most hair-raising noise I must say in real life, with no bars and only a stone's throw away. We speculated what to do if one decided to prowl about our tent or poke its head inside. They sounded that close. However they must have moved on because we drifted back to sleep in a short while.

Later that Monday morning something happened that I for one will always remember. It started about 10:00am when we spotted elephants on the ridge about eight hundred yards away. They appeared to be moving in a line that would bring them across the road directly ahead of us so we stopped and waited as they ambled slowly through the low bush. Another car came along and stopped at our signal. By now the elephants were near the road so we started up together and moved slowly forward hoping to get a closer view. They had seen us now and the leader broke into a run. The whole mob crossed the road ears flapping, trunks waving about seventy-five yards in front. We counted sixteen in all - a really grand sight and believe it or not within half a minute we couldn't hear that galloping mob in the bush. They seem to move with deceptive speed when they wish and are not half as clumsy as they appear, yet their terrific strength is evident everywhere in the big trees uprooted and tossed about.

A lone bull of huge size and sweeping tusks with three followers came over a few minutes later. I got what I hope will be a grand photo of him though the sky was a bit cloudy. We were soon to meet one at much closer range. The other car went on ahead and we followed soon after for perhaps a mile and rounding the corner we saw someone standing beside the car three hundred yards off waving furiously and pointing. We couldn't see anything for a few seconds and then we woke up on seeing an ominous grey bulk coming through the bush and heading straight for us. No chance of passing him on the road so George reversed in record time, turning the car around just as fifteen tons of meat, bone and worry came onto the road about twenty-five yards behind us. He came on down the road at us in a swinging gate not very fast but with flapping trunk, swinging head, curving tusks and pig eyes gleaming wickedly.

Photographing the charging elephant

We kept just ahead of him until I took a photo. Then jumping in the car we swiftly took off to the further bank of a nearby river. Another car came up then with a Canadian family in it. They turned around pretty quickly too when told what was just ahead. George and I reversed back to the river bank to see if he had gone and there was our big friend joined by a companion now standing on the road below. On spotting us once more he started up again with renewed energy. You would have thought he bore us a personal grudge. His companion stayed behind we thankfully noted. We started retreating again, the Canadians ahead of us and sure enough there he was when I looked out at the rear, his huge bulk was coming over the bank.

He came on top and stood still with his trunk swishing the dust about meditating on the next move, the magnificent bad tempered fellow Colossus, the very picture of Africa. Tiring of our elusiveness he presently wandered slowly off the road some distance away. We waited a safe time then turned around and continued our interrupted way. He was standing stock still in the bush as we passed, eyes gleaming and huge ears gently flapping. I'll never forget that morning or our encounter with God‘s masterpiece the elephant, and he was so disappointed not being able to turn the car over and playfully trample us out.

So much for that Alice it is really an experience that has to be felt. We were a little queer inside after at the thought of what might have been I don't mind admitting, but I guess it wasn't our time just then. We saw a lot more animals during the day - zebra, giraffe etc. but no more elephants and we left the unforgettable *Kruger National Park* behind at 3:00pm heading west for Louis Trichardt.

On the way we came across a motorist and his family beside the road with a puncture. He didn't have any puncture outfit with him so we fixed things up, being the only decent help. He had been three hours waiting. Being grateful I suppose we were invited to stay the night at his house in Louis Trichardt which we accepted only after a little hesitation. After all a soft bed when offered can't be easily refused even by such hardy types as us. So we drove behind him through the evening to the town and house where we were very hospitably received, quite a pleasant surprise in our journey.

After breakfast next morning (Tuesday) we bid everyone farewell, continuing north over the lofty Zoutpansberg Mountains and so to Beit Bridge on the Limpopo River. Here the Union Customs were sticky (just their usual form as before when we came down by road). We were sent back ten miles to Messina just for a special form to do with exporting the car. We were mad, and what we called those Afrikaans just isn't in any dictionary.

Camping on the way back to Lusaka

Letting go a sigh of relief that we were clear of South Africa again, the run through Southern Rhodesia was quite uneventful just mile after mile of road, Bulawayo and two night camps before the mighty Victoria Falls came in sight. Surely no one can describe these roaring, swelling cascading falls of the Zambezi properly. They are utterly awe inspiring to gaze upon tumbling spray covered waters a mile wide, falling far then dashing through the mighty canyon on its way to the ocean. We spent some time walking about that spray covered place taking photos.

That day (Thursday) after complying with customs and immigration people we got within seventy-five miles of Lusaka beyond a place called Mazabuka. It was 10:00pm by then over some bad roads and after a long sixteen hour day we slept without rocking. Next morning we stopped at the Kafue River for breakfast but mostly for a much-needed clean up as we were filthy. After a shave, a change of clothes and a full stomach we felt confident to meet our prospective employers later in the morning. So here we are at the end of the overland trail for now and installed in a government supplied, self-contained caravan in a government camping ground in Lusaka. The next move of ours, when out of the present financial crisis will be north. This is the point of no return - Tanzania and Kenya ahead or nothing.

4 August 1952 c/o Public Works Department, Lusaka, Northern Rhodesia. Here I am again better late I hope, than never having to answer for three of your letters, your last dated 8 July which I got the day before leaving Durban. I know you'll understand when I say we were terrifically busy down there. Firstly with work and overtime on the ship and secondly preparing for this trip we have just completed. Now back in the leisurely north we have time in plenty so no excuse for not concentrating on a spot of writing.

Government supplied accommodation Lusaka

9August 1952 Saturday. I'm starting off again six days later to finish this letter. I'm terrible aren't I? Perhaps I better explain that I've worked until 9:00pm every night since starting work, Monday included. Then to come back to the caravan and start cooking up is just about enough to make a fellow call it a day. No gas or electricity where we are here just hurricane lamps, candles, primus and an open wood fire outside.

I've got things a little organised now as I have a native boy to have hot water ready for washing and the billy boiling when I get home and to wash the dishes and keep the place tidy generally. I hate coming home to chaos and no hot water for greasy hands. Actually I've just got back from an afternoon of woodcutting with my African. He promises to be alright, willing enough and talks some rough English which is helpful. So now I have enough wood to keep the wolf from the door for a while. It is quite scarce about here and you must go several miles out for it.

George has been sent ninety miles down the road to relieve at a road construction camp for awhile so I am on my own. There are three African families camped near me and one of them reckoned I should find someone to share the caravan with me to have things ready when I get home. I replied it was not a bad idea but where would I find a girl to stay in the same room long with an ugly fellow like myself? What I really thought was that I'd sooner come home to some peace and quiet on my own than to go through what a lot of people here do - endless nagging and quarrelling and too much drinking seem to be the main trouble in homes out here. You just can't help noticing it everywhere. Drink is the main cause of half the strife. We've met not one or two, but lots of people who have broken up over it. George and I like a few glasses too but will never see the day it gets a hold of us if we live to be a hundred. In Africa the *Sundowner Party* is a custom and largely an excuse to drink too much. It makes you think when you see women and girls going to pieces because of it. More so in the country where white people go downhill earlier anyway, without other help.

Well Alice I've seen in papers over here quite a bit about the labour surplus starting over your side (as you mentioned) and the reduction in immigration but I still say Australia is a grand country. It must go forward not back. It's like America was fifty years ago and I'd go back any old time. If a lot of young fellows coming in could be persuaded to stay inland where the country wants opening up (with some encouragement of course) it would be a step in the right direction.

10 August 1952. I had good intentions of getting this away yesterday but I reckon another day won't matter now after so long. The light failed me before I could finish and kerosene lamps are a bit straining to read. It is dark in no time as soon as the old sun hits the horizon so I have to postpone writing or reading. It is 10:30am on a bright Sunday morning and the breeze is rustling the trees as I look from the caravan door. Church bells are tolling in the town half a mile away and altogether it is extremely peaceful. Half a dozen children are playing in the dust at the camp next door but they are very quiet. It must be very trying for families living like this especially for the women, even though there is a native help but I suppose they are living in hope of a house which are very scarce here.

Yes a mine did collapse killing some and a mine cage went down several thousand feet killing some more at another time, but both in the Orange Free State. There is always an odd one or two being killed, often through natives not being machinery conscious or because of rock falls. I was interested in the cutting you sent of the landslide and 'diver Johnson'. He was in New Zealand in 1947 when the ship *Wanganella* hit the reef. I was on that job at the time. Too right I remember the trip through the Dandenong Ranges that afternoon and how I enjoyed it. There are many things I could write from your last letter Alice but I'll put it off for now. As usual with all kinds of thoughts across the ocean, Bill. Until next time XXX

Steady job but not much money

9 September 1952 c/o Public Works Department, Lusaka, Northern Rhodesia. Dear Alice, You're welcome letter of 24 August came the day before yesterday so I'll give you the news of what is happening to us. We are still with the government civil service but uncivil at times with the form filling and running about with sheets of paper for a few engine spare parts. However this is an easy-going land so what we don't do today we might do tomorrow which suits us all.

George is back again now and he's glad too. I must say I'm not sorry to see his face about the place again though the change from one another didn't do any harm after being together so long. Everything is new again when you meet up. Well Alice, we are talking about our next move even though we've been here such a short time. It won't be for a few months though as we are flat broke right now having only just made it from Durban. If mates up at Howard's camp where we were before hadn't staked us, we would have been on damper and water, but George and I are well thought of here and can get almost anything. It's a good feeling that but we repay it, even if we have to wade through a river full of crocodiles. We are right again now but a month is a long time to wait for pay. When the time is opportune we will go north and try and work on the copper mines around Ndola two hundred miles away.

I had a dose of what everyone calls malaria a fortnight ago. I can't tell for sure because the family in the next camp fed me quinine and hot tea and brandy. The doctor couldn't diagnose properly after that lot but I'll know when it comes back again. I reckon it was the sun that got at me again because I had been out working on a machine that day. Anyway, I woke up that night with the most awful dreams and going hot and cold. Next morning after a bad night I was aching in my limbs and could hardly lift my head. The people next door saw I hadn't got out and came over to see why, though I wasn't very interested in anything. They dosed me as I said before and piled blankets on me and the perspiration was terrible it being a blazing hot day. It did the trick though and I woke up at sundown feeling a hundred percent better. The doctor next day said it was useless taking a blood test after the medicine given. A fellow can't go on forever without catching something, can he now? I'm waiting to see if it comes back again, interesting thought.

After that cheerful happening to me, please accept my sympathy for your recent cold and toothache as one sufferer to another we seem to be mates. The weather here is pretty warm and dirty which is natural after six rainless months. It might rain the end of next month to start the wet season off when everyone starts cursing the mud for a change. I won't, not 'till I get bogged out in it as rain will be a pleasant change even though so hot and humid afterwards. I'm glad for all of you over there that spring has arrived and the trees are waking up to the promise of another hot southern summer. I'd like to be on hand to pinch a few of those peaches when your dad's not looking too. My mouth waters for a taste, it's so long since I had one.

14 September. We met another young New Zealander in Lusaka the other day the same age as us, twenty-four and twenty-five and who actually lived within two miles of us for a time back home. We didn't know him. He was in Australia too for a while before coming to South Africa then drifting up here like us. There are four of them teamed up, the New Zealander, a Scotsman, Englishman and South African all working at the Rhodesia Public Works Department like us. They are learning to drive earthmoving machinery. They have an ambitious plan of getting a truck and going to Algeria from here, by way of Abyssinia, Egypt and along the North African coast. Some enterprise but what is there in Algiers except trouble I don't know.

They are trying to interest us as they aren't mechanics but we'd never get home if we joined up. We would be more likely to end up in a French jail and get deported broke as undesirables. It's no use pointing out the obvious lack of work or friendliness in these countries, to fellow adventurers anyway. Each of us only learns from his own actual experience of hardship and difficulties. We rarely take advice from others until confronted with the thing warned about and usually when our bridges are burnt.

It has been hot again today around ninety-five degrees and a hot wind blowing clouds of dust. It is torture cooking out in it. Well Alice this is it again for now. Holding fondest thoughts of you across the ocean and feeling just a little sad for myself. I am, Yours Bill.

12 October 1952 c/o Public Works Department, Lusaka, Northern Rhodesia. It has been a very busy weekend for me until this afternoon at four when I arrived back from the job - a water pumping engine I have installed at a native training settlement - thirty-five miles of bad road from here. I stayed the night there getting up early this morning to finish off and leaving for the return trip at midday. At the twelve mile post from Lusaka a front wheel came off. Quite a surprise and I had visions of sleeping tonight alongside the truck in case of native looters. However I sent the two natives with me back up the road to see if they could find the pieces and they returned with everything, bearing wheel, nut and washer. The wheel nut was completely stripped out. Having no jack we collected various large stones and using a long pole as a lever eventually got the truck up onto a pile of rocks. It was blazing hot out there squirming around in the dust but the wheel went on again and putting the nut on and swivelling the axle over I fixed it. After a drop of water all round we set off slowly and I was glad when the house came in sight after dropping the natives at their huts.

You notice I say house! That's it we're living in a big five room fully furnished place now – luxury, but there's a catch of course. It happened like this: The couple who live here are away on leave in Durban. He is an electrician with us and left the house in charge of another workmate who has gone away on a job lasting about two weeks. Knowing us as pretty steady fellows, not likely to hold wild parties or otherwise wreck the place, we were asked to come up and stay to eliminate the chance of raiders coming to the house. So here we are installed if only temporarily. It is a great change from the caravan with its cramped space. I am sitting on the sofa, legs out with this pad on one knee. There is a jug of cold drink beside me on a small table, radio going softly with George beside it reading and the cat on the floor, all very domestic.

There is a cook boy here who is a fair cook and we have just had dinner of some lovely steak I was given on the job today. The refrigerator is a novelty for us. Really they are an essential not a luxury in a country like this. At our camp we have to cook meat straight away or use tinned bully beef. Butter can be poured on despite being surrounded by water in a jar. We keep drinking water in a canvas bag which as you know keeps cool, even in the warmest weather but it's good to be able to have ice in your glass when the tongue is hanging out. In this weather it does a lot. This month is the hottest time of the year here prior to the rains coming and sticky with the promise of it. The evenings are hot too though the slightest breeze that comes in is appreciated. There is a nice breeze drifting in now through the window louvers.

10.45 pm Well surprise of surprises our friend Bart has just arrived back. That's the chap that asked us to stay here in his place. He has dumped his gear off and has just gone off to take his crowd of natives home. He appreciates us staying for him otherwise he would not have gone away on this job leaving the place unguarded. He and the foreman have just taken a forty by fifteen foot pontoon to a site on the Kafue River two hundred and fifty miles away. It is intended for ferrying cars across the river and has been somewhat of an ordeal getting it there.

Three weeks ago it started from here up the river, being towed by a launch with two of our men and a gang of natives aboard the launch. It lost its screw on a rock which they repaired, then rapids held up the pontoon until they got natives to manhandle it over. One had to go in the river with the natives for encouragement because of the crocodiles while the other stood on deck with a rifle firing at them. Quite exciting you say sitting in a chair Alice.

George and I are getting on our feet again now. Watching the pounds, shillings and pence rise from zero is fun actually, though you don't think so when it's down to zero pounds, zero shillings and ten pence. Now if the government says pack up and start moving we can drift off somewhere else, similarly if we tell them. They are more or less satisfied with us and this is a career job so we will be the ones to tell them to pack up when the time comes. It won't be this year now that we go further north, but after the wet season about next April.

20 November 1952 c/o Public Works Department, Lusaka, Northern Rhodesia. Your letter of the 25th last month came last week and I meant to get round to write a return straight away. I just didn't get down to it the main reason being I have been laid up with a wonderful cold, flu or something. It felt like all the things I haven't had for two years had come at once. Pains under and over the eye, absolute tightness everywhere and the doc says I had a temperature among other things. However we take a lot of killing and I am on the road to recovery.

Last week was the dirtiest bit of weather since we left England being cold, windy and raining most of the time. On the Monday and Tuesday I was out in it on a job at a water pump where I had to pull a lot of ball casing from the ground, fit on a new cylinder and foot valve and lower the lot down again, myself and six Africans. Nothing happened to the natives but I put my trouble down to getting drowned in wet clothes. So much for work and I'm glad it's more sunny this week. Today it was just on ninety degrees from 12:00pm until 4:00pm and I'm sniffing away. I don't know how I will stick it back in New Zealand.

I'm sure mum reckons I should settle into a nice steady job, perhaps the folks at home want to see a fellow bring a daughter-in-law into the family and maybe some grandchildren, Ed too. After you've been in a decent climate it's hard to put up with the cold wind and rain all the time and piles of clothes on, but it will be great to see mum and dad again after three and a half years. Yes a spell at home for a bit will be lovely. It was six months last time after I came back from the Northern Territory in 1949.

I still dream of that wide open place sometimes, a free and happy-go-lucky place. I just wonder how long I'll be back on our beautiful island this time. This time next year George and I will be home as at the moment we are nearly sure of being on the ship *Dominion Monarch* leaving Cape Town on 30 October 1953. Still a year to go yet to do all sorts of wonders, we hope.

'Little' brother Ed is up in Britain still, in the foggy islands as they are at the moment. He last wrote about two months ago and has owed me a reply since then. However he said that he was working on a hydro-electric scheme in Scotland in the highlands and it was as cold as charity and that he was keen to come down here. I sent him a letter I had from *The Settlers' Association* regarding him and of help and that is all I have heard from the terror since. However mum said he had written home in which he had teamed up with a young Scottish fellow just out of his apprenticeship and they were awaiting a C passage to South Africa so we may see him in this part of the globe before long.

Socialising for single blokes

20 December 1952 c/o Public Works Department, Lusaka, Northern Rhodesia. Dear Alice, your long and lovely letter got here the other day. I know I've been on top of the world for the last two weeks again and your get well kiss doesn't go amiss in any way. I think half my trouble is the need for a whole lot of that lovely shock treatment. We boys can stand a bit of that and hand it out too. We don't get a chance here but there's a good time coming. Well Alice it's just about another year again. George and I will be coming into the home straight then.

21 December. I have just finished looking through the Sunday papers from Johannesburg and Southern Rhodesia that George got when he met the South plane at lunchtime. It is now 3:00pm and as I'm tired of lying about I thought I would put time to some use. We didn't get up till 10:00am, which is the usual Sunday form.

Last night saw us in town and round about starting off at *Howard's Club* at the place we worked earlier this year. Saw a few people we knew and a lot we didn't and sampled the beer before leaving to have a look at the Rosedale Hotel a fairly notorious place five miles out, that we hadn't seen before. We stayed awhile 'till the official closing time 10:00pm then came back to town. Nothing much there except some pretty coarse women and a crowd of fellows in on the spree.

We took a companion of ours out of hospital to his home then called in at the *Regiment Army Headquarters.* Here we found a variety concert going on attended by the Governor General. After this finished and the more steady citizens had gone home a house game started for those who cared and we met an interesting young chap we know and adjourned to the bar where we talked guns and shooting 'till we rolled off to our camp a bit after midnight. So ended an unusually active evening for us in a town that socially doesn't get much further than the bottle. It makes a break to go out and listen to other people's worries when that 'wanting to do something' feeling comes on.

Well Alice so it rolls on. Ed is three days out from England now on his way down here. According to the paper there was a big gale on when he was due to leave so no doubt he had the dining saloon to himself as we did after leaving Adelaide last year. I envy him a bit rolling down at this minute toward the equator. A few weeks at sea is, my dear, perfect happiness - coming from a bleak land to tropical sunshine.

As you ask, my idea of a partnership is give a little, take a little and share everything. If two people want the adventure of love together, cooking well it helps. I bet when the novelty wears off the way to a man's heart is through his stomach. The old timer that coined that knew his onions Alice. What do you say? There is no room to say why I was sad last time. Maybe I was moody, but wishing your head was beside mine.

A lapse and brother Ed arrives

5 February 1953 C/O Public Works Department, Lusaka, Northern Rhodesia. My dear Alice, I have been sitting here for half an hour now reading your last two letters and trying to think how to make an excuse for the terrific gap since I last wrote. I started to reply on 20 December, but I won't tear up those two pages as I should. Actually they contain the start of what turned out to be a terrific bender, which is as near as I can get to it in writing. I asked George what excuse I could offer but he said, 'Don't offer any, you've just been too bloody drunk to care for anything most of the time', so I'll let it go at that Alice. They say you can't reform a bloke once he gets on it but there's one boy that's going to.

I hope I see you again one day. You mentioned once that you'd like to come over our way for a holiday. Why don't you wait till I get home to New Zealand and then come over with a girlfriend maybe. Mum and dad would welcome you and we could fix accommodation easily. It would do you the world of good I'll bet. I can't write any more now Alice so good night and God Bless. Yours Bill.

17 March 1953 c/o Public Works Department, Lusaka, Northern Rhodesia. George and I have just made a 3,000 mile trip to Bloemfontein and back to pick up Ed and his Scottish friend. They were joyful at the sight of us needless to say and the prospect of a start in this country. We tied up jobs for them before we left, just satisfied immigration people and now they are happily at work and have been for three days.

I am glad we pulled them out of the Union as it's not so good down there, especially if you can't speak Afrikaans. Anyway they're here now and happy as everything is okay. George leaves here on the weekend to go up north to try for work on the copper mines. They pay big money up there which he is after if he can get taken on. I will stay with the public works for awhile as shortly when it gets dry, some interesting construction jobs will be going and I wish to learn as much as I can. Mining work is the same all over the world but jobs such as we have here are not so easy to find. Ed and Doug are staying in our camp with us and it is fairly crowded, though George will thin it out a bit once he goes. They left England on the 18 February so they missed the big storm up there.

I am keeping pretty well. You know Alice I'm getting a bit into the 'don't care' attitude of Rhodesia. There's not a great deal to do outside of work here especially for us single fellows so we are liable to run a bit wild now and then. I suppose you can guess how it is. Up here you fall easily into the group that has no real home in the country and that move around like us, displaced persons more or less and one thing leads to another, usually starting at the hotels. I suppose I do you get lonely and bored. Sometimes I don't believe I'm any better morally then the next one, perhaps a little better than most, and a little worse than some I know. That's one thing a man can look forward to – an adventure into life with someone else – two people going forward as one.

Bill and younger brother Ed

21 March. Well Alice it's the end of the week again and George has left. I hope he gets on alright up north. The rains are at the last fling now and it has been coming down in sheets today and now it is dark the mosquitoes are out feeding. The other day I shot the head off a cobra which Ed thought was great work. Last week we got one in the workshop but they should be starting to hibernate shortly when it gets a bit cooler.

21 April 1953 c/o Public Works Department, Lusaka, Northern Rhodesia. Dear Alice, Your letter arrived the other day like a breath of fresh air. I could almost say correctly from a Victorian orchard. Glad to hear that everyone is cheerful down your way, excepting dad which I hope has come good now. I'm in top form as I usually am and looking forward to the future, though my future has changed a bit as I will outline shortly. Ed and Doug are getting on fine here and they like the country fine as well. Their jobs suit them alright.

I heard from George yesterday and though he hasn't managed to get onto a mine yet he has a temporary job, and he is boarding with a pretty good family in Ndola which is only two hundred miles from Lusaka so you mustn't think he's in the Mau Mau country. It's an awful long walk up to Kenya from there and I must say the outlook isn't too healthy round Nairobi with all the killings lately. That's Africa reverting back to its savage past before the white man came, which shows how thin the veneer is despite our teaching.

River crossing at Fort Victoria 1953

Yes that was my car crossing the river, myself at the wheel a gang of recruits to steady her and George taking the photo. It was actually floating in one place and steering was useless so it was a good thing the Africans were there or a man would've gone floating away downstream. It's a Vauxhall Velox 1949 and cost £350 sterling. I've had it about six weeks now, no troubles at all. George has the Chevy away with him.

You would have read Alice how Southern Rhodesia, Nyasaland and Northern Rhodesia are now federated states, the new Dominion of Central Africa. This country must go forward now. Progress is inevitable here despite native opposition. I can't see what benefits there are for them but if left to their own devices they would go back to where we first found them, the strong tribes killing the weaker, secret societies and slave trading. They live in peace now with no fear, famines or invaders but a lot don't see that - only 'get rid of the white man' they cry. Rhodesia is now peaceful and we hope it always will be.

Purchase of land

Dear Alice, I've given it some thought lately and discussed with Ed and we've decided to buy land here and build. We have seventy- eight acres in view and tomorrow we finalise it with the solicitor so we are now what are called 'settlers' with a stretch of virgin bush to call home and to do what we wish. I am signing up with the government for three years - nine months of which I have done already, and I'm quite certain I couldn't better myself as far as the job and conditions go. At the end of my term I get six months leave on full pay and my fare paid home plus a £300 bonus. There's nothing like this down our way. I will be due to go home then in August 1955, two years and three months from now.

It seems a long time but it will soon go especially now as we have a man size job of clearing land, building and farming. I think we're doing the right thing and personally I feel as though I'm at the crossroads of something big. Something I can't exactly put my finger on. One road leads to failure and the other to success. That now or never feeling is about as closest I can get to it.

I haven't a beard anymore and am respectable once more. It's a queer feeling without my beard now and I must say I puff out a bit for being called a nice looking fellow regardless of being unshaven. I am proud to hear that you have been trusted so far as to drive the new car and those Austin's are smart jobs, so Alice see that you treat her with respect young lady, because if anything happens you'll be on the carpet and for it.

One of the toys we play with is a Caterpillar D8, nice and handy about the farm, £15,000 each here. One went down the bank, left the cut about two hundred yards up the hill and careered away coming to rest down the cutting. The operator rode it out thank goodness which would take some nerve, otherwise it would've been harder for us to salvage upside down and weighing more than twenty tons. We had to make a road in to get to it. These jobs make an interesting change from the workshop.

We are putting this new road through pretty rough country to the hydro dam site on the Kafue River. The dam and power station will be ready in 1956 and will supply all Northern Rhodesia which shows what confidence there is in the future. A new town for 8,000 people is to be built housing the workers. I wouldn't mind being on that job if I'm here then. Time will tell.

14 May 1953 c/o Public Works Department, Lusaka, Northern Rhodesia. Dear Alice, Ed and I have begun work on our place now. We have had the government geologist out and he has marked a spot where there is a good expectation of water by drilling a bore. We are trying to arrange for a boring contract now. Meanwhile we are making a road in so that machinery can be brought in to the site. We are at a creek at present over which a log bridge is in progress. We camped there last weekend and were up before dawn and working when it was light enough to see, felling trees and cutting them into handy lengths, hauling them by ropes. We literally went to work for a rest on Monday.

Water is our first consideration, permanent water that is for though the creeks are still flowing most surface water dries up about June or July and there is none again ‘till November. Rather a long time to wait you’ll agree Alice. It’s rather like most of Australia in that the land may be as dry as a bone on top but underneath a hundred feet or so there is untold supplies of water. I was at a big government borehole recently which was being tested where 2,000,000 gallons a day was being pumped up, so you see why we need a bore and windmill first. The complete outfit will set us back about £300. We must have this before we do a single thing further, except clearing the land off. Meanwhile I have signed the government contract now for three more years service starting 28 July last year, 1952. I can only quit now by giving three months notice or by giving them one month wages, so my term ends on July 28, 1955.

15 May. I stopped writing last night. When I came home I couldn’t concentrate any longer. You know how it is. Well

George has been gone six weeks now and he's landed a job at *Luanshya Mine* near Angola. He said it took him a lot of trying though, but he's drawing between £150 in £180 a month which is big money. I think he'll postpone his return home for awhile. He'll be able to show his mother a good time (she's a widow) when he does go back anyway.

The last word I heard of mate Ian he was at home still. I wasn't back home a month before I was talking of going back to inland Australia and beyond. I gave George and Ian the infectious disease of the 'itchy foot' of course and it's exactly three years next Tuesday the 19th that we sailed out on that blustery afternoon from Wellington Harbour. I never remotely dreamt I'd be in central Africa three years from then. Of course I hadn't given a thought to where I'd fetched up really except probably back under the home roof.

The time has gone quickly when reviewed, but seems like a dream in another way when the towns you've passed through are remembered or recalled: Mount Morgan, Townsville, Normanton. Honestly I'll never forget that place we were held up in for two weeks, Alice Springs, Darwin and Melbourne when I stayed at your house. Then the Dandenong Ranges, Perth, Colombo, Suez, Naples, quiet villages in Devon, London, Glasgow and the plane trip across Europe and Africa to Johannesburg the city of gleaming mine dumps. Our trips up and down here, Zululand, Swaziland, Mozambique, the Kruger Park and the bull elephant (I won't forget him), Southern Rhodesia, Bulawayo, Salisbury and the mighty Victoria Falls, the stamping of passports and now here I am in Lusaka in a caravan the paraffin lamp hissing, African drums heard faintly in the distance.

The two suitcases George and I each left in Durban last July in storage, have been sent up to us in Lusaka. I opened mine yesterday and everything was in perfect order. I had expected things to be a bit mouldy after that humid climate. I put naphthalene in so nothing was moth-eaten. That big jersey you knitted me awhile back is in perfect condition. I don't need it here but it will come in handy when we get down New Zealand way. I'll be there to do some moaning about the weather when I get home. It's no South Sea island paradise for climate down there, though it's beautiful country.

An interesting proposal

15 May. Alice, remember the day we all fell into the train carriage in Sydney going north, just a few days short of three years ago? What I've seen since has steadied me up a bit. Here we are still writing away exactly as we did at the start, except for a few lapses on my part. Still it's nice to be forgiven and be able to creep back in the fold again with that ashamed feeling. It gives a sense of starting out on the right foot again.

Though I've only seen you for less than a week altogether in these last three years, I count you as a best friend. You are a woman I am a man of course, and the natural instinct between the two arises, as it should. What I'm trying to say now, or ask, Alice is that I consider you as my possible future wife. I have never, or hope I have never, said anything I didn't mean anywhere in the world and I'm not starting now. This is in all seriousness and I'd like your feelings of the idea of you being my offsider for better or for worse, for richer or poorer, 'till death. I know many promise plenty before, but give nothing after. I promise nothing except love and shares in everything. It takes two to make a marriage. Until I hear, I am ever yours through words. Bill. XXXXX

9 June 1953 c/o Public Works Department, Lusaka, Northern Rhodesia. My dearest Alice, I had your letter handed to me this evening at 6:00pm as I climbed into the Land Rover going home from the workshop. I've read the four pages through a few times now and my heart's honestly so full that I couldn't see for tears that suddenly came just now, thinking of what the future holds for us now that you have accepted marriage with me. It's now 11:30pm and I'm going early down to Chirundu tomorrow on the Zambezi River where the road crosses into Southern Rhodesia. I will be back in two days when the water pump to the police camp is fixed.

12 June. I got back this afternoon from the job which took longer than expected so I'll carry on from where I left off more or less on Tuesday. I know letters aren't as satisfactory speaking face-to-face but I think we're both sufficiently literate to get by alright. In fact I can explain better in writing I think than talking and if something is in black-and-white it's definite.

Natives take a little bit to get used to after an all white country on account of the large numbers, but you soon get the hang of it. In South Africa and the Rhodesias they are quiet and still very civil to the European. No, it's my honest opinion there's not much to worry about Alice in the matter of life and limb. Life can get pretty monotonous here too I know, especially for single people but this is a grand country and the climate I think superb. I don't know how I would get on in a place of cold wind and rain again. Fever is all but stamped out in the settled areas too so there's not much to worry about on that score.

Bill by the Land Rover

It rains heavily in the wet season, November to March, and the roads are a bit intolerable at times, but the rain and thunder comes quickly and goes just as quickly and the hot sun is out drying up the earth. This is the best time of the year in May, June and July and it is quite chilly at night and in the mornings 'till 10:00am. The days are beautiful. I think you'd grow to like this country too Alice.

I am entitled to a house and have my name in. These are allotted according to length of service and though they are building, completion is slow. By next year I should be well up on the list though. Meanwhile caravan accommodation is supplied. These are quite luxurious affairs, very well fitted out with a large tent slung from the side. They are very cosy for two people without children. There are many people living like that here with two or three children as well, all waiting on houses which is not so good in this country.

This country has only woken up since the Second World War after a sleep of countless ages, when there were only scattered grass villages of Africans, and prior to 1945 only small European centres. Lusaka for instance has 5,000 white people now, buildings are going up everywhere and the town is spreading out rapidly. This country has a great future now that Federation with Southern Rhodesia and Nyasaland is here. Good night and God bless and as the old Southern Cross is shining down from the clear night outside, it's over to you in Victoria. Perhaps you're even looking at it now as I did a minute ago. As yours before, so for always, Bill XXXXX.

3 July 1953 c/o Public Works Department, Lusaka, Northern Rhodesia. On Tuesday I go up to Ndola to see how George is going. It will be great to see his face when I tell him about us, don't you think? He used to pull my leg often when I got letters from you. Tomorrow the three of us here now leave for a 1,500 mile round trip to Bulawayo where the big Rhodes Exhibition is being held. They say it's a good show though accommodation is short. The Queen Mother and Princess Margaret arrive there on 1 July so we will probably see them.

It is 2:00pm now and I have been getting things set for our tour to Salisbury and Bulawayo all morning. Ed and Doug are working today but we are leaving about 4:00am tomorrow for a week and an early start is the best way. Get on the road before dawn.

You didn't seem to make out too badly with the shipping company. The *Dominion Monarch* is a lovely ship though a bit pricey. £132 is about what they quoted us to go home from here but then we had to wait for a cancellation. The *Arawa* is an older ship and one class I think. It will be less formal probably and that usually means more fun and the whole run of the ship. Apart from the fare difference I'd take the *Arawa* every time. 'B' deck is alright, not like us away down below on the *Orontes*, not that it worried us as we were only in the cabin to sleep and had a very good crowd of young people on board. If you have the same sorts as we did you will enjoy the trip immensely. I saw the immigration this morning and everything will be okay. I will send a letter later. Definitely take the berth Alice and ask Shaw Savill to write to Anderson's in the Cape letting them know I will be sending the fare down to them. Everything should be alright. I can understand them wanting a letter from here because things like that are a bit sticky in South Africa these days. You will only be in transit however, Cape Town to Lusaka.

You'll enjoy the trip back up through Africa Alice where the primitive and modern rub shoulders. It's a continent of contrast. If you haven't got that little bit of pioneering spirit still in you well there might be complaints. This country is still building and you have to do things for yourself here like outback Australia.

If you like a little travel you'll like Africa and its sights. You'll see on the 2,000 mile ride up from the Cape. Well Alice it's 9:00pm now and as we are all getting up at 3:30am I will turn in now. Well my love, looking forward to a future together forever, Bill XXXXX

16 July 1953 c/o Public Works Department, Lusaka, Northern Rhodesia. Dear Alice, Another letter or the start of one hoping you and the family are all well, as I am here. I have completed my two weeks holiday and return to work in the morning. The next holiday will be in eight months time when I come down to meet you off the ship. We had a good week away to Salisbury and Bulawayo seeing the exhibition, though not the Queen Mother. On the way back we went through the *Wankie Game Reserve* on the way to Victoria Falls, seeing only antelope, buffalo and pigs which quite disappointed us hoping as we were to see elephants, lion and giraffe. However, we saw the falls which never ceases to make one gaze in wonderment. None of us were sorry to get back to Lusaka though as it is rough riding having had the springs set up just before we left which made it a bit solid, even with two sacks of sand in the back for ballast.

I saw George on the mine before we left and everything is fine with him, still in the big money up there. The last few days I have been busy out on our block sinking a shaft in the hope of striking water. I thought I may as well try as it will be some time before we can get a boring machine in and if I do strike it we can start brick making straight away. The scene looks like what I would imagine an early Victorian gold mine looked. It's mighty hard work in the sun, a native and myself swinging shovel and pick. It's truly a case of returning to work tomorrow for a rest Alice.

On our place I intend building a small house first, starting soon - two bedrooms, dining room, kitchen and somewhere to live while we get on with the main place which we intend making a fair size. The first place will always come in handy as houses are in extremely short supply, the increasing population much exceeding the housing being built. It's easy enough to bring people into a country but not so easy when it comes to finding them a place to live. Later on we will build the second place as finances allow, a little at a time. You'd be surprised how expensive it is starting a place up but I don't suppose it would be very interesting if we could just whistle money up from nowhere. It's literally hacking a home out of the bush as you will very soon see. It is nine miles from Lusaka which I don't think will be a joyride in the wet season, but then many roads are like that in this country, the same as outback Australia. Nothing could be worse than some of the tracks in Northern Queensland, not much anyway.

I hope our temporary show is complete by the time you arrive. I will sketch roughly what we have in mind as a plan if you like. You will see it is not very large but quite large enough for us and Ed to live in for the time being. It looks quite alright on paper and now we must keep our noses to the grindstone and put it up. The cost should be about £400 - £450. The initial outlay on the property here is great because of the need for permanent water. This will run into around £300 including an engine, so you can appreciate that things must be done in easy stages if we are to keep our heads above water and not go piling debts up around town, which is quite a common thing in this country. I can't rest if I have things like that on my mind.

21 July. Well Alice I'll write a little more this evening to mark time more or less until your letter arrives. I've persuaded myself to wait until it does before posting this off. I posted some papers and pamphlets last week. They will give you some further ideas about the country. I included a Centenary crown piece in the package. I got it at Bulawayo. It will be some time before it reaches you going by surface mail.

You would be surprised how cool it does get here at times, this being winter now of course. A lot of people imagine Central Africa as sweltering in perpetual heat but not so. I always thought of it like that but now I know better. We are over 4,000 feet in altitude here which makes for a healthy climate. October is a very sticky month just before the rain breaks but actually nowhere near as humid as Darwin. This is a better climate, something like Cairns or Townsville. There are mosquitoes in the wet season but malaria is practically stamped out except for here and there. I'm sure what I had once before was heat stroke, the sun catching the neck while working outside. The heat here is not great this time of the year. From May ‘till September it is lovely warm days and cool nights. October is humid before the rains but not as bad as Darwin. I like a place of extremes myself, of two seasons wet and dry. You appreciate rain when it comes. The last rain here I’ve about forgotten now. I think it was the beginning of April and was a vicious short, heavy shower.

There will be plenty for you to do Alice, not manual work but plenty to occupy. Apart from the kitchen I haven’t mentioned it before but in the average small house it is usual to have two native servants, one the houseboy who cleans floors, dusts, does the washing and the other the kitchen boy who chops wood, peels vegetables and washes the dishes. There is a garden boy too. It’ll be a bit strange at first but things are made fairly easy for the European here. You’ll soon get the run of it as we did. Some women come down from Britain who are used to doing everything for themselves, then in a few months are too bone lazy to lift a finger, just shout out orders. Servants do the lot from cooking to looking after the children. A little bit of authority and cheap labour goes to their heads and they become petty tyrants. The average native in Rhodesia responds best if treated fairly and firmly and if promised something expects to get it, whether it is a dressing down or more wages for hard work. You’ll see for yourself and form your own opinions, it’s very interesting really. Would you like me to send you a booklet on the international African language? You may feel like studying now and then in your spare time in preparation. If you can learn a little you will find it a great help in getting ideas across to natives. I am very poor at it yet.

17 August. An international certificate of smallpox is a good idea Alice and lasts three years. It is not always required but it is annoying if it is and you haven't had one. Yes get it in the holiday. You only get one injection and you go back a few days later to see if it has taken. The doctor will write you out a certificate then. Yellow fever, typhus and cholera are unnecessary for South Africa to the best of my knowledge. I don't know about what notice is given for a marriage but I'll write down shortly and enquire of the church. I will also write to Anderson's which I haven't done yet. They like a monetary advance early as a sign of good faith, otherwise they can re-allocate the berth which we don't want to happen. There is plenty of time.

I hope the parcel of books and papers I sent turns up okay, the crown piece with them. It is a Rhodesian Centenary one I should've said before, we can't get English ones here either. I'd love to see some photos of the centre again. I was going to ask you once if you came across *Walkabout* magazines, to send them across so that I could further the education in our workshops. They often have some beaut photos in them. Well Alice, I'll make this finished and pack up as it's late. Lots of love as usual and sweet dreams, yours always Bill. PS enclosing the engagement notice from home that mum sent. Love Bill.

24 August 1953 c/o *Public Works Department, Northern Rhodesia.* Dear Alice, It really is amazing when you think of it what we find to write about. Sometimes I think quicker than I can write and end up losing the gist of what I originally intended to put down, however usually end up with about six pages which is a fair night's homework. I'm glad you're a country girl Alice you won't miss the bright lights and cars over here. For all I know you might like Africa as much as I do. It'll be strange at first but then again you might take to it. Rhodesia has got something about it. Backwards as it still is there's a feeling of promise for a great future if its immediate problems can be solved very shortly.

There's a full moon over Lusaka tonight Alice it's nearly as bright as day. Crickets are singing and the air is lovely. It's times like this that a country grows on you a little more, but I'd like someone to share it with me as it only gives me half a satisfactory feeling. I'd feel the same at this minute in the Northern Territory or in Queensland, anywhere the sun shines.

Hot by day and the nights are cool, even humid a little. If this country doesn't turn out the best for us there is always Australia or New Zealand. I can get a job mostly anywhere in the world. I think we should give this country a trial though as there are more opportunities and chances of success here than in either Australia or New Zealand. I'm still pro Australia of course and maybe will get around there later on in life.

I still have a rather vague ambition to circumnavigate by land working on the way. Imagine it starting from Melbourne, Sydney, Brisbane, Townsville, Cairns, the gulf country, Cloncurry, Tennant Creek, Darwin, Wyndham, Broome, Perth, Adelaide and back to Melbourne. A truck, self-contained and independent for living out and working here and there in the mines, mills, logging, cattle and sheep stations, workshops, meat works. No time limit, stay as long or as short as you like and finance and inclination dictates. As free as the kangaroos themselves that bound about western Queensland. I'm only daydreaming now but didn't you ever think you'd like to do something like that? To see some of the three million square miles you live on in Australia? I did and I'm not even Australian. I'd love to camp by a billabong or beneath a mountain or on the beach by the Great Barrier Reef or on the never-ending plains of grass. You and I could do it wonderfully together Alice counting out children or a home of our own of course. So it looks as though I'll just have to do it on a map.

I've just got wondering what happened to the three Melbourne boys left in Darwin. I've lost track but I guess they're all well home safely by now. They were great lads - my idea of real Australian mates. I still laugh at some of our exploits at times.

26 August 1953 c/o *Public Works Department, Northern Rhodesia.* September is nearly here, time is flying toward Christmas and once that is over it will be no time before you are Africa bound. Darling Alice we will have a wonderful time before we get back to Lusaka, the most lovely three weeks that you or I have ever had, or ever likely to have again. The light is very bad here tonight. I have a battery being charged and the pressure kerosene lamp is out of order. It is quite hard writing at times. You don't miss electricity until you can't put a switch on, especially for reading. I should be quite used to it by this time.

It is thirteen months since I started with the Northern Rhodesian government now and still going strong. I can honestly say it's the best job I've ever had yet. I'm on outside plant construction now and getting that sunburnt look. There's an interesting job coming off, involving the fitting out of a steel motor launch in the workshop then transporting it and launching it on Kafue River thirty-five miles away. From there we go about a hundred and fifty miles upstream to a place called Namwala where we have to bring up a pontoon, fit engines etc for ferrying vehicles across the river. The country there teams with game but I want to have a shot at crocs which are numerous and to which I have an aversion.

I like the open-air life of my present job working here though I could get twice the money on the mines I wouldn't be happy for long. Money isn't everything in life. I really and truly wish we could do without it at times. A good job to do, a good rifle and a good wife - that's my basic idea of a full life. I've got the first and the second. The rifle, though hardly used gave us a feeling of satisfaction. All I want is the last which is rapidly approaching and I should be set for life almost, together with the belief in God running through it all. We've been working steady on our land weekends lately. Ed and I are digging the foundations of a small house now. This will be the first before we start bigger. It's a big enough spare time job believe me Alice.

27 August Sunday. We have got 10,000 bricks to start with and quite a bit of stone on the property but transport is quite a problem. The bricks are only two miles away but it is hard getting a contractor with a truck to deliver them and sand which we need.

Brick making for the Lusaka farm

We have hopes of getting some satisfaction during the coming week. We have a pumping head in the camp now. That was given to me at work, just needs a little work on it. All that is required then is an engine. This pump can be worked by hand if necessary.

I don't think you will find a woodstove too hot, not if you've worked one in Queensland because there's little difference in the climate. I can honestly say that and I bet it's not as warm as Townsville or Darwin. A lot of kerosene stoves are used here too, like the one you sent in the cutting. You'll be using these things Alice as you say and of course I welcome any suggestions - just the sort of interference I welcome and you know more about this side of it than me. If I do any boasting about your cooking at work, and we ask someone to dinner, you'll need the right gear to produce the goods. I still say leave your money in Australia for the future though. We'll get things here alright.

13 September 1953 c/o Public Works Department, Northern Rhodesia. Dearest Alice, Received your latest yesterday and so I wondered what I had struck at first glance at the colour pink, but you must admit it has a rather more romantic appearance than the common black colour. Someone had evidently taken a liking to the stamp on the envelope too, which was missing. You'd be interested to hear that I have bought a refrigerator, an Electrolux three and a half cubic feet paraffin kerosene model. It belonged to our machine shop foreman who is getting married and whose future wife has one already. At £40 it was too good to pass by, the new price being £85 here and I beat three other chaps at work to it, giving him a cheque as soon as I saw it. One of them told me his wife is after my blood for getting in first, but he who hesitates is lost.

I made another acquisition this week, a cocker spaniel puppy and he is a little darling, so knowing and full of life. You'll love him I'm sure. His mother and father have a pedigree as long as my arm I'm told. I've seen them both and they are beauties. I'll bring him down on the run to the Cape for company. He will take a back seat later of course after the *Arawa* gets in. He was born on Coronation Day 2 June, and I thought of calling him Hilary but I thought against that. It's a girl's Christian name really besides being a bit of a mouthful to call out, so I've called him Sherpa after the hill tribesmen that climbed with the Everest expedition.

Some setbacks

15 September. Here we are again. Sorry I finished so abruptly but I was interrupted suddenly. On Sunday (last night) Ed and I spent some time at the police station which spoilt the evening. We went to report the theft from our caravan of a pair of shoes and most serious, an automatic pistol of mine. We have a strong suspicion about who it is - a native houseboy we had to recently fire - and I only hope they pick him up and get it from him. We're pretty worried about it all.

18 September 1953 c/o *Public Works Department, Northern Rhodesia.* Dearest Alice, I received your lengthy letter on Wednesday afternoon. Also the parcel of engagement cards which I will read to eliminate any risk of me wanting to see them as soon as you leave the ship, also the two *Digests* which I have nearly read. It's been a bad week for us here perhaps the worst luck I've ever had in one week before. I told you about the other things stolen. Now on Wednesday evening one of our brick makers walked in nine miles from where we are building to tell us that the tent that they were sleeping in, and which contained most of our tools, was completely burnt out there. Story is that three Afrikaan speaking Europeans came in a truck during the night threw petrol on the tent and set it alight. One set of tracks led off into the bush but there should be two if someone came and went. The stories are very mixed and the police are working on it now. The police say it is a very puzzling affair. I thought at first they may have burnt the tent accidentally and wanted an excuse but the tire tracks rule that out coming from the bush where no truck has ever been before.

The brick makers appear very frightened to talk and the police told us that they had also lost everything they had. There is something fishy somewhere but will try and get to the bottom of it. I've got to explain to the government now about their tent. We have no enemies we know of here but if they're trying to scare us off for some reason they will have to try something better than that. Very shortly we intend moving from this government camp site in Lusaka out to our place permanently, water or no water. There is water of a sort in the creek and I've possibly drunk worse in the Australian bush. So much for our troubles here, if they never get any worse it won't be so bad I suspect.

22 September Tuesday. Sorry I'm slipping up again over getting this letter away. All the same, there's such a lot doing here lately. Your latest letter reached me today. I read it sitting on a fallen tree a little way from our camp this evening. We have moved out to our land now lock, stock and barrel. Everything is chaotic, can't find a thing hardly. It'll take a week to settle down, always does when you make a new camp it takes awhile to find a place for everything.

Glad to hear you still love me Alice, in absence although the weeks are going steady towards that day in April. I feel the same toward you and always thinking of us and what it will be like when we are here together and able to discuss things big and small. I mightn't be as rich in worldly goods as some but I'm certain we will get by alright Alice.

6 October 1953 c/o *Public Works Department, Northern Rhodesia.* I felt dog tired last night, didn't get back from work 'till 7:30pm and by the time I've eaten it's getting fairly late.

That's something you will need to bear sometimes. It doesn't happen very often except when there's something to do a good way out of town. We cover country a hundred miles either side of the workshop in Lusaka so there's a bit of travelling to do at times and I don't always get back within regular hours. It'll be lovely to come back home to you after being out on a government job somewhere, dinner waiting and able to relax. I promise not to bore you with stories about work except outstanding ones Alice. All I will want to hear is how you, the house and farm are going on.

I have a pretty ambitious program of development next year which will give you plenty of scope too. It will still be fairly primitive here when you arrive, though we've made an impression since May. We are held up for cash more or less now as far as the house goes. The three natives we have are making a garden and tree felling at present. Ed and I are hurrying along building a small storeroom and bathroom, also a cooking shelter (all brick with iron roof), before the rain comes which will be in about three weeks. It is a bit trying in the open then as you can imagine.

You will have your hands full bossing up the garden. Do you know anything about chickens Alice? I have an idea that may be a good thing to have a go at if it's done properly. If you have an ambition to be a farmer at all there's plenty of scope here. I think it'll be wonderful building something up out of the bush to something approaching civilisation. I don't think there can be too many places in the world that you can do it as easily as in Rhodesia, especially with the future prospects under Federation.

14 October 1953 c/o Public Works Department, Northern Rhodesia. Hello again Alice my dear, Since Tuesday I have been away in Broken Hill installing an engine and water jumping plant and only got home about an hour ago. I'll see Ed when I go to town in the morning so just now it's still and quiet for writing to you Alice and I should say right now that I love you so and I won't need much practice to tell you so either next year.

I must tell you about the two men I met at Broken Hill in the hotel. One is from Hobart and had been on the line there for twenty-two years, last back in Australia two years ago for a holiday. I know the Hobart Derwent Valley fairly well from when I worked there after I first left home, so he thought I was a great fellow. The other chap, much younger is a South African who stowed away on a ship to Australia so that he could go into the army there. He was fined £10 and allowed to do so, meeting a Melbourne girl later whom he married and brought to Rhodesia when the war ended. She is on her way from Melbourne on the *Arawa* after a holiday and gets into the Cape on the 28 October. I told him about you and I Alice and that you were also coming on the *Arawa* next March. It is only five months now you know dear, until we sign up for life.

17 October Well Ed arrived home last night on a bicycle and he was full of woe about his van. Some bolts had broken on a shock absorber. Anyway we went in this morning and I helped him fix things up again. It is very warm tonight, sticky and I am sitting here in the caravan without a shirt on, the kerosene light throws off a lot of heat. I am alone. Ed has gone to town but Sherpa is frisking around chewing a sock of mine which if it's smell was any indication when I took it off, must be very tasty. There is half a moon out and it is quite light. Everything it's very still except for a dog barking in the distance.

Everything is progressing fairly well on the place and next week three natives are starting to make bricks for us by contract, even though they must roll water by the drum. Tomorrow we are starting to roof our temporary quarters and by the time you arrive we will have quite a respectable camp. The next thing will be a room for Ed to sleep in. We think the house may be ready next October or thereabouts, but the temporary place should be cosy enough until then. There will be no rain for six months after your arrival which will be all the better. I will make a sketch to give you an idea of the setup. We will use the government supplied caravan as a bedroom Alice and I assure you it is very comfortable. It is the latest design and I have had it since new. The tarpaulin fly is of generous size and could be the living room. The tent that went with it was what I had burnt down - still an unsolved mystery.

22 October 1953 c/o Public Works Department, Northern Rhodesia. Lusaka is growing fast. You can notice it month by month, always something new being started. The main street, Cairo Road is chaos right now, has been for six months and will be for a lot longer as there are drainage and water pipes being put down. New buildings are going up fast on either side and the town has a distinct progressive air about it. You'll see what I mean next year. It has still not been decided where the federal capital will be. It may be Livingstone being on the border. Lusaka is the northern capital or state capital you would say in Australia, Salisbury the southern and Nyasaland is the junior partner of the Federation of course.

No further rain has fallen yet and it is extremely humid. We want rain in one way but not in another as the roads become very bad and muddy. I went outside just now and what I thought to be a bushfire for a second or two turned out to be a nearly full moon resting among the trees and a golden copper colour and a lovely sight. I wish you were here to share. Instead I have to dream away on my own and take ages to write like you do. Sometimes I think of all these little things we will share together one day. It's getting pretty late now and I see this is page seven so I'll knock off for the time being. A lot of work here tomorrow so good night Alice dearest, my thoughts are with you now, as they are so often.

25 October 1953 Sunday evening. I have been hard at it all day long setting the new camp in order. I guessed right about Sherpa he's in everyone's way and has been called lots of names today. We haven't had any more rain yet but it won't be long by the feel of that humidity. It's this weather especially that you appreciate the fridge. It is luxury to have cold water and ice instead of lukewarm though the water bag isn't too bad. It's luxury to hear ice clinking after being in the sun for a few hours. I'm glad you're okay now after the vaccine. You must certainly be allergic to it after the trouble you've had, and it must've taken well.

Just thinking, it's five months almost now until you land here and I'm wondering what your honest impressions of Africa and Lusaka will be. I'll feel like Lochinvar riding over the southern border into this country with you. I only hope you're not put out by the quietness here and get used to seeing so many black faces about. It doesn't worry us a scrap now of course and it's amazing how soon you become used to everything though the first month or two are strange, until you find your feet among a race of a different colour.

There are two European races here as in South Africa, English and Afrikaans, speaking the only official language English. Most of the farmers here are Afrikaans and about half the population. You'll notice the names outside farms along the roads. Africa is quite a mixture and a lot of people have no love for the other. It's all very puzzling to a stranger to follow, but you can feel the atmosphere in South Africa especially.

25 October 1953 Springvale Road, Donvale. Dear Bill, Here I have been writing for weeks and weeks and at intervals telling you to take care of yourself, and you promptly burn yourself with a welding torch and get sunstroke too so please take care of yourself. I hope this letter finds you well. Anyway talking of sunstroke I'd better be moving myself. The sun is rather warm and as I'm in a sun frock and hatless my bareback is no doubt a little roasted. As a matter of fact it is still a bit brown from last year. Sandy is becoming attentive again. I'm afraid this letter will smell rather doggy for he has just licked the pages and tried to push it off my lap with his nose. You'd never recognise him as the pup mum got last Christmas. He has grown and is a beautiful golden colour.

Talking of your plans in one of your letters written from Springs in January 1952 you say, 'George and I are full of ideas of getting out into the bush here up to North Rhodesia where the copper mines are paying pretty well. We have set our mind on not going home too. We have a car each and something besides a sort of souvenir to show we haven't been knocking about for nothing'. Well I've been thinking you've got your car now and there is something besides, for one thing you'll have me to take home and probably a child, so maybe your friends will think you haven't been knocking about for nothing. After all life sure is interesting.

31 December 1953 Springvale Road, Donvale. Darling Bill, I really can't give much of an answer to the question about whether we'll end up in Aussie or not until I've had a taste of African life. On the surface it would seem more reasonable to stay put in your job with the assurance of six months leave every three years with your fare paid than be somewhere in the north of Australia with none of these extras. What I'm saying is if we have to go as far as the Gulf country we might as well go back to where your prospects are better or at least stay there long enough to get a bit behind us. If we have to leave Rhodesia because I'm a home sick Aussie then I should think I'd be just as sick in the Gulf country, but as I said before Bill I'll have to try Africa first and by the way the natives may be the deciding factor.

5 January 1954 Broken Hill, Southern Rhodesia. Dearest Alice, here we go again answering two of your letters this time, one of 13 December starting 'Hello there' and the other just received dated 16 December, written after you had received a late addition from me. It's really no novelty for me to be answering two of your letters and we've had words over that before. (I had better let sleeping dogs lie anyway). It won't be long now and we will be saying, 'hello there' every day Alice my love - anyway for the rest of this year and always. It will certainly be a lasting year in both of our lives - the most important single thing we've ever done, once we've pitched in together for better or for worse. Time is getting close now and we will soon be knowing what it all means I guess.

I've had a very quiet Christmas and New Year holiday really, exactly the opposite to last year I must say. As far as work goes it has been busy. On Monday 28 December three of us were called out to Broken Hill hospital on the water supply breakdown. From 6:00am Monday none of us slept until

9:00pm Tuesday. That's thirty-nine hours straight working. Then from Wednesday 6:00am through to 6:00pm Thursday, another thirty-six hours. You can imagine we were pretty done in. However, it's all in a day's work and I do hope you won't feel too browned off about my sudden disappearance say if I'm still in this department when you arrive. Actually I'm away now in Broken Hill again, left Lusaka yesterday and hope to be back again on Thursday. That's if the job is finished and not much time is wasted.

Letter To William Latimer, Esquire C/O P.W.D. Lusaka. 19 January 1954. Dear Sir, Thank you for your letter of the eighth instant together with a Northern Rhodesia money order value £53. Our official receipt is attached hereto, and I will notify the principles in Melbourne that they may issue a passage ticket to your fiancé Miss Alice White who should present her passport when she calls on them for identity purposes.

Regarding sailings from Cape Town to New Zealand in 1955: We wish to advise that the Arawa is being withdrawn from service at the end of 1954 and although a new tourist all first class passenger liner of 20,000 tons is at present under construction and is expected to commence service during 1955, we regret that at this stage we do not have any indication of sailing dates. Should you be interested we can offer you definite accommodation by the all first class liner Dominion Monarch which sails outward from Cape Town on 15th of April and 2nd September 1955. Yours faithfully, W. M. Anderson and Co Pty Limited.

23 January 1954 c/o *Public Works Department, Lusaka, Northern Rhodesia.* Yes Alice camping out in Africa must be made with discretion depending on what part of the country you are in. Between Cape Town and Durban it is as safe as your back garden as far as hungry animals go. In other parts if you can't get to a hotel you sleep with an easier mind inside the car. I would say there is more danger, if it exists, from humans more than animal prowlers. There's no real need to be uneasy about Southern Africa dear as you will find out. I should mention I am going down via Salisbury, Southern Rhodesia, Johannesburg, Bloemfontein in the Free State to Cape Town. This is a monotonous drive but the shortest route. The Orange Free State is flat featureless country with very few trees.

2 February. Well dear here I go again. I'm taking long enough about it this time too. I've been down at Choma a hundred and seventy-five miles from Lusaka and one hundred and twenty-five miles from Livingstone, installing an engine and electric power plant. So that's my excuse this time. I could've finished this down there but I didn't have the right atmosphere at the hotel so I let it slide 'till I came back. Still haven't got the right atmosphere really and won't have until I feel you in my arms at long last. Next month will soon be here now and Melbourne will slip behind you for the time being. You will find Africa excitingly new after living at home and me as well probably.

3 February 1954 c/o *Public Works Department, Lusaka, Northern Rhodesia.* The most important factor here is the African who out numbers us so vastly and who is becoming more politically conscious as each month passes. We are all used to them now but to a woman from an all European country they may seem different. I personally would go anywhere within reason and I obviously wait for your outlook after say one week in Lusaka and out where we are. You'll probably be quite happy about everything and my fears are groundless. That's how I want it to be because this isn't a country of fear as yet, and we hope never will be. We'll have plenty of time to talk about that after you've arrived.

You've got one big advantage dear and that is to start off as a country girl. At least you're just as much at home out of a city. A city to me now is a place to visit and they're not a place to live in if it can possibly be avoided, a place of work but a person wants peace and quiet where he's living and sleeping. Lusaka can be quite busy enough at times as small as it is and Cairo Road is a nightmare in a car quite often. I wonder what you will think of Lusaka. To me it's a fairly happy go lucky town. A one horse town that's outgrown itself is my impression. It's got just about everything you could want really even a few neon lights as well.

13 February 1954 c/o Public Works Department, Lusaka, Northern Rhodesia. Hello there Alice dear, I nearly wrote Mrs Latimer! Another letter arrived from you on Tuesday. A parcel of magazines came today which up to a few minutes ago I have been looking through. The royal tour article about New Zealand makes me dreamy about the old homeland. Nice colour photo of Wellington - looks better than it really is. Of course pictures of Waitomo, Lake Wakatipu and Rotorua make me think that we'll be back there together shortly when I'm on long leave. I had grand times there with the boys in our holidays. I'll have an even better time next when we see these places together. Probably bore you with stories of my past excursions before I left home.

21 February Sunday. I've been working on the car today Alice and Ed has been putting iron on the roof in the blazing sun. It has been a really hot and rather unusual day. I woke about 5:00am this morning to hear a wind roaring in the trees and thunder. I rushed outside closing all the windows and throwing some bricks on the sheeting and just made shelter again as rain started to lash down on my bare skin – it really came down for an hour before moving on at 6:00am. Beautiful morning, then at five this afternoon another heavy shower came down but now it is quite humid again. The rains finish next month and then really beautiful weather begins. The nights can be chilly but the days are always cloudless, warm and sunny. Even if the nights are chilly, isn't that one of the advantages of having a wife Alice? (I guess I'm getting cheekier as our time drawers nearer!)

We hope to have work started on a bore hole about July. It'll be a great day when water comes up first because it's quite inconvenient at times. There's so much to do that progress seems slow but we've made quite a show in comparison with six months ago. I'll feel so much more like doing things after you're here Alice so all my love again. It won't be long. Yours always, Bill.

Letter from the Principal Immigration Officer. P. O. Box 6, Cape Town, South Africa.. PJT/MJ. IM.2104/52. 25 February 1954. Sir, I have the honour to advise that Mr William Cecil Latimer, engineer and fitter with the Public Works Department

Lusaka, states that his fiancé Miss A. White formally of Donvale Melbourne Australia is scheduled to arrive at Cape Town on or about the 8 April 1954. Mr Latimer intends meeting the ship and will be marrying Miss White in Cape Town and I would confirm that there will be no objection to their entry to this territory.

I have the honour to be your Obedient Servant, Chief Immigration Officer. cc Mr W. C. Latimer (whose letter of 17 February 1954 refers). cc Chief Immigration Officer, P.O. Box 583, Bulawayo.

PART 2: ALICE ARRIVES

6 March 1954 c/o Public Works Department, Lusaka, Northern Rhodesia. I have been up at Broken Hill since Monday. I will start to moan about all this travelling after we get back from our honeymoon. Some of the others might get their share of travelling then. As it is I'm the only single fellow so I don't mind much. I can earn a bit extra too. So this is the month the merry, merry month. I've just noticed I've put February on the heading must be getting a bit dreamy these days, more than usual. This is my last letter to you at home Alice do you realise that? It will just about reach you the day before you sail westward-ho.

Just now we are paying £40 a month between Ed and me for land payment so have got to take it a bit easy. Ed is definitely going to get started building whatever happens. Norma isn't keen on living in the bush out of town but Ed's going on with building whatever happens and he's a pretty stubborn fellow, won't be pushed around much. He's changed a lot since you first saw him briefly. Well I think so anyway. It's no use to be worried over Ed at all. He's got his own way to go but at present it suits both of us to put in together. We don't get on so well together either at times. I guess we are opposites as far as natures go. He is inclined to be the impatient, hard driving kind. I'm more easy-going and lazier I suppose. I've always liked the company of friends like George and others and some of the fellas I've worked with here too. They'd do me a good turn any time and I'd do the same for them.

Married in Cape Town

9 April 1954 Letter from Alice to her parents. Durban South Africa. Dear Mum and Dad, Yesterday I saw land for the first time for two weeks since leaving Australia. It really was an event. We tied up about mid-day at Durban and soon afterwards the ship was alive with natives carrying parcels, running messages or preparing to unload cargo. The ones unloading were the most interesting. They chant the whole time. I suppose it means something to them for they all heave at the same time. I've been watching them in the hold. The gang bosses are dressed in khaki uniform and carry business-like weapons, one being a long stick with a round knob on the end. It is surprising how quickly one gets used to seeing the natives working everywhere. At first we felt we were watching a film, now I find it very easy to pick the Indian from the

African native, sorting them into their tribes is another matter though.

Yesterday we went ashore and had a marvellous time. Durban really is a wonderful place. I'll send some photos later. Marine Parade is something never to be forgotten with its tall buildings of flats, each one being of a different design to its neighbour. Well cut lawns in the centre of the Parade and across the road the sea-front with its snake pit, sunken gardens, fun parlours, swimming baths and anything else one could wish for. Rickshaw boys all dressed up put on quite a dance to attract the attention of the tourist and Indian women walk the streets with baskets on their heads and bead bracelets and necklaces in their hands selling to anyone who will stop. We were looking at some and within minutes we had twelve or fourteen around us so had quite a selection.

I was very thrilled when I got back to the ship and received a telegram from Bill. 'Happy land-fall - see you Saturday.' Poor me, we evidently don't leave here 'till some time tomorrow. Cheerio once again, love Alice.

Bill and Alice marry in Cape Town 13 April 1954

18 April 1954 Tuesday. From Alice's Diary, Cape Town South Africa. A middle-aged couple travelling on the *Arawa* from New Zealand came to our wedding in the Methodist cathedral, Green Market Square, Cape Town. He, Mr Baker by name, gave me away. The Methodist minister drove me to the ceremony and afterwards we were invited to the manse for an afternoon tea wedding breakfast. Another lady was at the ceremony, I think she must have been a friend of the minister.

Bill had been living at this hotel Rhodesia by the Sea for a week before I arrived and the staff and a few guests he had been talking to were most interested. This hotel sits with its back against the hills and is most attractive. The service is very good, all servants being natives. Our room overlooks the front drive and rockery. The view finishes with the mountains on the opposite side of the bay. It is a lovely spot twenty-five miles from Cape Town. One couple told us last night just before they left that we had given them quite a thrill, took them back fifteen years to their own wedding. Leaving Cape Town we passed through the suburb where Mr and Mrs Sanderson live. We are going to go there tomorrow for afternoon tea and will then go on to Cape Town to the Sunday church service at the church where we were married.

Yesterday we went for a drive to Cape Point. The last few acres of the Point are a reserve for animals. No wild game of course just some kind of deer and baboons. We didn't see any deer it was a bit early in the afternoon, but we were most excited to see a whole lot of baboons. They are an average sized monkey, not very big and were most cheeky. A few cars had stopped to look at the old man one sitting on a post and two others nearby, so we stopped too – we looked and saw ever so many more among the undergrowth. We quickly shut the car windows and then had a wonderful time watching these monkeys in their natural home. Someone had thrown away a piece of paper and one monkey was busy chasing it and tearing it to shreds. Another sitting on a post feeding her baby was methodically de-fleaing it and giving herself a scratch at intervals. I put a piece of biscuit through the car window on the side of the road but quickly pulled my hand in as a big one landed on the bonnet. It sat there looking through the window at us and scratching itself. Then along came the one with the brown paper up onto the bonnet and then onto the luggage rack on top, dragging the paper behind him.

We drove slowly to watch several others playing about, still carrying the one on the bonnet. It had seen the biscuits on my lap and grabbed the car door handle in an effort to get them but I had hold of the handle on the inside. They are as cunning as could be. It was a wonderful experience. Can you imagine it? Driving along with one monkey on the luggage rack jumping about and another one sitting on the bonnet looking in? It really was amusing.

18 April 1954 Sunday. Bill says two more pages won't make this overweight so I'll tell you a little more about this hotel. It sit against the mountains, as I said before. The mountains here look very weather beaten and rugged with very little growth around the base and nothing at all higher than halfway. From Cape Town to Cape Point is a distance of about forty miles. It is very flat land. It is a peninsula with the Indian Ocean on one side and the Atlantic on the other. The mountains rise from the water on both sides and the draft through the valley seems to draw in the clouds. They hit the mountains about halfway up and follow them along through the valley from one ocean to the other. Because of this the scenes are continually changing. The hotel dining room windows show an uninterrupted view and I find it fascinating to watch these changing scenes as we eat. At night, the scene changes once again as the lights from the surrounding beach towns begin to twinkle as night approaches. The dining room waiters are a source of interest to me. They are dressed in suits with white jackets and under these are blue and white striped waistcoats. I'll leave the rest of this page to your son-in-law:

Message from Bill. Hello everyone over there at Donvale. I'm happy to have become one of the family on Tuesday and thank you for everything you've done and so many lovely presents that were given. Especially I would like to thank you Mr and Mrs White for giving me Alice and seeing that she eventually got on the ship after the unfortunate delay. I know it must be a little sad for you that we couldn't be married from your house but I promise she'll be looked after throughout her life with me and look forward to seeing all of you towards the end of next year. We are very, very happy together and having a wonderful time here. We are looking forward to starting the long journey to Northern Rhodesia on Tuesday. To each and all of you I send my thanks again. Very Sincerely, Bill.

Honeymoon drive to Lusaka

20 April 1954 Tuesday. Dear mum and dad, This is the letter in diary form I promised to send explaining our trip and I know that you will show it to others who are interested. No doubt you'd find it more interesting if you followed our trip on the map marking the places as you come to them. I think the atlas was left in the bottom cupboard of the bookcase in the boys' room. (Suddenly writing that bit I felt very far from home! I could hear dad calling out for his dinner long before you finish reading this.)

It is a week since we were married and we picked up our luggage and left *Rhodesia by the Sea* at Simonstown. We've been very happy there. Through the huge window on the east wall we had a lovely view of the sea and each morning as we drank our early morning tea we would watch the sun come up over the mountains on the other side of the Bay. We took a photo of the sunrise one morning and are keen to see the result but now that part of our honeymoon is over and we felt a little sad as we left that lovely hotel. As we moved off down the drive we promised ourselves we would stay there again in August next year.

We drove the twenty-five miles into Cape Town where we stocked up our tucker box and bought a few cooking utensils. As we travelled through the ever changing country we saw very few Europeans. We had a glorious view of the sea as we climbed the mountains on the highway known at that point as Sir Lowry's Pass. The mountains are very rugged and have very little vegetation, just a few scrubby trees. The mountains rise 1,500 feet above sea level there and after reaching the top we went on through mountains where thousands of pine trees have been planted. The whole of the Union has concentrated on planting pines, Australian gumtrees and wattle trees making these districts very Australian. Pines are planted on the mountain or where huge washouts are forming due to heavy rains and erosion. When the pines are planted on more level ground they are surrounded by several rows of gum trees. Some of the bigger trees are felled and are cut into props for the gold mines.

Coming into flat or undulating country we saw several farms and apple orchards. We met a few trucks loaded with apples. The top cases had apples piled high making it look more like a load of stones. I was able to understand why fruit in the shops were so bruised. One farm had a flock of most unusual sheep known as Karakul. They have white wool on their bodies and black wool on their head and neck. Their wool is valuable. They are a hardy breed which is fortunate as they would never survive otherwise.

Caledon, a hundred and nineteen miles from Cape Town was the first big town we came to. We stopped and had tea there boiling the kettle beside a stream - our first meal on the road. It was a most peaceful setting far removed from the days when I learnt about 'darkest Africa' at school. We might have been having tea on the banks of the Yarra River at Warrandyte. We travelled another sixty-seven miles to Swellendam where we stayed the night at the Commercial Hotel. Afrikaans is spoken in all these towns set back from the coast. They can speak English too for it is taught in the schools but Afrikaan is spoken most of the time. Well, that was our first day and we were only a hundred and eighty-six miles from Cape Town.

21 April 1954 Wednesday. We did two hundred and forty-six miles today and stayed the night in a very nice log cabin high in the mountains. This place is known as a forest wayside place for travellers. The cabins are very comfortable and all furniture is made of pine milled in the forests surrounding it. We had an interesting day. The first unusual sight was fourteen miles from Mossel Bay where we saw four ostriches feeding with a herd of cattle. We stopped at Mossel Bay at 11:15am where we bought a few provisions. We took a snap of a Dutch Reformed Church there for its unusual design.

George was very pretty town on the Western Cape with oak lined streets, then came Knysna and we were almost on the sea again, the mighty Indian Ocean which stretches back to Australia. At Knysna we noticed a native cart being pulled by six native prisoners instead of the usual oxen or donkey, then on through the *Garden of Eden* and into more mountains. We stopped in these mountains to cook our tea and Bill took a snap of me as I bent over our frying pan. It was 7:30pm when we arrived at Forest Inn and its twinkling coloured lights looped from tree to tree was a welcome sight.

Cooking on the honeymoon trip

22 April 1954 Thursday. This morning we took a few snaps of Forest Inn before leaving. It was 8:45am when we left and we made Jeffrey's Bay, eighty miles distant our stopping place for lunch. We picked a lovely spot where we had a picnic ground and beach to ourselves. We climbed the sand dunes which separated the picnic ground from the sea and slid down the white sand on the other side and looked for shells for about half an hour. This place is famous for its shells and we found some pretty ones but so many are broken as the surf hurls them against the rocks.

Next stop before reaching Port Elizabeth at 3:00pm was when we met a native driving a team of oxen, his wife beside him and his small son pulled and tugged at the leader in a vain attempt to hurry those beasts with their terrific horn span. We took a snap of them and drove on. Port Elizabeth proved to be quite a big and thriving place. We stayed there about an hour then drove on, climbing once again. We saw several pineapple gardens. Then the light began to fade so we decided to have tea and camp in the car on the side of the road about six miles south of Nanaga.

23 April Friday. By 7:00am we were ready for the road again. This time the destination was East London, a hundred and fifty-three miles distant where we were to stay with Mr and Mrs McNally (Norma's parents and Bill's brother Ed's new parents-in-law). We passed through Grahamstown then through a native reserve where we saw quaintly painted rondavels (traditional huts). Each had tried to outdo his neighbour in artistic work and the result was somewhat like our so-called modern art. The next big town was King Williamstown where we stopped and had a look at the Museum which is well stocked with stuffed animals native to Africa. Leaving there we went on to East London arriving there about midday and stayed the night at the McNally home.

24 April 1954 Saturday. Next day was Saturday and we wanted to be in Durban for a week so we left McNally's flat early hoping to do the four hundred and thirty-one miles to Durban by nightfall. The sights on that journey proved very interesting for we travelled through the Transkei where the natives have changed very little. They still paint themselves and wear very little clothing, although they have a fancy for bracelets, anklets and necklaces of every variety. Small, naked children minding herds of cattle would run to the road side to wave and shout a greeting, yet if we stopped they were too shy to say a word. They seem to like to build their huts near the roads and we saw several funny sights. One young woman was carrying a baby's bottle on her head complete with teat and they carry everything on their heads, from one pound of butter to a flock mattress. I have seen them carry huge cans of water on their heads and quite often they have real struggle to get it up there, but once there they never spill a drop. Usually they have a baby on their back as well. Some of their farms look quite prosperous, due no doubt to help from the government agricultural schools for natives. Others are very primitive.

Peering through a cloud of dust, I found it was caused by three natives driving eight oxen. They had the oxen hitched to a huge bundle of sticks which they tied together with rope. One native man I saw had his face painted orange and he really looked hideous as he looked at us, his white teeth and round eyes seeming to gleam in his orange face. They build round kraals by interlacing sticks where they keep their cattle at night. A native is prosperous or not according to the number of cattle he owns and woe-betide the boy who loses any of the stock he is set to watch.

Goats are very plentiful. We found herds of them grazing everywhere and quite a lot of sheep were on these farms too. The native women seem to be continually washing. They meet at a creek or waterhole and laugh and talk. When washed they spread the clothes on grass or bushes to dry. What clothes they do own seem to be all worn at the one time. One small boy we saw had two jackets on but no trousers. The roads through this hilly native country were rather rough and very dusty and it was 6:00pm before we reached the coast again at Point Shepstone.

We were looking forward to the highway drive along the coast to Durban, a journey of eighty-four miles, but came to a detour just out of Point Shepstone and had to bounce along on it for about thirty miles. Eventually we reached Durban at 8:30pm where we had booked a lovely room, complete with bathroom at the Killarney Hotel, just a short distance from Durban‘s famous Marine Parade with its ultramodern hotels and flats, swimming baths, fun parlour, amphitheatre, miniature golf course, bowling club and snake pit. It is a most interesting place. No one seems to have anything to do except enjoy themselves. We watched the lifesavers training on the beach on the Sunday morning. Lots of other folk were watching too and most of them hire deckchairs which they erected on the sand and in no time there were rows and rows of deckchairs with their canvas tops waving in the breeze. Everything about Durban spells money and leisure, except perhaps the native markets where one can barter with the salesmen, mostly Indian, for almost anything.

25 April 1954 Sunday. Explored Marine Parade and ate at *The Doll's House* - a drive-in tea room.

26 April 1954 Monday. Before leaving Durban today we did quite a lot of shopping and also secured a visa to allow us into Portuguese East Africa. At 4:00pm we were on the road again travelling through the sugar cane fields of Natal then on into Zululand where the natives have changed very little.

There are times when one sees amusing contrasts as a native adopts a European way of doing things. One native man we saw had very little covering his body except numerous tails from all sorts of animals mostly fox tails, fastened onto a belt around his waist. He was quite confidently riding a bicycle and how these tails managed to keep from being caught in the spokes of the wheel as they floated about in the breeze I'll never know. A native who owns a bicycle is a very proud man and the loads they carry on it would amaze you. I've seen one with a huge bath tub on the back of his and another had his wife on the bar and his child on the carrier and often these passengers will be carrying a bag of something. What they carry in those odd shaped bundles, covered with a brightly coloured piece of material is anyone's guess.

Well we put a hundred and nineteen miles behind us that day and when night fell stopped about twenty miles from Eshowe and slept in the car. Next morning we enjoyed the curious stares of natives as we prepared breakfast. Most of them were on their way to their respective jobs but found time to stare at us. We travelled through hundreds of acres of wattle trees that morning and near Melmoth passed a tanning extract factory. The roads are rather hard on cars. During the day we stopped three times to adjust something.

We reached Golela at 3:40pm and then crossed the border into Swaziland which is also populated mostly by natives. In both Zululand and Swaziland *Employment Recruiting Stations* are quite common. There are native signs for work on mines in and near Johannesburg where they will live in a compound with hundreds of other natives from all over Africa, until their term has ended. He can then return to his tribe where he will flaunt his newly acquired knowledge and his pounds, shillings and pence until such time as his wealth runs out. Then the cycle can be repeated. Wild game is quite common in the sparsely populated parts of Africa, all types of buck being the most common. We startled an impala grazing near the road causing it to bound along in front of us for some distance. He was beautiful to watch as he leapt along covering yards with each graceful leap.

The native villages in Swaziland are more often than not quite close to the road as in Zululand, and the native children delight in running to the road side to wave and shout to the passing motorists. Their houses are most unusual and most unsubstantial being built of sticks interwoven then patched with grass, looking exactly like the old-fashioned beehive. They have no chimney as cooking is done on an open fire in the centre of their circular home and smoke makes its way out as best it can, quite often giving the impression the whole place is on fire.

That day we travelled two hundred and fifty-three miles stopping at 9:30pm to sleep once again in the car. However at 4:00am we were awakened by thunder and lightning and as the rain began to fall we decided we had better move on for the dirt roads can be very troublesome after rain and it proved to be a real downpour. We travelled to within five miles of Stegi the town which separates Swaziland from Portuguese East Africa, where we waited until daylight at 7:00am.

27 April 1954 Tuesday. When the garage opened we filled the petrol tank for we had no wish to buy expensive Portuguese petrol. It took about an hour to move the hundred yards or so across the border. First we drove through a gate and signed papers to satisfy the African Customs. Then another gate was opened and we drove about fifty yards to the Portuguese custom's shed where Bill had great trouble trying to make an official who couldn't understand much English realise we had only just been married, and although we had two passport books and mine still bearing my maiden name, we were legally married and the one visa was all that was needed. Well the marriage lines were produced and the fat little fellow poured over those. After convincing him that this visa, obtained in Durban, was all we needed to allow us to enter his country he sent his offsiders to search our car for anything dutiable. Fortunately they were not very thorough and we were eventually allowed to move on.

The country as in Swaziland is pretty poor looking. Forty miles from the border and we were in Lourenco Marques. We drove through the city and around the foreshore to the Chinese cafe where we managed to get a room for the night. I had some trouble finding the ladies' toilet but eventually stumbled on a door marked 'Senorita' and there it was. We couldn't even read the road signs, for naturally enough everything is written in their own language. After getting tidied up a bit we made our way into the city again intent on finding a place to eat. Unfortunately it was still raining so we did not see the city at its best for most cafes serve the customers in the open. Tables and chairs line the pavements, and walled-in gardens weather permitting, is where the population enjoys itself at these tables. All shops close at midday reopening around 3:00pm and toward evening the city usually wakes up and becomes as colourful as portrayed on the films.

28 April Wednesday. Early next morning we left the Chinese cafe and made our way back to the city passing through the camping area on the foreshore again where monkeys were having a wonderful time chasing one another around the rotunda and tents. It was a lovely sunny morning although the roads were still very wet and slippery on the outskirts of this fascinating city, with its houses and buildings of unusual and often quaint design. We stopped to buy fruit from natives here and we bought fifty-eight beautiful bananas for two shillings, paw paws and wooden hand-crafted ornaments from two little boys for two Afrikaan shillings apiece.

Next stop was the border where once again we spent an hour filling in forms, this time at Ressano Garcia, the border town between Portuguese East Africa and the Transvaal. We cooked a lunch at Marracuene on the banks of the Crocodile River. Moving on again we passed through lovely fertile valleys, for the Transvaal is farmed extensively. I was very interested in the orchards. Acres of citrus fruit are grown in these areas. Some have stalls on the roadside tended by natives and we stopped at one of these to buy oranges, lemons and grapefruit, all a penny each.

White River, one of the towns we passed through was very nice with lawns in the centre of the main street. It was here we turned off the main road for we intended spending that night at *Kruger National Park* . We arrived there at 4:30pm and secured a Rondavel (hut) at Pretorius Kopp. These camping sites within the park are very convenient and comfortable and are protected by an ordinary barbwire fence which seems to be sufficient protection for no fatalities have been reported.

We were ready for a cruise around the southern portion of the park early next morning, anxiously scanning the bush for wild game. We were very thrilled to see four cheetahs basking in the early morning sun about five miles from where we had camped. We sat in the car and watched those huge spotted cats playing and stretching or just basking there in the sun. Driving on again we saw zebra, giraffe, monkeys, buffalo, ugly looking wart hogs and even a harmless old tortoise making his way across the road with his usual slow gait. We saw hundreds of Impala too. They are so prettily marked, timid and very graceful in their movements.

By this time it was mid morning and we had arrived at the hippo pool where we were met by a native who carried a rifle. We left the car and were escorted to the water by the native and there we saw four huge hippos and a baby one which was really amusing. He would go to sleep for a little while with his head resting on his mother's ungainly body then he'd wake up, give one or two yawns opening a very big mouth for such a little fellow, then dive under the water coming up near one of the sleeping hippos and he would then try to wake one of them up, for he wanted to play, but no such luck they were all much too tired. For all this apparent lazing, hippos have been known to upset native canoes and bite it or it's occupant in half just for fun. We stayed quite a while watching these monsters of the river then made our way back to the main gates.

Once through them we were once more on the open highway and travelling through or around very mountainous country. (The author of *King Solomon's Mines* found material for his book in these mountains.) At 4:30pm we stopped to cook our tea on the banks of the Selati River. On our way again and darkness soon overtook us. At Tzaneen we took a shortcut to the main North South Road, bypassing Pietersburg. It was rather a rough and dusty shortcut with many detours of its own, and also narrow bridges. At one of these bridges we saw a very nice car on its back in the middle of the road, its lights still piercing the darkness. It had passed us a few miles back travelling rather fast and had evidently hit the inevitable hole near the bridge and overturned right outside the garage and Red Cross First Aid Post at the little town of Makutsi.

It was quite late when we finally stopped to spend what was left of the night in the car. We had done two hundred and eighty-three miles for the day, or at least what was left of the day after roaming around the park and we were just ten miles from Louis Trickardt. We camped at the side of the main Cairo to Cape Town Road.

27 April 1954 Dear mum and dad, I wrote a note to you the other day but haven't got a stamp for it yet so thought I'd write one of these letter cards just to let you know we are still safe and sound and enjoying our trip around the east of Africa. Yesterday we arrived in Portuguese East Africa and stayed at the capital in Lourenco Marques. We had a huge dinner at a cafe in the city: soup, boiled fish and vegetables, sausages fried in cabbage leaves, half a small round loaf of bread each and two beautiful bananas. It is the home of bananas and they are really beaut, not at all like the ones we buy at home. We bought five bunches for two shillings.

While Bill was in an Indian store several native boys came up to me selling souvenirs. They waited for Bill to go in the store. I had no more excuses but they said South African money would do, just two shilling six missus, so I said two shillings and got a nice little ornament of birds carved from wood and wired to a little log, also carved. It really is quite nice. Rain spoiled a day there really but this afternoon we are well on our way to the *Kruger National Park* and now here we are settled in our Rondavel - a round thatched room with two beds, table and two chairs and a few shelves. A native boy brings water and generally makes himself useful. We made pancakes and banana fritters on the community stoves and the native boy washed up. We have eaten about eighteen bananas between us today. Travelling through Transvaal today we saw acres of oranges and all citrus fruits also pawpaw. We bought oranges and lemons and grapefruit one-pence each. Flowers common in Queensland are growing everywhere. Hibiscus trees line the roads in many parts, the size of which would amaze you. They are as big as our peach trees. Travelling through Swaziland we saw hundreds of acres of wattle trees.

It is nearly time for bed now. All this travelling is rather tiring. It is hard to believe that African wild animals could be just the other side of the fence. I've yet to see them. Maybe we'll have some luck tomorrow as we cruise slowly around the park's roads. Unfortunately the northern part of the park is closed due to the rainy season and reopens on 22 May. I believe the game is more plentiful there. Good night and love to all from both of us. Alice.

29 April 1954 Thursday. From Alice's diary. We camped at the side of the main Cairo to Cape Town Road and were up early and had breakfast there much to the amusement of passing motorists. A few hailed us. Louis Trickardt was just waking up as we passed through the main street and as we climbed the Soutpansberg Mountains on the far side we had a lovely view of the town spread out in the valley below and of the highway beyond running straight across the plains on its way to Johannesburg - the 'City of Gold'. Pines were planted in these mountains as in most others we passed. It was about 8:30am when we stopped at Messina, a mining town and the last town we were to see in the Transvaal. Our next stop was the South African customs post at 10:00am on the south side of

Beit Bridge on the Limpopo River, then over the bridge to the Southern Rhodesian border. It was here I filled in a form giving all particulars of myself as Alice Latimer, wife of William Latimer then signed the thing A. White! By the time all this was over it was 11:00am and the sun a little hot.

1 May 1954 Saturday. Our destination today was the Zimbabwe Ruins one hundred and seventy-four miles from the border where we intend spending the weekend. We arrived here in time to have tea and get settled into the Rondavel allotted to us before dark.

2 May 1954 Sunday. We explored these remarkable ruins which were found about sixty years ago. Prospectors and wild game hunters have ripped quite a large area of the ancient walls in an effort to find gold, for it was quite obvious the original occupants had dealt it gold. Each wall is built of stone, each one placed on another with no mortar or anything else holding them together. They made use of and built around the huge boulders already in the hill and from there is a wonderfully clear view of the valley, reaching to the mountains some miles away. At the foot of the hill is the temple, the walls of which are ten to sixteen feet thick at the base, narrowing to eight or nine feet at the summit. Inside are several smaller walls and two conical towers, the largest of which is thirty-one feet high. Well, we did a lot of speculating as to the history and inhabitants of these ruins as have countless others before us. Then at the caretaker's hut we signed the visitor's book and bought a small wooden native carved axe.

3 May 1954 Monday. This morning we packed up and were ready for the road again at 8:00am. Native prisoners guarded by native police carrying rifles were already working near our Rondavel cutting and preparing grass for thatching. We stopped at Fort Victoria, twelve miles from the ruins and it was there I saw a funny sight. Evidently it was moving day for one family for down the street came a native and on his head was a cupboard and behind him two women. The first had a baby on her back and a cot on her head and the second one had a table and two chairs on her head. No one seemed in the least interested in their progress. Another native sticking to the native way of wearing all they possessed wore two hats on his head.

Next place of interest was a small town named Balla Balla where I had my first view of the asbestos mine which was just as white and dusty as a lime quarry. We did two hundred and five miles that day slipping into the Bulawayo camping area with engine trouble at 9:30pm. Thanks to the help given Bill by the garage man we were mobile again at midday, but we only did eighty miles when we decided it was too hot for driving so pulled into the side of the road and rested under the shade of a tree with the intention of travelling well into the night instead of in the heat of the day.

About 9:00pm we stopped at Wankie, a mining town and had a thermos of tea. It is there where one can visit the Wankie Game Reserve and although the highway does not go through the reserve the animals don't seem to have any respect for boundaries and often wander onto the highway, so notices such as 'Beware of Elephants' are quite common. All through this danger area I kept gazing into the shadows sure a herd of elephants would lurch onto the road in front of us, but all we saw was a few rabbits and two foxes who, dazzled by our lights ran for some distance in front of us. We were amazed at their speed for we did twenty-five miles an hour behind them all the way. We also hit and killed a young duiker (deer) that night which hurtled down an embankment and as our torch globe had fused, we were unable to find it.

A bit of excitement was at a detour when we had to drive down the bank of a river then across its stony bed to the opposite bank where I saw wet imprints on the sand, obviously made by a crocodile in hasty retreat at our approach.

Altogether a most interesting night and I didn't feel at all safe when we pulled up at 2:30am to wait for daylight. We were eight miles from the border between southern and northern Rhodesia and the mighty Victoria Falls. The roar of its falling waters could be heard from where we were quite distinctly. In daylight when we moved toward the border the cumulus cloud caused by the mist which hangs continually over the falls was clearly visible for miles, giving a preview to the sight awaiting us.

4 May 1954 Tuesday. We passed the Southern Rhodesian Customs and after more form filling booked a Rondavel in the camping area. Then we went into Livingstone and obtained a pass from the Northern Rhodesian customs gate on our way. Both forms were filled in there too of course. Later we admired the falls and walked about photographing them from different angles. It was still early morning and as the sun shone on the mist two rainbows perfected the picture. The Zambezi River is running high now being just after the wet season so that most of the time it was almost impossible to see the actual falls for the mist which fell like rain on the highway some distance away and also caused small waterfalls on the opposite side of the canyon.

A statue of the missionary Livingstone, who was the first European to see this wonder of nature, stands on a small clearing in full view of the island in the centre of the falls where he stood and no doubt marvelled at the size and beauty as we did.

At the camping area I saw two young men who had been on the ship *Arawa* with me, one an Aussie and the other an Englishman. They had brought motorbikes from Australia and their intention was to travel on them from Cape Town to Cairo, a rather hazardous journey on a motorbike. The roads in Rhodesia are often corduroy and very dusty but I'm told the roads here are much better than the roads further north which quite often are nothing more than bush tracks.

4 May 1954 c/o Public Works Department, Lusaka, Northern Rhodesia. Dear Mum and Dad, We are held up in Bulawayo today with a bit of car trouble but should be on our way again late this afternoon. We've about six hundred miles to do yet before we see Lusaka, maybe on Friday (9th.)

Last Friday as we drove around *Kruger National Park* in search of wild animals we really had a marvellous time. We saw dozens of Impala (a small kind of deer, very pretty) zebras and buffalo. The zebras were lovely, so sleek and fat too. So were the giraffe. They are much bigger than ones we have seen in zoos. We rounded one corner of the road and surprised a huge giraffe on the road and three others were standing behind a tree gently leaning down to nip leaf buds from the top of the tree. Bill stopped the car and I put one foot on the ground leaning out of the car to get what I hope will be a good snap of the one on the road. I felt about as big as threepence as it turned and looked down on me. They are very gentle animals and graceful and I believe harmless. We saw a wart hog which looked anything but harmless, an ugly looking thing like a pint sized hippo with two tusks protruding from its jaw. Later we stopped and had a cup of tea. Imagine having a cup of tea in a wild game reserve - sounds so matter of fact doesn't it! But really I could quite believe we are in Australia most of the time the country is so similar.

While waiting for Bill I have our washing hanging native fashion on thorn bushes. Of course the native life soon makes one realise this is not Australia. I haven’t yet got used to the way the native children run to the road when they hear a car and shout and wave as we drive by. I feel like the queen or something as I wave back. We noticed it most in Zululand and Swaziland where it is almost impossible to find a white person.

Our trip is nearly over. We've done 2,676 miles so far and are not even half way through Africa. It certainly is a huge country. Most places we have cooked our lunch and tea on the road, breakfast too on the few times we have slept in the car. Don't worry about us for we get along fine. You should see Bill he is singing most of the time. I tell him he looks like a kitten that has just had a basin of cream and he just gives a silly grin.

We have been through seven customs gates so far and filled in endless forms and still have the Northern Rhodesian one to go through. I wrote my name as Alice Harriet Latimer and then signed one 'A. White' which I had to cross out and sign again. Love to all. Take care of yourselves. Love Alice and Bill.

5 May 1954 Wednesday. From Alice's diary. At Livingstone, we had a disappointing drive around the three hundred acre game reserve seeing only one zebra and a few buck. We were now only two hundred and sixty miles from Lusaka, the capital of Northern Rhodesia which is to be our home for the next eighteen months.

6 May 1954 Thursday. We started out on the last lap of our journey. At Kaloma Road surveyors were busy and had a beach umbrella attached to a long stick protecting them from the hot Rhodesian sun. It looked really funny and rather out of place to see a beach umbrella hundreds of miles from the sea. Later we surprised a band of monkeys playing on the road. Not far from Choma we overtook the motorbike travellers and stopped to talk with them for about half an hour. They had left Livingstone the day before. They didn't look much like the young men of ship board days for apart from the dust covered clothing, helmet and goggles they wore they were also sporting beards. I've since heard they have passed through Lusaka. Well after that little chat we moved on again stopping at Monze for lunch – a typical Rhodesian small town with stores run mostly by Indians and the usual cluster of two or three natives lolling about.

We had a wonderful seventeen days on the road and a lovely week at Simonstown but now the job of living begins, and for me learning to adapt myself to housekeeping in a new country. Ruben the native boy came running from the compound which is a short distance from the house to welcome Bill and await orders and I suppose to have a look at the new *donna* that *bwana Bill* had bought home. I felt very strange, rather an alien really but now we've settled in quite nicely.

Culture shock

6 May 1954 From Alice's Diary: It was 8:30pm and dark when Bill and I finally pulled up at his home nine miles from

Lusaka (the capital city of Northern Rhodesia). The next morning we looked around the property discussing plans for the future - the borehole being the immediate priority - and then on Monday morning Bill left for work at 7:00am and I made a home for Bill, cooking, organising and writing letters home.

Accommodation on Bill's bush block

10 May 1954 Lusaka Farm. Dear mum and dad, It is very hard to describe Africa it is much too big. All the groceries I buy all the notices, in fact everything in the Union is written in two languages, English and Afrikaans. That is just one of the things I'm getting used to and I'm growing to like it all too. At 7:00am every week day Bill drives off to the Public Works

Department in Lusaka leaving me to my chores. Ruben understands a little English.

17 May 1954 Lusaka Farm. Yesterday Bill's brother Ed and his new wife Norma were here for the day. Ed's car has so much wrong with it that it has finally refused to go so Bill spent the day working on it while Ed did a bit more to the room they are building. Later it will be a garage but he and Norma will live in it until their house is built. The bricks are made of the red soil here and then burnt. The mortar is dirt from ant hills mixed with water which sets like concrete. After the walls are done they smooth the mortar on for a nice finish, a most economical way to build for the native brick makers don't get paid very high wages. The wood used for burning is from the bush block and the bricks are made on the place. Water is the main problem as we haven't got a bore.

Bill buys milk and bread each day on his way home from work in Lusaka and I do the rest of the shopping on Saturday mornings. I go with Bill and meet him at 12:30pm when he finishes work. He is quite busy doing different things here to make us more comfortable. I don't know whether we will be keeping Ruben or not yet. I sometimes think I'd find it easier to do things myself. The trouble is he wants more pay and he already gets as much as a town worker and he only works four and a half hours each day. Anyway we'll see how things go later on.

24 May 1954 Lusaka Farm. It's Monday again and a holiday from work for Bill. He is busy making brick-boxes. Each box holds four bricks. Six natives have been employed to make 40,000 bricks at two pounds per thousand. Then when they have been made and baked they'll be ready for use. The native workers are setting up the camp at the moment near the creek and have cleared quite an area of flat ground ready for laying out the bricks. Bill says the workers seem quite good and anyway, there is nothing to lose when they are working by contract. It is up to them how much they get done. They were lucky to find an ant hill right near the creek so we will soon see the bricks piling up.

We are taking only one third of the total bricks. Ed is paying two thirds of the bill because he wants to build a house as soon as possible. We'd rather stay where we are and save some money before we think of building.

We are getting our little shack quite comfortable. By that I mean Bill can now go to a shelf or cupboard and get what he wants without asking first, 'What did you do with . . . . ?', or 'where are my papers now?', or 'have you seen . . . .'? Poor man must've felt a bit bewildered at first. I have now finished one curtain and have it hanging up. It makes the other windows look a bit bad. I didn't realise what slow work hand sewing is. I have to sew right across each curtain four times which makes one curtain a day's work. I'm still waiting on a letter from home. It is two weeks now since the last one arrived.

26 May 1954 Lusaka Farm. While I'm working around the house I often think of things I should tell you, then when letter writing day comes I've forgotten everything I wanted to write. So today I decided to put down everything as I think of it. Maybe the result will be a bit of a jumble - however I hope not.

9 June 1954 Lusaka Farm. You hoped we'd get more water before long. Well it won't rain before the end of October. We will be right for water in Lusaka for they can't get rid of it there. They are having trouble with their sewage scheme having struck an underground stream at six feet. Here nine miles out we would probably have to go down about a hundred feet, maybe more we are yet to find that out. Lusaka is flat with slight inclines, not hills exactly but it isn't flat. Several channels are taking water away from Lusaka and it is flowing all the time. The water is very hard but there is one soap powder on the market which will lather up without forming a scum on top of the water. Bill says the water is full of lime and the kettle now has a coating of lime about one and a half inches deep in the bottom of it and takes quite a time to boil. As a result we have a new kettle and new saucepan and cake tins.

23 June 1954 Lusaka Farm. You'd never believe that one would crouch over a fire in 'darkest Africa' but that is what I'm doing. It is 8:00am and sunny and a cold breeze is blowing and by lunch time it will be quite warm. The weather is really ideal cold, bright moonlit or starry nights and mild sunny days. Sometimes clouds gather real rain clouds too, but they don't drop here but move on to some other place. Sherper and pup Butch are at my feet having the usual early morning tussle for ownership of the bag mat.

Yes Bill goes to Lusaka every morning to work. He leaves home at seven and gets back about five. He's never late getting home. He thinks it's lovely to have someone to come home to and tea ready. I'm always out looking for him too. Sometimes I take the dogs and we go for a walk to meet him. He reports to the Public Works Department (PWD) each morning and maybe works in the yards there or takes his four natives out to do some local job. Just lately he has been putting in a new pump at Government House. We have a new Governor just out from England who is hurrying up improvements there. The last one was a wily Scot who didn't even spend the government funds. Bill says if he has to go away on any jobs he'll take me with him and I can stay at the hotel. He gets a living out allowance for himself which pays for the hotel so he would only have to pay for me. So far though, they've given Bill's previous jobs to someone else.

A Move to Lusaka township

24 June 1954 Thursday. Bill came home with an extra big grin last night and I said, 'you haven't got news already?' And sure enough he had and even had the key of the new government house we are to have so after tea we drove in to see it. Honestly you would think it was a mansion the way we go on instead of the aluminium temporary building it is. The government put up a lot of them to ease the housing shortage and when the new homes are completed these will be scrapped but in the meantime they make cosy homes. A bit like an oven in the summer I should imagine. I'll leave a description of the new place (in Rhodes Park) for my next letter for we will be settled in by then.

Today I've got the awful job of packing to do. My big box is once more being filled with china and glassware. I hate packing, but it could be worse, the things packed in the caravan can stay there and we'll tow it to the house and unload it there which will save a lot of time and energy. Bill hopes to get the day off tomorrow, also the use of a government truck and a couple of workers so we should be in by the weekend. We will be two miles from Bill's work and milk, bread, meat and groceries are delivered to our door. The rent is about £2 a month, electricity and water extra. We found out now that the only other houses available at the moment are at Woodlands extension which is eight miles south from Lusaka. They are new homes and about £7 a month with no hope of electric light for at least two years! So we are very satisfied with the one we've got. The new houses on the East Road haven't any light yet either. I must get on with my job of packing now. I stopped to have a cup of tea.

28 June 1954 Monday. Lusaka Town. We are now settled in our new home, more or less anyway. We still have to hunt for things we want but will soon be organised. I'll tell you all about it in my next letter as I have a couple of snaps to put in then. I don't want it to be overweight today. I had a letter from you written on 21 June, it arrived in seven days (a record). Bill thanks you for the boot laces and now has them in his boots. It's time for bed now and I'm very tired due to all the scrubbing and various household chores that have kept me busy from early morning to dusk.

1 July 1954 Lusaka Town. These houses are long and narrow and divided into two flats each having a bedroom, living room, pantry, bathroom, spare room and a wired-in veranda. The kitchen and a little storeroom are in the back yard with the roof covering the kitchen and storeroom next door as well. Luckily there is no one living next door so Bill is putting up a fence between the two flats first.

On our back fence we have the Lusaka radio station and at the front less than a quarter of a mile away is the aerodrome. We can't see it for houses but can hear the planes as they arrive and depart. On the opposite side of the road in front of the house is the Public Works Department's apprenticeship's hostel.

Bill is working at the Lusaka hospital for a while now putting in a new laundry. It is not very far from us. Most of the town is built this side of the shopping centre. The other side which we pass on the way to our block is reserved for heavy industrial sites. There is room for huge factories there. Last night Bill and I paid a first visit to the church which is just a few minutes by car from here.

11 July 1954 Lusaka Town. A kitchen is not a woman's castle here, she only does it on sufferance. Most of the women work and so can't be bothered cooking. Norma and Ed were here for tea last night and we enjoyed having them. Bill and Ed spent most of the evening trying to work out how many bricks are in the stack that has been made. They are stacked in a huge square with a tunnel through at each end, where they light the fire. When the fires have been burning about three days they pile on more wood and seal the tunnels, then pack the outside of the walls with mud and seal them. The weather is warming up now, although June and July are the winter months with occasional frost.

Bill's addition: Dear mum and dad White, I'd like to write a little on to Alice's letter though I've got nothing particular to say. We are very happy and very much in love as we always will be. We have been busy the last few days straightening up the garden and I've been home yesterday and today for the public holidays here.

26 July 1954 Monday Lusaka Town. We went out to the farm on Saturday. As usual I packed our lunch, put it and the dogs in the car then drove to meet Bill at the workshops and we went straight out to the block and had a picnic lunch. The dogs love that trip and they seem to know when we are preparing to go and hang about the car. Bill worked yesterday (Sunday) as he has the job of preparing three big trailers in readiness for the Public Works Department exhibits at the

Lusaka Show, which is to be held next weekend. There is another holiday next Monday, English bank holiday and the show is open Saturday, Sunday and Monday with night events. Bill has to put these trailers side-by-side then build a canopy over the top of them to keep the hot sun off the folk as they look at the trailers inside. He has finished the laundry at the hospital.

Has Grace been to see you yet? She said she was going to. I'm glad you enjoyed the thirty-six page letter diary I wrote on our honeymoon. Mr Daws may be interested in it and perhaps you could send it to Casfords in one of those brown envelopes from Coles as I can't write much on the letter card. I wonder if you found the *Outspan* magazine interesting. I've been sending them fairly regularly as we get it nearly every week.

3 August 1954 Lusaka Town. Yesterday we went to the Lusaka Show. Bill left here about 8:30am as he had to start up the engine which generates the light for the Public Works Department's stands and he got back about 12:30pm. I spent the morning in bed and didn't want to move but was glad later that I made the effort. Bill showed me around and we saw all the tractors and deployment cars and trucks, cattle with terrific horn spans, some of them could scratch the middle of their backs with the horns. It wasn't 'till later when I read it in the paper about the cooking and needlework exhibits that I realised we had missed seeing them, also the flower show although I examined corn, oats, lucerne, tobacco, oranges, lemons, limes, grape fruits and lots of other things.

In the evening about one hundred native police recruits put on a show and they were really marvellous and they had had only four month's training. They marched on in threes. The first three had red shorts, next white, next blue and they all had white athletic singlets, white sandshoes and white gloves. It was really most impressive. The police band is all natives too. Last year they too were recruited out of the bush and in three months they could all read music and play their instruments. They play beautifully. The natives love a uniform and loved showing off and you could see they enjoyed doing their bit last night. (They don't seem to treat physical training with contempt as the Australian soldier does.)

The mounted police were lovely to watch too. They were white men not natives. There were eight riders and each one had two horses, one in front of the other. The rider sat on the back one. Each of the eight front horses had a candle fastened between their ears and they nodded and bowed to the crowd and then went into their show with their feet moving in time to the music. When the tune changed to a fast tempo the horses changed step and galloped around the ring. When the act was finished they lined up and the front ones put their front feet on boxes and bowed again. I could've watched them for ages.

A native has just arrived selling fowls and eggs. I couldn't be bothered with a fowl this time so bought eggs at one shilling and nine pence cheaper than in the shops. Earlier today another native came, selling carrots and lemons and two others were looking for work. Then an Englishman and five natives came to fix the sink pipe. We have not been able to use the sink since we've been here. The Englishman diagnosed the trouble then they all went off to get a screw. They all came back and Wally the Englishman, talked to me. The five natives crowded themselves under the sink to fix the pipe.

After they had gone Dusty M from the hostel came to borrow some dripping. Now at 4:00pm Bill and a workmate have just left. They came for a cup of tea as they were very thirsty. They are working at the Showgrounds taking down what they put up last week. Altogether I've had quite an array of calls for one day. The days are very warm now but the nights are cold. We were shivering at the Showgrounds last night and I had an overcoat on. Bill brought two mugs of soup and we drank that while we watched the arena events.

10 August 1954 Lusaka Town. I wrote to Bill's people last week and Bill also wrote to George to tell him about the baby. Bill is busy at Government House again laying all new pipes this time. I don't think he has quite finished at the Lusaka hospital yet but has done as much as he could for the time being. By the way don't worry about me or the baby for they have a very modern and efficient hospital here and we are less than two miles away from it.

12 August. When you see Mrs Pittard you can tell her that I've only seen one snake in Africa and that was dead. Someone had just run over it at Cape Point. She told me gruesome tales about snakes the night Auntie Alice and I went to see her.

Evidently the *Arawa* is still going strong because Mrs Latimer says it reached Wellington on its second last voyage. I think George must be on her last trip for he sails on the *Arawa* from Cape Town on 2 December. We'll hear more from him at the end of this month for he is spending a night with us on his way to meet the game reserve man in Mazabuka who is taking him big game hunting.

30 August 1954 Lusaka Town. Another month almost gone, this time next year we will be in Cape Town heading for our holiday at home. By the way George stayed the night with us last night and he sails for home on the *Arawa* on 2 December.

He just might be in Melbourne for Christmas. I told him to go out and see you and sample a few peaches. Has Lin got the phone on yet? I was thinking I could give George the phone number to ring and he could ring up and tell you when to expect him. Maybe you could meet him at Box Hill or Mitcham station? He will be staying a couple of days with us in November on his way south so I can give him final instructions then. This morning he left here to travel another hundred and fifty or so miles further south where he will spend his two weeks leave tramping in the bush with the Game Ranger in search of big game and excitement African style. He'll stay a night with us again on his way back.

We are settling down into a routine now with Ruben doing all the house work, washing and ironing except for my things which I wash and iron myself so I should have nothing much to do, yet I'm on the go all day. I have about two hours rest after lunch but apart from that I'm always busy doing something. Ruben has a place about four miles from here and on Saturday morning Bill bought a bike so he'd have no excuse for being late. He's almost finished his jobs by 11:00am and with nothing to do between 10:00am and 12:30pm I gave him an hour off to play with the bike telling him to ride only on the roads near our house or the police would get him as the bike was not registered yet. All bikes have miniature number plates which helps the police when looking for a stolen one. Ruben was like a dog with two tails as he wheeled this treasure to the road. Sherpa and Butch sat at our entrance for awhile and watched his antics. (I was watching through the window.) He proudly displayed it to neighbouring servants but never let go the handlebars himself.

6 September 1954 Lusaka Town. I'm feeling much better and even cooked a cake this afternoon. Dusty M came in with Bill after work and we had a cup of tea and now I've only got half a cake. Poor Bill hasn't seen a cake since I've been ill. I have to make more. George will be back on Saturday. We have been wondering how he is getting on. I guess he'll have quite a tale to tell. I wonder if you managed to keep the news of our baby a secret until we had written to Bill's parents. Bill says he met a man tonight he hasn't seen for ages and he said, 'How are you going? I believe you'll have an arrival in March', and a week ago another man he hasn't seen for ages said, 'How's the wife? I believe she's been sick'. And then you'll hear it said men don't gossip! Yet each of these was told by someone who had heard from someone else, so there you are!

14 September George got back about 3:00pm on Saturday and he definitely had an exciting two weeks. He said about sixty elephants passed within a few yards of them once. The

Game Ranger is trying to tame some lions. Every evening he kills a zebra and takes it to a certain spot and George said a lion, lioness and three cubs came charging out to get it and he sat and watched them eat it. The lion turned the zebra right over with one paw. George says that last year this game keeper had to kill a lioness and so he took her two cubs and reared them in his house. However, as they got bigger they began killing cattle so he took them to the East London Zoo where he stayed for a week to feed them because they wouldn't take food from anyone else.

I believe he caused quite a sensation among zoo visitors because he used to put his head in the mouth of one and one arm through the cage at night cuddling. This year he went to see them and they remembered him and cuddled him again. During George's two weeks at the game ranger's home he was taken right into the bush where the natives seldom see a white man. Most of them had never seen a car and the women and children crowded around and George pressed the horn for fun and they scattered in all directions. One native offered to direct them to where they wanted to go and they got completely lost for the native didn't know the way and had only offered because he wanted a ride. They will do anything to have a ride.

Bill has been busy building a chicken run and has ordered one hundred day old cockerels which we hope to sell about Christmas time if we can keep dogs and rats away from them. They are £30 for one hundred so we won't lose much even if the venture is not a success.

Not so nice neighbours

16 September 1954 Lusaka Town. The more I hear of our new neighbours the less I want to see them. She comes in here often usually when she wants to borrow something and we are quite friendly but she has a dreadful voice and choice of words. She talks kitchen kaffir like a native and intersperses it with English words. A friend has just arrived next door and he and Mr B next door are busy testing his motorbike engine. The noise is terrific. The wife has just broken a cup and is having trouble with a smoking fire and he is swearing away above the noise of the bike so things are not too good.

The weather is warming up now. And although the houses here are aluminium there is a breeze going through all the time which helps keep them cool. In the afternoon I like to sit in the shade at the front of the house where so far I've always found a cool spot.

21 September 1954 Lusaka Town. It is a very gusty day today the dust is blowing up the road in a cloud about twelve feet high. The dust is like fine sand and seems to be everywhere. Bill made cement with some of it yesterday, we had no sand and we wanted to make a front path so that we can keep our feet dry when going to the car during the wet, so he took the wheelbarrow and shovel and got the dust from the road. We smoothed the job with a piece of broad board and my tiny gardening trowel. We are quite pleased with the result, even if it isn't a real professional looking job.

Yesterday we took a small table onto the brickwork at the front door and had our dinner there. It is cool and shady there. We had roast chicken, potatoes, turnips and beans and pawpaw and ice cream. I had also made several bottles of orange cordial from Dot's recipe and we drank that instead of tea. We both went to sleep in our chairs after the meal. No worry about washing up, Ruben did that.

I spend very little time in the kitchen these days as it's outside and rather like working in an oven. I cooked a fruit cake and some biscuits early on Saturday morning. By this you'll see I've improved in health. When I get the sick feeling now I have a drink of creamy soda and it makes me feel okay again.

Yesterday morning Bill was working in the front garden and I was in the kitchen when I heard the dogs barking strangely so I went to the front door intending to ask Bill what was wrong with them and found he was bending over a native who was lying on the ground, his bicycle nearby. Several other natives were there too. I was very relieved to know our dogs had not caused the accident. It appears this native (I recognised him as working next door) often has blackouts and apparently had one while riding his bike. His face was all cut and bleeding and Bill said his eyes were rolling as though he had concussion. Dusty M came over too and between them they helped him to the hostel kitchen with the other natives attending to him. Later I saw him walk past our place and I asked him if he was alright and he said he was. I see he is at work this morning. They rear them tough out here!

This morning the Northern Rhodesia Regiment left for service in Malaga. They marched from the barracks not far from the hospital to the railway, a distance of about nine miles. I was going shopping and stopped to watch them pass the Secretariat where the Governor took the salute. Native men, women and children lined the streets near there and European school children were also massed there to wave them goodbye.

After they had passed I took the backstreets and continued with my shopping and had only bought my vegetables when I heard the police band again. The main street was cleared of traffic and the soldiers marched into town as I had seen them before but this time with the police native band. It was almost impossible to see the band and the first fifty odd soldiers, for the native children were running alongside waving branches and chanting, others clapping their hands in time to the music. Native women and men were running along beside them too. Apparently they picked up these admirers as they passed the second class area which is always overflowing with natives.

The native soldiers marched in threes and each group was led by a European officer and then a native officer and they were all dressed in jungle battle dress. There must've been at least two hundred native soldiers and about twenty European officers, rather a colourful parade. Lusaka is looking quite colourful now. It is Jacaranda time and huge trees covered with the lavender coloured flowers line many of the streets and quite a few people have them growing in their gardens.

10 October 1954 Lusaka Town. Bill is working again today still at the hospital. He and an Australian Mr M are working on it together. They have about four native boys each to do the labouring. Two of Bill's workmates were inmates at the hospital last week and Bill popped in to see them in the afternoon.

2 November 1954 Lusaka Town. I am enclosing a newspaper clipping which appeared in the paper after that meeting Bill attended at the Governor's residence. It seems the Public Works Department (PWD) employees are the only ones who have had to wait for government supplied houses. All other government branch employees get a house immediately. The waiting wouldn't be so bad if there were no houses, but lots are empty and others have been leased to the council or some private firm. So the PWD decided to check on all empty houses then attend the Civil Servants' Annual General Meeting in strength. The current committee didn't think that the other workers would turn up, especially the Secretariat who run things to suit themselves. The Secretariat are now fuming, especially as a PWD man was appointed to the committee to represent the Secretariat, as none of their members were there. Now the previous committee want to call another meeting to right matters to their previous state again. I'd say it should be called the uncivil servants meeting. The chairman was heard to say that the PWD would soon make a mess of things for those fellas haven't a clue. If they are so incompetent then why are they so worried? We are now interested to hear of further developments.

LUSAKA, F

'GRAB' CONTROL OF CIVIL SERVANTS ASSOCIATION

Bitter Complaints About Housing Conditions

C.A.P. Reporter

BY "packing" (as they openly admit) the annual general meeting of the Lusaka branch of the Civil Service Association, employees of the Public Works Department pulled off a coup d'etat this week and now control the committee.

And because, we are told, there was not one person from the Secretariat present, the P.W.D. workers decided to appoint one of their own mechanics to represent it in future.

The decision to attend the meeting in force was made by the P.W.D. in anticipation of usual apathy being shown by the 1,100-odd members. Last year only nine people turned up at the annual meeting. Tuesday's meeting was attended by between 60 and 70, and more than 90 per cent of them were from the P.W.D.

It is reported that neither the chairman nor vice-chairman were present at the meeting, and that the secretary presided.

DETERMINED

Last year the committe numbered 18. But on Tuesday the P.W.D. vote doubled this after being told that only about five ever turned up at committee meetings.

P.W.D. went to the meet-
Hill' towards it.
ing determined to deal with the attitude which it claim has long been adopted by "t

They say it is a case of ' white collar versus the dir overalls'.

MAIN COMPLAINT

Biggest bone of contention in P.W.D. is about housing. Some 20 families are living in caravans at the Municipal Camping Site in the central area between Church Road and King George Avenue.

There are another 20 non-Government families there, and P.W.D. say the whole area is a slum and a menace to their own and their families' health.

Some of the men say their marriages are being threatened by the appalling conditions they are forced to live under. They complain of the sanitary and washing arrangements; many families walk more than a mile each way to the municipal lavatories in town rather than use what is provided at the site.

EMPTY HOUSES

When the rains break the whole area becomes a bog.

While conceding that the P.W.D. men living on the camping site were employed on a no-accommodation-provided basis, they say that there are as many as 91 Government houses vacant in Lusaka, but that Government refuses all appeals to let them use the houses.

One house in King George Avenue is said to have stood empty for seven months.

All these points were raised at the meeting on Tuesday.

Mr and Mrs M are living in the camping ground in our old caravan and she has told me some of the things that happen there. Some of the campers are pretty rough (not PWD employees). Natives of course are always wandering around too.

9 November 1954 Lusaka Town. Bill is anything but well just now. He was complaining of his tummy on Sunday then that night it was very hot so yesterday I got the doctor to look at him and he has a form of flu. Doctor is coming again this morning. He looks much better today for the fever has left him.

A lot of the native labourers at the Public Works Department have had this tummy trouble and Ruben has been away for two days with it. When he turned up this morning I asked where he had been and he put on a pained expression and with his hands clasped to his tummy he said, 'oh much trouble donna'. I hope I don't get it from him. Just feeling well again now and sometimes I'm sick in the mornings, but it doesn't last.

Last Friday night we went to a Guy Fawkes barbeque and had a beaut time too. One of the Public Works Department workers put on the evening and the neighbours' kiddies all had a wonderful display of crackers and an old Guy Fawkes in the fire. We met a New Zealand family and I believe he came over here as a missionary but found it very disheartening and is now a carpenter. He said a prayer. When the evening ended he was telling Bill that he had built a house in Khandallah (where Bill's parents live) before coming over here. I might say he and Bill spent a lot of time chatting together.

The *Lusaka War Memorial* was unveiled at 8:30am last Sunday morning. We went along to the service then in the evening we went to church. The doctor has been and Bill is much better. He has gastric flu and his tummy is still troublesome but the doctor left tablets so he'll be right in a day or two. Bill ordered a cup of *Milo* a few minutes ago so I went to light the fire and now he's asleep one hand on the cat which has moved in with us. The cat which has moved in thinks it is marvellous to have someone in bed all day and there's no moving her.

24 November 1954 Lusaka Town. Saturday. Bill was moving a few sheets of iron in the backyard and killed a small brown snake. He chopped it with a shovel. It is the first I've seen here. Now that the rains have started the number and variety of insects that come around us is amazing. I almost walked onto a six inch centipede in the bathroom the other night. I always put my shoes on now. We witnessed an amazing sight one evening last week when the yard seemed to be alive with flying ants. The earth had cracked in about four places, just narrow openings and about three inches long, and these ants were swarming out and taking to the air. Yesterday lunchtime we had our heaviest downpour so far. I had gone shopping and in no time the streets were small rivers. On one side of the main street is a huge open drain about four feet wide and six feet deep and it had about four feet of water in it as the side streets are not drained so well.

Several of the Public Works Department employees from the camping site have now been allotted houses, one of them being a man with a wife and three children. By the way since the rain, the road to our block (farm we now call it) has been graded and is much better. Even with all the rain there is still a little dust rising on the roads.

Frugal living

30 November 1954 Lusaka Town. Ruben didn't return from his holiday yesterday so I asked the native next door if he knew a young person who wanted to work. I might add here that quite a lot of natives came looking for work during the two weeks of Ruben's holiday but I expected Ruben back. However the native next door came over with another in the dark and I told him to come at six this morning and when Bill got up the fire was going well and the kettle boiling, so all was well. He's not much good at cleaning so I'll have to show him everything but that's better than having one who thinks he knows all. He is very eager at the moment but by next week will have settled down I guess, and I'll know then whether he's worth keeping. I will probably give him two shillings a week (ration money) and £2 at the end of the month. Ruben got more than twice that for doing the same work but he was experienced. I've just asked his name and he says 'Gek'.

I am looking after a four year old boy for his father who works with Bill and my neighbour is much quieter since I've had little Ian staying here. He was imitating her and one day when she shrieked and swore at the dogs. Ian called out to me, 'why the piccanin say that? Why the piccanin shouting?' and I suppose she heard him. He doesn't know it is a woman who kicks up all the noise.

I've had a rather hectic morning so far. Sherpa has a sore ear and today it is quite swollen so off I had to go to the vet and it cost me nine shillings and nine pence for an injection and four shillings and six pence for ointment. I'll be broke by the time I'm finished for he has to have four injections. Talking of money I wonder if you could send me a State Savings Bank withdrawal form as I would like to have £250 of my money sent over. We are paying 8% interest on the land payment so I want to hurry it up a bit. I thought I could fill in the form and dad could collect it, then send a cheque through his bank. I hope this won't be too much nuisance for you and I wouldn't ask if I could see any other way out. We want it all paid off before we leave here in August next year and with my money should be able to do so. I'll sign the form in my maiden name and send my book home too.

We haven't been able to save anything or make extra payments so far for Bill has had just his wage since we married with none of the overtime received as before when he used to go away on jobs. £23 a month goes into the land before we even see his wage and last month Bill had to pay £22 income tax on the year 1952 - 1953 and this year's is due this month I believe. With one or two other extras like that during the year, it has kept us pretty short. We live very quietly too, seldom go out. Reading through this again it sounds as if I'm complaining but I'm not at all. Shortage of money is nothing new to me and we are so happy we don't really worry about money. It's just that we've got to have something behind us by August or we won't get home.

11 December 1954 Lusaka Town. I don't think I mentioned that Bill is away on a job just now. He flew to Mongu the capital of Barotseland about five hundred miles west of here a week ago yesterday. I'm finding it awful without Bill. I had a telegram on Saturday saying he'd be home Wednesday afternoon and that is tomorrow. I'll go to the airport and meet him of course. I don't think any other mechanic at the Public Works Department has been flown to a job, they usually go the hard way along almost non-existent roads at times so of course they were chipping Bill before he left calling him the 'flying fitter'. He flew off in one of those little one engine *Beavers*, the only other occupants being the pilot and a small boy who was clutching a thermos and a parcel of sandwiches. Bill has to check the diesel engines which run the light and radio transmitters at the Mongu airport.

I've never heard of Mongu 'till Bill was sent there and when I took Sherper to the vet I met a man who knew Mongu very well. He told me of the good fishing there. It is in the Zambezi Valley and how by February the Zambezi River is lapping at the doorstep and one only has to throw a line from the door and the natives hold a sort of festival. It is very primitive out there of course with few whites. I believe the District Commissioner there is a New Zealander.

I guess Bill will have lots to tell me when he comes home and I'll be able to tell you more about the place then. I had made arrangements to stay with Alf and Avis (Norma's sister in Lusaka) or even Norma when Bill was sent away, but with young Ian as company I didn't need to go there. (I'm now looking after Ian full time for his father). Dusty M from the hostel over the road comes and talks to me for about ten minutes each lunch time. I miss Bill most when I see all the others coming home for lunch and again at night. On Sunday Ian and I went to Norma's and had tea there. It made a nice break.

11 December 1954 Lusaka Town. Thursday. Yesterday Ian and I went to the airport to meet Bill. We were there almost an hour too early and the plane was an hour late due to storms on the way. Bill was on board anyway and quite pleased to be home again. Ian keeps telling me, 'I happy Uncle Bill home again' so evidently he found life a bit dull too. Bill stayed at one of the two houses near the Mongu airport about two miles from the township for the ten days to be near his job.

One day he met the folk who used to be our next door neighbours. They had driven the seventy-five miles from their new home to get their truck fixed at the government garage. Bill says they look well and happy and the baby is doing well. There are about one hundred and twenty Europeans at Mongu and an endless number of natives. Things which are grown locally are very cheap but groceries and things like that are very expensive. I think he said sugar was two shillings a pound. They all make their own bread with hops. Meat is about one shilling a pound, chickens about two and six each and milk very cheap too. Where Bill stayed they used to send a brandy bottle (about one and a half pints) to the milking shed and pay two shillings for that much milk. They have no milk bottles. I can't think of anything else he told me just now.

20 December 1954 Lusaka Town. Just a few more days until Christmas, I can't believe it. It has rushed on me here just the same as at home. Having young Ian here will make it feel more like Christmas to me but even so it will be a strangely quiet time for us. Bill has invited two bachelor friends for Christmas dinner. We did ask Norma and Ed but they are going to Avis and Alf. We have a new houseboy and he asked if he could stay in the little storeroom next to the kitchen as he had to move from his 'kyoa'. After a lot of thought we decided he could, although neither of us like a native hanging around the house all the time, but this one is clean if lectured occasionally.

24 January 1955 Lusaka Town. Yesterday we went to the regiment grounds and watched a game of cricket - typical country cricket with the Public Works Department playing a

Lusaka firm. Ian‘s father was with us and we had a picnic basket. It was quite a nice day not too hot and the trees nice and shady. We really enjoyed it.

Managing houseboys

The new houseboy we have been employing since Ruben left is slipping back with his work and it has got to the stage where I'm calling him back to redo everything. Of course Ian misses nothing, even if he seems to be absorbed in a game of some sort.

31 January Lusaka Town. So far our new houseboy Hassan is proving to be good. He just gets about quietly doing what has to be done without any fuss. He sees what needs doing without me chasing him up all the time. He had only been here a few days when he asked if he could live here so a tent has been erected at the back away from the house for him and his wife. While we were out yesterday they acquired a child from somewhere and he and Ian are playing together just now. He is a bit bigger than Ian and looks a nice little boy.

7 February 1955 Lusaka Town. We had a lovely day yesterday, went for a picnic to Chirundu ninety miles away. Before Federation it was where all cars were stopped by customs as it is the border between North and South Rhodesia, the Zambezi River separating the two. We drove across the bridge into Southern Rhodesia then back again. I haven't been on this road before as we came here via Bulawayo and the customs at Livingstone. The way we went yesterday is in the direction of Salisbury.

Yesterday's trip wasn't exactly all pleasure. Dusty M was down that way the weekend before and the bearings went in one front wheel so he drove the car into the hotel yard and left it there. Then yesterday we drove him down there to get it. However they only took outside bearings to fix it and on investigating he found the inside one had worn too. However, as there is no garage at Chirundu they decided to try driving it back to Lusaka slowly, but it made such a noise we stopped after only driving twenty-nine miles. It was 5:30pm by this time so we decided to have picnic tea on the side of the road before going further. Two other men came along a little later with something wrong with a generator (one of them works for the Public Works Department) so they had tea with us then the four of them set to work to try and put Dusty's generator on their car but it wouldn't work.

While this was going on Ian and I were reclining in a couple of deckchairs on the side of the road. Eventually they decided to leave Dusty's car where it was and get the other one back stopping every so often to let it cool down. It was 9:15am when we left in the morning and 9:30pm when we got back in the evening so it was quite a day, full of variety too. We didn't see any wild game although we did see where an elephant had been. I wouldn't like to live near Chirundu for it is very hot and humid there.

There is a rabies tie up on until further notice, according to the paper on Saturday. The dog catcher was around this way and took the dog next door as it was not tied up. They were out so he told me to tell them they could get it back by going to the pound. This of course means paying a fine which no doubt will be rather high for it had not been injected against rabies either. I met a lady at the hospital Monday and she said their dog had been bitten by a dog suspected of rabies so she and her family were all having a course of injections to be on the safe side - sixteen injections around the naval. All dogs are supposed to be injected against it and most of them are so there is little chance of an epidemic, especially as it is almost five weeks since the one and only case was spotted. The only dogs which have been shot (over three hundred) are the ones without registration or a rabies free ticket on their collars, mostly native dogs. Well I've used a lot of paper explaining that but hope I've made it clear. There is not much to worry about here really.

Yesterday we had a letter from Bill's home and George has arrived there safely. Even got his name mentioned in the paper as it was the last trip for the *Arawa* so there was quite a write-up about her and some of her passengers.

New baby and a visit to Salsibury

4 March 1955 Lusaka Town. Today you will have received the cable telling you of your grandson's arrival. I hope you're as pleased as we are with the arrival of Andrew William. I only wish we could show him off to you. Still the day will come soon. He is a fine healthy little boy and always has his mouth open when given to me.

8 March 1955 From Bill's mother, Khandallah, Wellington, New Zealand to *Alice's mother Springvale Road Donvale, Australia.* Dear Mr and Mrs White, George Hardgrave was thrilled with his visit to you in Melbourne and he was quite taken with Alice too. He's a nice young man always happy and cheerful. He is working down at Cable's (in Wellington) where Bill used to work and everyone was around him to get news of Bill as soon as they knew he had been with Bill and just returned from Africa. Yes he was mentioned in the evening papers too.

Mr Latimer is house building for the *State Advance* and others as well at the moment, three of them on a share basis and they seem to be doing well at present. They are building a new home for my friend's son newly married too. Everyone needs homes these days and it's hard to get builders. We have had a beautiful summer and a beautiful autumn so far. I hope this finds you still in good health. God bless you and yours very sincerely, Laura and Cecil Latimer.

12 April 1955 Lusaka Town. Dear mum and dad, Since my last letter to you we have travelled seven hundred and thirty-two miles so I will have quite a lot to write about this week. We went to Salisbury for the Easter weekend and left here on Good Friday morning at 4:30am. We arrived in Salisbury at 4:45pm after quite an interesting journey. Now that Federation is here there is no need for a passport when going to and from Southern Rhodesia. At the border on the Southern Rhodesia side we were stopped while the car was sprayed in case we were carrying tsetse flies as Southern. Rhodesia is afraid the fly may be brought in from the north. Three times we were stopped at these gates, the last one being rather interesting as we had to drive into a big shed and we were shut in there while the wheels were sprayed. Then we were released again. Ian didn't like that one much because it was rather dark with the doors of the shed shut both ends. We saw lots of tobacco farms on the Southern Rhodesian side and it looked very prosperous.

We arrived at Linnoia about 1:30pm and had lunch there. After leaving there we ran into rain, the first we'd seen for two or three weeks and it pelted down. We intended attaching the fly of the tent to the car and camping but we decided to try for a hotel room but there was no luck because they were all full so we drove on to Lake Makliwaine twenty-three miles out of Salisbury and set up camp. It was dark by this time but the rain had stopped and we had no more. Saturday was a glorious day and we really enjoyed lazing about and watching the picnickers who had to come for the day. The boating club is on the opposite bank and were having a regatta so it was quite a day. It is a huge lake and the nearest Rhodesia can get to the sea. Launch trips run every hour and there are swings and see-saws for the children also a sandpit and paddling pool.

Salisbury is a lovely city very up-to-date. We had a cup of tea in the gardens, they are very spacious and in one corner they have a scale model of the Victoria Falls. From there we drove to the suburb where Ian's mother is staying and there she and Ian met for the first time since November.

As it was 2:00pm when we left we had no hope of getting to Lusaka before two on Monday morning so we decided to stop at the nice new hotel at Karoi for the night (Karoi is about halfway). Well we got there about 7:00pm and the place was crowded. We were amazed as it looks a real one horse town, just the new hotel and a service station and a couple of shops just being built. As we drove up the hill to the hotel a black cat ran across in front of us and I said, 'Oh mind the cat isn't it supposed to be good luck when a black cat crosses one's path?' Bill didn't know but thought so. Anyway we couldn't get a bed at the hotel so we decided to have dinner there then drive on to a likely looking place to stop for the night. Neither of us was looking forward to that.

The dining room was crowded and at the next table to us was a party of six. About halfway through the meal one lady leaned over and asked if we'd been fixed up for the night - her friend had heard Bill asking for a room. I said no so she said if we cared to wait until the film is over (the hotel shows a film every Sunday night) we were quite welcome to stay the night at their farm which was twelve miles away. We thought this extremely good of her and decided to accept. They have 4,000 acres mostly bush but they've cleared quite a lot and have planted tobacco. We had a look around the sheds next morning and found it all very interesting. They have sixty natives working there so their wage bill would be no less than £180-£200 a month. They had a beautiful Alsatian dog. Up to last week they had two but one had been taken by a leopard. The room we were given had its own bathroom and in one corner of the bathroom three guns were propped up. One was just a light one but the other two were heavier. This information I gathered from Bill. We left there about 10:00am and arrived back here at 6:00pm very glad to be home again. I forgot to mention there are mica mines at Karoi. After leaving there we climbed the mountains around the Zambesi River then descended into the valley and my were we glad to climb out of it again on the Northern Rhodesian side as it is hot and oppressive in the Zambezi Valley.

21 June 1955 Lusaka Town. Sir Edmund Hillary was in Lusaka yesterday and gave a lantern lecture on the climb up Mount Everest. Bill and Ed went along and Norma and I stayed home with our babies.

2 August 1955 Lusaka Town. Lusaka Show was held last Saturday, Sunday and Monday. We went on Sunday. Remember last year I wrote and told you of the wonderful events at night when the Southern Rhodesian mounted police were here? Well they were to come this year but there was an outbreak of foot and mouth disease at Choma between here and Southern Rhodesia, so they didn't come.

Holiday to Australia and New Zealand

18 August 1955 Bulawayo. Dear mum and dad, We are on our long service leave at last. I was really glad to leave Lusaka and be on our way home to see you. By the time we finished packing it was midnight Saturday night. We had twelve visitors during that last day, two stayed for lunch and three for tea and I sent to the shops for fish and chips for tea and we ate them out of paper bags, kitty and Sherper too.

On our second night away we stayed at a real country hotel. The owner has a farm and in his day was a real hunter. At the entrance are two elephant skulls and just inside the door are stuffed crocodiles. On the walls were mounted heads of all sorts of buck and leopard skins on the floors. Between there and Livingstone notices say 'Beware of Elephant' and although we saw fresh spoor and fresh leaves on newly broken branches we didn't see an elephant. We saw three Kudu (huge buck about the size of a pony) with lovely big horns. Well we are well on our way now but a long way from halfway yet having only done seven hundred and twenty-four miles.

The roads are not too good until we get to the Union - shakes us up a lot so we decided to rest here a day or two then on into Kruger Park where we hope to spend six or seven days. These Matopos Mountains are hundreds of miles long - just huge boulders one on top of the other. Most of them look anything but safe too but I guess they have been like that for thousands of years. It is in these mountains about twenty miles from Bulawayo where John Rhodes is buried. Tomorrow we hope to visit there.

We arrived at these new government rondavals last night and at first lazed around being the only ones here - and only the second ones to stay as these rest huts are not officially open yet. The American consul stayed here on 1 July I believe. Quite a lot are expected on Saturday and tomorrow government officials are coming here to inspect them and have lunch here. We are now sitting at a table writing letters by the light of hurricane lamps. Although we are only twenty or thirty miles from Bulawayo this is primitive country. We asked the Ranger about wild animals and he said there were very few lions but leopards took two hundred native cattle a year.

2 September 1955 Simsonstown. I don't think I wrote a letter last week and now it is this week already gone. I just don't know where the days are going. There seems to be so much to do and settle up and so much to remember. We buy a paper each day now for we could never tell what day it was. When we arrived here at Simsonstown there were two letters waiting for us from you. We were two days late arriving here owing to trouble with tyre tubes in the Kruger Park, one puncture after another. However all is well that ends well. We can't complain when one realises the thousands of miles those poor wheels have done.

19 October 1955 Letter from Bill's brother Ed in Lusaka, to Bill's family in New Zealand. Dear mum and dad, Bill, Alice and Andy, Sorry I've been so long writing. I suppose Bill and Alice are there now. They should be anyway. Is young Andy behaving himself? I expect he's quite a handful by now. It's been horribly humid and hot here the last few weeks the heat is awful tiring. We had a good shower of rain early this morning which cooled the heat out a treat.

I received my income tax demand today for year ending March 1954 and I have £63 to pay within thirty days. I reckon it's grim. It sort of puts a hole in our bank balance. I think it's cheaper than New Zealand though as a single man. We are planning a holiday now for December, only another eight weeks before we leave for East London. We reckon on taking four weeks off as the trip down will take six days alone. It's an awful long way.

Bill the car is still going fine and no adjustments have been necessary. It should be nearly run in by now. I've had my car's speedo repaired at Proctors for £3.10, quite reasonable I think.

I am now doing about a hundred miles a week by the speedo. I can hardly believe that. I've put all new woodwork in the back and done away with all the rattles putting new corner posts and floorboards in. It's a good job as the body had dropped about one and a half inches at the back and was resting on the chassis which caused a lot of noise at the back. I've jacked up the body and put in two bearers.

They are now working on Bothas Rust Road and the dust on the detour is wicked. I'm sure in the rains it will be unusable. At present the detour puts miles on the trip out to our plot. There has been a commotion lately by Lusaka citizens because one of the government officials is making a township out on the Bothas Rust Road called *Lilanda Township*. It won't make things too good for selling our land. There have been several protest meetings here but there is no law against him selling it out.

My job's going alright, work is picking up again now. Things were very slack before. The trouble now is that there is only myself and three kaffir butchers to do the carpentry work. The boss is trying to get another man but joiners are rare up here. Plenty of rough hands but no joiners, it's too much for me to do by myself. There are quite a lot of jobs a kaffir cannot do.

Do you still use some of the furniture I made mum? How is the radiogram, is it still going? Well I can't think of much more to write as things are quiet here except for riots now and again. They had a good riot at Nchanga copper mine the other day, nobody killed. Be writing later. Love to you all.

25 November 1955 Letter from Alice c/o Khandallah, Wellington, New Zealand to her parents. Dear mum and dad, I received a welcome letter from you and was pleased to hear you are both getting better, it must've been miserable for you. I can't believe our stay in New Zealand is almost over. We leave here next Thursday and arrive in Sydney early on the morning of Monday 5 December. I don't know yet what plane I shall be on but hope to get one for Monday afternoon and Bill expects to be in Melbourne on Monday night's train arriving in Melbourne about 11:30am Tuesday morning. I'm afraid our luggage will need the services of a truck as we have now got a tin trunk as well as our cases. We bought it last week hoping it will take our overflow.

Last night we went to George Hardgrave's home and had a chin wag. He thinks Andrew is like that bunch of children at my home and Mrs Latimer thinks he looks like my father so he must be more like the White's than the Latimer's. I believe there is to be a party here in our honour on Saturday night.

Bill's mum bought Andrew a lovely teddy bear the other day and he loves it already. Just now we are busy making goodbye calls. I'm afraid Andrew is a bit of a mischief mum. His grandad found him chewing a Savoy sausage the other day that he had taken out of a parcel. He never wastes time crying over what is taken away he just goes off and finds something else. He has a box full of toys but they are not half as good as the rubbish tin or the basket of potatoes. He bites everything even the lovely polished occasional table that Ed made. I'm always trying to teach him not to bite the furniture or scratch the wallpaper but he's pretty persistent. I hope to be able to take the pram on the plane as I'm afraid it would get a rough time in the luggage van of the train.

Friday. I had another letter from you yesterday so will answer it too. I'll send an urgent telegram from Sydney to let you know the time of my arrival in Melbourne then if Bale's rings through to you, you should have it before the plane arrives. (That is if I can get a plane Monday afternoon.) If you're not there I'll ring from the airport and wait for you there. I'll probably get another letter written before we leave here. I'll have to start packing in the next week. It is a lovely day today and Bill and I are sitting on the lawn overlooking the harbour. We watch the ships go on the floating dock. Andrew was with us but is now asleep.

6 March 1956 From Bill's mother to Alice's mother. Dear Mrs White, These few lines are to say how sorry Cecil and I were to hear of your accident. However we hope and trust you are getting past the shock and the worst is over. Yours is far worse than my accident, I could get my shoes on. We shall look forward to knowing you are back on your feet again. Wasn't it nice to have Alice home again? We enjoyed having them around and to see our Bill again was a real thrill and a great event after such a long absence. The time seems too long before we shall see them again. The same will apply to you all I am sure. Kind regards to everyone. We remain yours very sincerely, Laura and Cecil Latimer.

A move to Mazabuka

13 May 1956 Mazabuka. Dear mum and dad, Bill is now in charge of the Public Works Department workshops here at Mazabuka. We have received a temporary house and we move into a permanent house next weekend. That is a step up even though it is only a small town. The man who was in charge will stay next week to give Bill details of his work then he is to go to Livingstone and we move into his house which I understand is known locally as *The Castle* as it is a huge place, more about it in my next letter. I haven't seen it yet.

19 May 1956 Mazabuka. As I mentioned in my last letter we have moved. It is quite a big place and has a large ground surrounding it making it a pleasant situation. From the front we have a view over the Kafue River Valley and sometimes in the morning it's like looking at the sea from far away. We have two native boys to help in the house and outside.

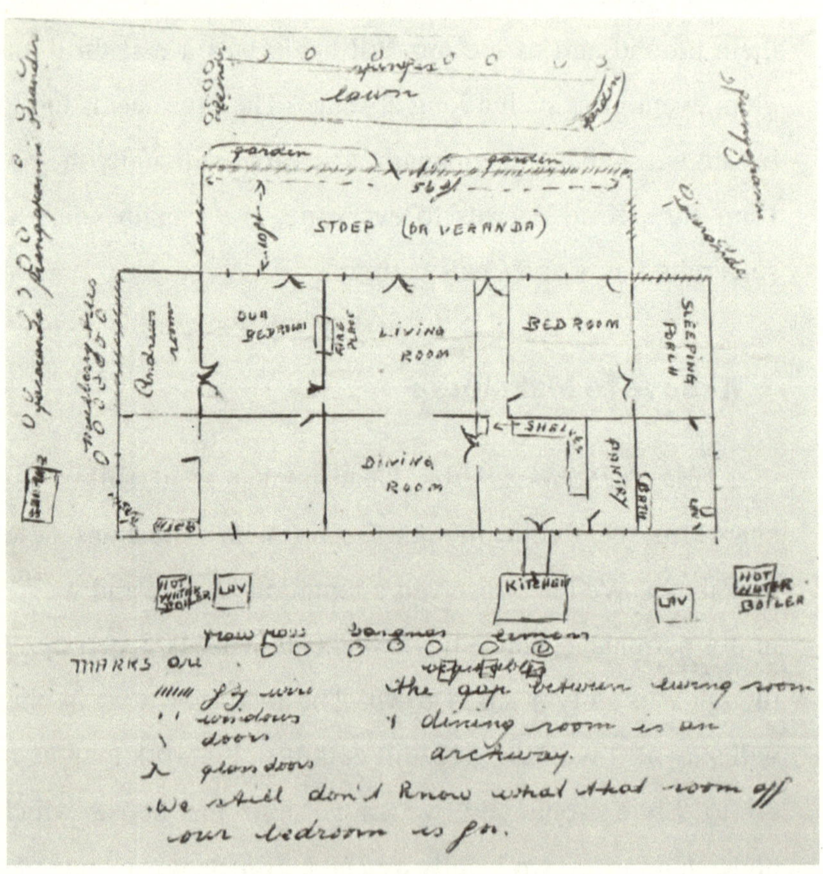

Plan of the Mazabuka house

We won't have any trouble with neighbours here. On one side is a police Crime Investigation Department and on the other is the game ranger, (the man that George did a trip with) and he's hardly ever home.

We haven't heard anything of Hassan yet so I've put on quite a good help called Pencil. I think I'll have to put on another one for both Pencil and myself are on the go most of the day. Pencil is a middle-aged man with a limp and he seems such a lonely type. I feel quite sorry for him. Pencil and Domino gave us a great welcome after we'd been away. They rushed around doing everything at once with big smiles on their faces.

24 June 1956 Mazabuka. Bill was telling me that the man from the Health Department went into the Public Works Department the other day and asked him to look at his Land Rover as it was spitting and backfiring and making funny noises. They found everything, carburettor and so forth all whitish and it turned out a native at the Health Department had put in a tin of mosquito repellent instead of petrol! Life is never monotonous here! Bill is soaking stamps again tonight and one was posted at Salisbury Plains and Lark Hill in 1917. He must've got those from you.

6 July 1956 Mazabuka. Bill made arrangements today to have a bore hole put down on our property out of Lusaka. He thinks it may be better to build a small house there and toward the end of the year ask for a transfer back to Lusaka. We would not be moved to other towns if we are living on our own property. I like it here but of course one never knows how long we can expect to be in one place with the government. Apart from that there is a new housing grant of an extra £300 a year to employees living on their own property. This is to encourage a more stable type of employee. They have been mainly a floating population in the past. This of course will help us considerably.

8 July 1956 Mazabuka. Bill has a pile of books all over the dining room table and he is ordering stores for the workshops. What it is to be the boss - he is never still a minute now. This is a holiday weekend with work starting again on Wednesday. Bill came home yesterday and remarked, 'A holiday, ok I hope it's a quiet one' and just as we finished lunch a man came in to say his Public Works Department truck had broken down so off Bill had to go. We are quite happy here though. I've got a lot more to occupy my mind here too with a big house and grounds. The garden looks lovely.

20 July 1956 Mazabuka. Bill's brother Ed and Norma are talking of going back to New Zealand permanently next year. It means selling their half of our land first. Land around there is bringing £7 an acre now, more than Bill and Ed paid so they hope they can make something on it. We are going out there this weekend and they will discuss what is to be done. I was thinking this morning of the difference between here and home.

Nearly all cars here are new or near new, we seldom see one older than eight years and yet beside that will be a trailer pulled by ten oxen which passes here nearly every day. Makes one realise there is still a large gap between the old life and the new.

Sunday. Well we're back home again from Lusaka and we bought baby Keith and Norma back with us and they are going to stay one or two weeks. It will be great company for Andrew and me. I've been feeling a bit off colour so went to a doctor up here and he said I'm a bit rundown and gave me a tonic. He says I should get a servant to look after Andrew as he is too big for me to handle all the time. I should be doing that of course but Norma has brought her native and he can watch Andrew and Keith if they are outside and give us a bit of a break. I think Norma looks a bit rundown too.

Incentives to build

Bill and Ed have decided to divide the land they bought together and each do what he wants with his own half, which is really more satisfactory now they are married. Another thing, Bill thought it might be an idea to build a small place and live there as the government are trying to encourage the workers to live on their own plot. They get steady employees that way and also the employee doesn't get moved around (which is a big thing to consider). There is also to be a £25 a month housing grant to be paid to employees living in their own home. All this is just talk yet. Of course our land in Lusaka is surrounded by blocks all being sold around us now and the telephone is out past the place. Also a tarred road is halfway along and a good dirt road the rest of the way. Lusaka is spreading like a bushfire. If we did get a transfer and move it wouldn't be 'till next year though. Bill says he will build a convenient place to live in before we did move which shouldn't be difficult as our bricks are still lying there.

16 August 1956 Mazabuka. Bill saw his Lusaka foreman the other day and he asked if Bill would like to go back to Lusaka. He said, 'I was on leave or you never would've been moved'. Bill thinks it might be a good idea if we could build a small place on our property while living in a government house in Lusaka, however there is nothing definite yet and even if we do move it would not be before next year. A liveable house would add to the value of our property when it comes time to sell. Ed and Norma haven't put their place on the market yet. It isn't legally divided yet. Ed didn't want it cut in half, he said it would cost too much so Bill said he'd pay the fees if he could have the choice of blocks.

That was agreed so we took the half which has had some of the timber cleared from it. Later we hope to plant veggies and sell them. This is just a dream yet which will probably burst all too soon when the money runs out. A native boy would do the hard work in the garden. It would be nice if we could keep the two we've got now but it remains to be seen. They may not want to leave Mazabuka. They get lonely when they are not near the other members of their tribe.

Last week Bill needed a haircut. You'll remember how he loves having his hair cut. Well Saturday morning he took some change with him and said, 'I might be late for lunch Alice I'm going to get my haircut'. Come lunchtime and Bill was on time as usual with no haircut. His explanation was that a native Methodist preacher came to the workshop collecting for the mission so he didn't have enough left for a haircut.

Sunday evening. We had a typical Aussie dinner today: roast mutton, green peas (home grown) and apple pie. We both agreed it wasn't Australian or New Zealand mutton as it was so tough I think it had walked the 1,500 odd miles from the Karoo Desert. Still it was a change. Bill and I have been sketching plans for a house and now Bill is busy trying to work out an economical roof. We've still got the bricks which we had made when we were there before so they'll be a help.

Tragedies & lifestyle

One of the natives under Bill at the Public Works Department came here one morning last week before Bill left for work and told Bill his little boy, aged about seven had died at the African hospital the night before. The Public Works Department carpenter made a box for the little fellow and later when we were having lunch we saw this father and another boy walking away from the native burial ground with a shovel on the boy's shoulder, so very sad.

21 August 1956 Mazabuka. A dreadful thing happened ten miles from here last Saturday morning. A Public Works Department man put petrol around his house to kill ants then walked inside with the four gallon tin. The heat from the stove ignited the petrol and as he ran to the door the tin exploded in his hands and he was burnt from head foot. He wasn't expected to live but he's getting on fairly well now. I met the wife today. She is expecting a baby in October and has two others one eleven months old and the other about two years. The house and all they possessed was burnt to the ground. Everyone here has given something to help them.

24 August 1956 Mazabuka. Don't worry too much about the decorative transfers mum, just send them when ready. I should think we are more likely to receive parcels here at Mazabuka than we were at Lusaka. The post office in Lusaka is a real hovel and in two buildings on two different streets and with the population increasing in leaps and bounds they are in a bit of a muddle I should think. Foundations are laid for a new six story post office so when it is completed things should improve. Here in Mazabuka the post office is a new building, small of course but quite nice about the size of the Mitcham one at home.

Each day Bill gets the milk at the dairy which is opposite the Public Works Department, Mazabuka. Sometimes I have the car and on those days I go in for the milk. Sundays we all go for the drive. Well, one old gentleman there has taken a fancy to Andrew (in fact they all make a fuss of him) and he has seen the bottles washed, filled with milk and the caps put on (all done by machines) and he has also seen the cheese being made but didn't like the taste of it. One day this week I went there and as I was giving the old milk bottles to the native this old man came to the car and lifted Andrew out and Andrew started telling him, 'chackta chackta' and pointing to where the tractor stood. The old man took him and sat him on the tractor and showed him the horn and Andrew had a lovely time turning the steering wheel. When I was ready to leave the old man insisted on carrying Andrew back to the car and as we drove off Andrew gave him a lovely smile and waved 'ta ta'. I suppose they like Andrew because he is friendly.

Lusaka is the capital of Northern Rhodesia but now with Federation they want a federal capital as in Australia and they have the same arguments as Australia had with each State wanting the capital in a different place. Because of the copper mines Northern Rhodesia has the money. Southern Rhodesia was about on the rocks when Federation came in. The north is annoyed at the moment because the big hydro electric scheme is being built at Kariba on the Zambezi River instead of on the Kafue River in the north as after all, the bulk of the money for it will come from the north.

1 September 1956 Mazabuka. Bill has just been reading from a local magazine and it states that property in Lusaka is now four times its 1952 value. In 1954 Lusaka became a municipal council and elected its first mayor - a builder Ed used to work for. There were only 4,600 Europeans here when Bill arrived in January 1952 and now there are over 10,000. The African population has almost tripled in that time and is now estimated at 60,000. Rates for land in Lusaka are now £8 on buildings. We do not pay rates as we are outside the municipal area in what is known as the farming belt.

Some time ago they called for tenders to wreck a market building but now they've decided to allow anyone to sell their produce on a vacant block near town so they can judge whether a market is necessary or not. There is a native market already in the second class trading area. I told Bill of the marketing experiment and said it just might come in handy if we grow more veggies than we can eat. He just laughed. Today I used our own carrots, parsnips and silver beet for Andrew's lunch. It is lovely to have the time to make a veggie garden especially here when the supply in the shops is so uncertain.

Last weekend the Lusaka Public Works Department gave Bill Andrew's Christmas present from last year's tree. It was a surprise to us as being away we didn't expect anything. It was a lovely toy Irish terrier dog, one of those with long straight legs. He loves it and wanted to take it to bed so now when he lies down at night he'll say, 'Pat, pat, pat' and then he lifts his arms and I give him the koala bear, the teddy bear and the dog and he does his best to put his arms around them all.

9 September 1956 Mazabuka. Bill has some odd jobs to do with his work sometimes but I'm glad he isn't a police man. The police inspector asked Bill for a towing connection so he could tow a trailer behind his Land Rover. Bill said he hadn't one on hand but would send to Lusaka for one, 'Oh don't worry, that will be too late. One of the fellows has to go into the bush and bring back a native who was drowned four days ago. He'll just have to put the body in the back of the Land Rover as he can't take the trailer.' Just imagine how nice that would be in this climate! Bill just read this through and tells me this boy was a fisherman and he was killed by a hippopotamus.

16 September 1956 Mazabuka. One day last week the grass paddock opposite our place caught fire. I've never seen anything go so fast. The wind was behind it and it even jumped the two roads which lead from here to the main road. Usually even a cow track will stop a grass fire but not this time. Then yesterday a whirlwind got started and gathered up all the burnt grass, leaves and dust and swept them through my neighbour's house. I was thankful it was not mine. It was about fourteen feet high and as black as could be. The fires are a big help here more often than not for they burn the dusty old grass which must be full of germs and snakes. I was watching the road in front of our house and nothing escaped this fire it was too fast. In the bush the fires do a lot of damage killing lots of wild animals and making survivors short of feed but here near the towns they don't do much real damage. Sometimes native thatched huts are burnt but that is often helpful. It kills lots of vermin.

20 September 1956 Mazabuka. It is Monday morning here and Andrew is full of beans so I don't know how long I'll be able to write this. Bill made him a lovely semi trailer (being a piece of wood with five nails to hold cotton reels). He loves putting them on the nails and off again. Bill painted it red so it is quite a gay affair. Later we gave him cotton reels of different colours. On Saturday I planted Jacaranda seeds. If they come up we hope to plant them on our land in Lusaka.

Ed wants to sell the land so that he can go home to New Zealand but there are so many places on the market just now it would really be better to wait awhile. I've just put Andrew down for his morning nap and now Bill has just rung to ask me to cut his lunch as he has to go to a job about sixty miles away. This is a huge area with roads, bridges and so forth being built all around to say nothing of bore holes and add into that a new town where hundreds of native from the Zambesi Valley are being housed to make room for the huge hydro scheme at Kariba Gorge. Bill has to attend to vehicles from there too and all the metal trucks and bulldozers and everything else which goes to road making. He is feeling a bit displeased as he has been given all this added responsibility without a rise in wages. An Irishman's rise he calls it. He gets less than the man under him so is doing quite a bit of agitating. The book work is enough without anything else.

30 September 1956 Mazabuka. A friend of Bill's came yesterday and stayed the weekend with us. He has been away on a job near the Belgian Congo border for a couple of months. There are only a handful of Europeans there. He has been putting extensions on an ice plant which is part of the *Native Development Department Scheme.* The natives catch lots of fish in the lake there and now the ice plant is there they are able to pack the fish in ice and send it four hundred odd miles to the Copper Belt to be sold. Before the ice plant was built they were not able to market their fish. This chap once brought us some fish from up there. The place is Lake Mweru.

18 October 1956 Mazabuka. Your postal employees in Australia must've been a lot of casuals while the strike was on

I should think, for this week I received a letter from Nell thanking me for the telegram for her birthday. It was posted in August but had been sent to Canton in China before being sent here!

3 October Mazabuka Sunday. We had a nice lazy day today and this evening took sandwiches and a thermos and had a picnic tea on the side of the road about two miles away. It was a nice change as we seldom go out. They hold pictures here every Friday night in the *Letters Club Hall* and about once a month in the hotel but we've never been. We've become real stay-at-homes. We had a telephone message from a driller in Lusaka last week to say he has started on our bore hole. Fortunately the geologist pitched on a spot only twenty feet from the small house Bill built when I first came here so the piping won't cost too much.

11 November 1956 Mazabuka. Last Monday we had a very nice letter from the water boring contractor saying the bore hole is finished. They struck water at seventy feet then continued drilling to a hundred and ten and the water rose within fifty-five feet of the surface and when tested pumped six hundred gallons an hour. This is very good considering it was the end of the dry season and no rain had fallen at the time. He said it was a good bore hole with stone nearly all the way down and they only needed thirty-three feet of six inch casing near the surface. It cost us £157 altogether which we've paid, so that is over. Now we will start saving for a house.

We are able to save more now that I am running a child minding nursery from here at home and we are still waiting to collect nearly £300 from the government for our fares while on long service leave. Fortunately Bill knows all about servicing bore holes as he has done a lot for the government and in Australia. We have a second hand pump which Bill is working on now.

17 November 1956 Mazabuka. Bill went to Lusaka today to put cement around our bore hole and started a tank stand. He left at 5:00am and will probably be back about seven this evening. There is no talk of us leaving Mazabuka as yet but we want to get the essentials ready on our block just in case. I'll be surprised if we are moved before next June. In the meantime I'm quite content here. We have our view back now that the rain has washed away the smoke and it is even more like a view of the sea. It is forever changing too with the light and shade. The grass and trees are so green now and when the sun shines it looks so nice and clear, like spring time at home.

Andrew is still a bundle of mischief learning new things every day. Instead of saying, 'eh?' he now says, 'What did you say?' and waits for an answer too. One evening Bill wanted to check over the car so Andrew was after him at once. Bill wasn't too keen on having help and I said in a rather hopeless voice, 'Will you be a good boy?' and Andrew shaking his head said, 'no'. I wish you could see Andrew today. He has on a new pair of pants with pockets on the front and as he has a cold I put a handkerchief in the pocket and he keeps pulling it out and blowing his nose. He has such a fat little tummy he has to draw in his breath to get his hand in the pocket.

24 November 1956 Mazabuka. Andrew and I are going to Lusaka with Bill after lunch today and are staying the night with Ed and Norma. We have some scrap piping we left there when we were on leave and Bill has managed to get a mate to take it out to the plot tomorrow. This will be a great help as we couldn't possibly carry it on the car, even one piece at a time, as some of it is quite long.

17 December 1956 Mazabuka. We heard, not officially but reliably, that we will be moving from here about the middle of March next year. A man we know, Harry M, is due back from leave on 7 March and our good friend Mrs Evans happened to type the letter telling him he was being transferred to Mazabuka. This suits us nicely as we will be able to go straight onto our plot and live in the three rooms already on it and the rains will nearly be over by then. We are going to stay there over Christmas from Saturday to Wednesday and start the brick boys on making a kitchen on the end of our three rooms and also they are to build huts for our native helpers. Bill will also get the pump working on the bore hole. We have a second hand stove and sink towards our kitchen and hope to pick up a table and chairs at a sale. The sales in Lusaka are pretty good.

28 December 1956 Mazabuka. We can't start building a house yet mum, we are going to put a kitchen on one end of our existing three rooms and live there while we save up. It is a comfortable little place and we intend replacing its present iron roof with corrugated asbestos and then it will be much cooler. There is an asbestos factory near Lusaka. I hope to make a little extra from fowls when we get settled. The shops can never get enough eggs or dressed poultry, in fact anything is saleable as the population in the town has increased enormously and nearly everything has to be imported. There are a few small farmers and the big farms are mainly cattle, mealie corn or tobacco.

10 January 1957 Mazabuka. The phone has just rung again - the Mazabuka hospital is having trouble again. The fluorescent light bar has given out in the theatre and the doctor is operating so Bill has to race off to put in another one. He has been there three times this week, one night from nine 'till eleven and last time from 2:00pm 'till 4.00pm. At least we are not in bed this time.

20 January 1957 Mazabuka. Bill is in his element just now. He has managed to buy two seven horse power engines from the *Mazabuka Management Board* for £20 and hopes to make one workable, to pump water from our bore hole. Both pumps are still full of oil so are in not too bad condition and he has quite a few spares thrown in. We also have the offer of a two hundred and forty volt lightning set for £40. All these things make a hole in our house savings account but will make us more comfortable in the small existing cottage on our land. We've decided to add a kitchen and bedroom to the existing three rooms for the time being and replace the iron roof with corrugated asbestos.

28 January 1957 Mazabuka. Yesterday we met the folk who have bought the place in front of our farm block. They seem very nice and hope to build a couple of rooms and live there by April. Our block is higher than theirs and a road separates the properties. Our house will overlook where they propose putting their house and they were quite envious of our block although they have paid £7.10 an acre more than us. There have been thirty blocks sold around us in the past couple of months and it is becoming quite common to see a man and woman with a tape measure stretched between them, obviously planning a house or digging among the trees to make a garden. We all seem to be thinking of going in for fowls too. Andrew loves it up there and insists on helping so we try to give him something to do where he can't do too much damage. Although the sun was under cloud most of the day we all got sunburnt.

We went to see Ed and Norma after we left the farm. Andrew had a lovely time playing with Keith. He had no sleep from six yesterday morning 'till we left Lusaka at 8:00pm and was as good as gold all the time. We made a bed in the back of the car and he slept all the way home not even waking when he was moved into his cot. He is rather grizzly today of course. It is rather amusing to hear him raise his voice and call, 'Bill, Bill' when his daddy gets out of sight. On Saturday he stepped backwards into his little cart and the side of it bruised him in a line right across his back. This morning he was standing on the barrow trying to reach a cake tin and fell. Fortunately he wasn't hurt that time. Last Monday Domino's child had a fall and her tooth went right through her bottom lip. It really needed two stitches inside and out. However I put a band-aid on the outside and told them to keep it clean. She seems alright now. Our garden needs watering again. Lusaka has had heavy rain. There is a range of low mountains between here and Lusaka and the rain seems to finish before it gets here. It is even raining either side of us and we have only had a few drops.

2 February 1957 Mazabuka. The other day Domino asked me when we are going to live on our farm. I said I didn't know and asked if he wanted to live there too. He told me in kitchen kaffir, 'Yes, here it costs a lot of money always buying food but on a farm I can grow my own pumpkins and mealie corn.' It is their staple diet and they can live much cheaper. He would like a bicycle too. He can't afford a bike of course so it would mean we would have to buy the bike and he would then have ten shillings a month taken from his pay 'till it was paid off.

Being on the farm nine miles from the town he would really need a bike so I promised to speak to bwana Bill about it. We are quite pleased to take Domino with us really because he doesn't mind what he is asked to do. For instance the cook boy may refuse to clean rooms and a houseboy would not do the garden. Well Domino has done all these things when he has been asked. We always give him something extra of course.

You asked about neighbours. Well there is a nice couple going to build on a plot in front of us. The plot on our south boundary is sold to a bachelor who has done nothing there, then next to him and over the creek is a nice little house, actually about a quarter of a mile from us. We expect our plot to be surveyed and cut in about six weeks time so Ed will probably sell when it is fixed up and it remains to be seen if the folk who buy it build there. There are people living behind us about two miles away but I've never met them. The telephone now goes past our place and when we can afford it we shall have it put on. No one is allowed to cut plots smaller than twenty acres out our way just yet so I'm afraid Ed will have to sell in one piece as half will be thirty-nine acres, same as ours.

The Public Works Department maintains the road from our boundary to Lusaka and I hear they intend tarring the road when there are enough plot holders as it would be cheaper than keeping the grader on it as they do now. Five miles of the road is already tarred. I've drawn a rough plan of our plot and surrounding plots which I hope you will understand. All the plots have lots of trees but it is not the best firewood as it makes too much ash. However, it is the native timber and is one of the few types of trees to resist the numerous grass fires.

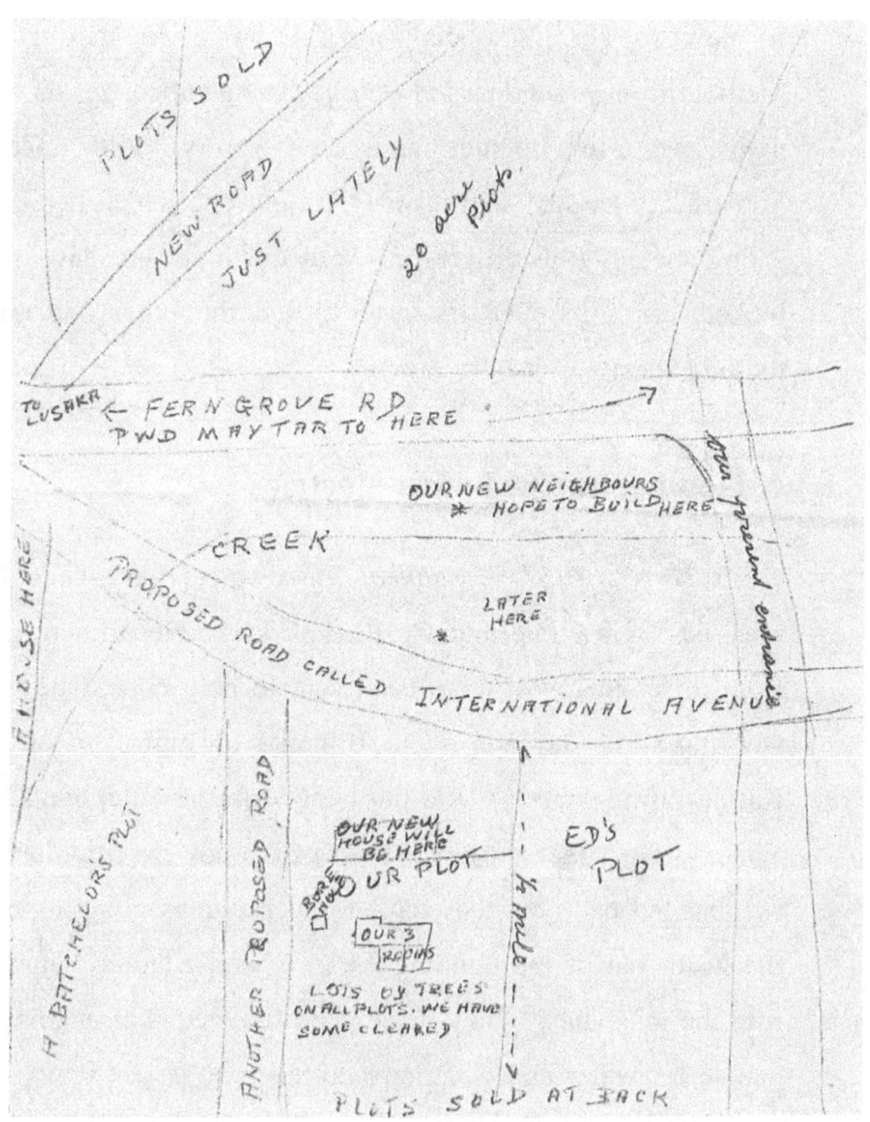

Farm block Lusaka

Ed says he has a booking on the *Southern Cross* for June 1958 and is definitely going home then. I wonder how Norma will get on doing her own work over there. Everything will be so new to her. You may meet them when they reach Melbourne as you did us and George. The game ranger sent his native over a few minutes ago to see if we would like to see a lion's head. He had shot it today, an old one which had been eating sheep. Its teeth were all worn down and its claws also looked very old. One eye was closed the other one open looking at us.

Flood at Kariba hydro-electric

23 March 1957 Mazabuka. Floodwaters have caused a crisis at Livingstone and the Public Works Department men from different towns have been sent to help cope. They are working shifts day and night. Bill was on night shift at the Kariba Power Station flood but is now on the afternoon shift. Water is eight feet above the floor of the power station and is sandbagged back but they have to keep pumps going to keep the water out of the building itself, where it would naturally ruin the machinery. They've stopped the electrical engines of course for water and electricity do not mix as you know and now the water supply is also threatened.

Bill rings up each day to see how we are. He left at 5:30am Wednesday morning and I've had a lady stay with me for these first four nights. Sunday, Monday and Tuesday nights I'll be staying with the New Zealander's Smith's at the Research Station two miles away. After that my neighbour Mrs H (who had Andrew while I was in hospital for my vein operation) is coming with Jane to stay each night, as her husband will also be away for a week. I'm hoping Bill will be home by then. They told him he'd be away a week but there is very little sign of the river subsiding.

30 March 1957 Mazabuka. Bill got back on Thursday evening and I can tell you we were pleased to see him. Andrew skipped about singing, 'Daddy, mummy, mummy, daddy'. He seems so happy to have us together again. Bill said he was glad to get back from the Kariba dam flooding and that the job had been no joke. He had to walk across a cable swing bridge then get down into the power station where all the doors and windows were bricked up and it really is a wonder the building didn't wash away as the water was seeping through the bricks in the walls. As a fresh swell of water would hit the building small geezers would spring up through the floor.

They had twelve pumps pumping the water from the building all the time. However the power is on again now as the worst danger is over. Bill said the river and falls were an awe inspiring sight. The force of the water washed an island down the river and wild animals were running frantically round on it as it came to rest on an obstruction, then slowly it broke to pieces and hurtled over the falls.

Friday lunchtime. Bill left for Lusaka to get some spare parts needed for the Public Works Department here and while he's there he's going to go out to our farm and see how the brick boys are getting on. He wants to start them on our bedroom. Domino has everything cleaned up around the house here in Mazabuka so Bill took him with him and he will get a bit cleared for more garden on the plot. He'll probably stay a couple of weeks or until Bill goes up again. Bill is due back this evening.

Sunday evening. Bill says everything was alright on our plot. The brick boys hadn't done as much as he expected but they had run out of cement so that was why. What they had done was well done.

All the men who worked during the Livingstone flood crisis received a letter of thanks and congratulations on a job well done and were told it would be entered in their personal files so that's a feather isn't it?

Letter from Acting Commissioner of Works to Mr W. Latimer, Mechanic, UFS Provincial Engineer, Southern Province, Livingstone. Subject: 1957 Zambezi Floods, Letter of Appreciation. Flooding of the Kariba Hydro Electric Plant. Dear Sir, The following excerpt from a letter from the Provincial Commissioner Livingstone quoted for your information: 'Now that the crisis in Livingstone seems to be over I hasten to write and thank you very warmly indeed for all the assistance given by the Public Works Department in the emergency.

The Public Works Department has had a very good reputation for some time in this Province and their efforts over the past fortnight have greatly enhanced this. I am directed by the Acting Commissioner to convey to you his appreciation of your good work in connection with the flood emergency and to say that a copy of this letter will be placed on your personal file'.

I am Your Obedient Servant, Johnson, Acting Commissioner of Works, Office of the Commissioner of Works, Lusaka.

Flooded Kariba power station & footbridge 1957

Flooded Kariba power station 1957

5 April 1957 Mazabuka. The Game Ranger (our neighbour) gave Andrew a serval cat skin this evening. Andrew had been rolling about on a lion skin at Johnny's and he said, 'Here Andrew, take this little one home for yourself'. It is three feet long and about eighteen inches wide at the centre, but much wider at the hips. Andrew lay down on it but can't bear the feel of it on his bare toes. It is spotted like a leopard and very savage I believe. Johnny and his brother were out hunting yesterday and shot an elephant. Tonight they went to the circus. What a contrast!

The snakes are bad around here just now. The cat has bought two dead baby ones to our door and the boy missed a big one near the fowl yard. I think they are looking for water as my neighbours complained of finding them in the outside toilet. I think the cats keep them away from this place a lot. One of my neighbours who wouldn't have animals (one of these very decided people) came to see if we had a spare kitten. She hoped it would grow up to keep snakes away as they had had a puff adder on their front path and a cobra in their toilet. Needless to say I keep a close watch on Andrew and bless this large veranda which is so airy it is almost like being outside but much safer. He's sitting on the floor right now packing small stones into one of his trucks.

28 April 1957 Mazabuka. We are in the money this weekend by way of a change. Bill sold his second best suit which he has outgrown to one of his workshop natives for £5 and he was so thrilled with it he wouldn't accept paper to wrap it in but carried it over his arm. I've no doubt he'll be sweltering in it all week. Then in the post yesterday was a government cheque for £303, £50 more than we expected being a refund on our fares home at last. £200 of this is to go into a savings account in my name and we will add to it as we can. The other £100 will be spent on the plot. We have been wondering how we will pay for the roof on the new room. The cheque has arrived just in time. We pay as we go and have no bills owing and that's how we like it. It is nice to know that what we have is paid for.

30 April 1957 Letter to Bill from the Office of the Commissioner of Works, Lusaka. Dear Mr Latimer, Now that all the shouting is over and the Livingstone incident is fading into the background I would like to express my personal thanks to you for all the work that you did at the time. You proved once again that the workshops could get cracking in a crisis and save the situation. It does not matter whether it is a large scale derailment, a boiler explosion or a flood you are the chaps that we rely on to pull us out of the mess and so far we have never been disappointed and I am sure that we never shall. Thanking you once again, Sincerely S.F. Gauron.

A new tractor and a new baby

5 May 1957 Mazabuka. A very sad thing happened here on Friday. One of the District Officers shot himself about 11:00am and died at five that afternoon. His wife is very well known and liked and both work hard for the district and its interests. They were due to go on leave in July. It is hard to understand what caused him to do such a thing. He left no note and to all outside appearances seemed a happy-go-lucky, likeable person. He was buried yesterday. He leaves a wife and three young children, two boys about eight or nine and a little girl Andrew's age. He used to bring her here each day when I had the nursery. I believe it was one of the little boys who found him.

Last week Bill heard of a farmer who wants to sell a *Case* tractor 1949 model I think, so went out to look at it. The farmer had six tractors and felt this one was surplus. He wanted £150 for it. The engine was done up twelve months ago and it seems in reasonable condition, still has its original paint. After talking and driving around on it and generally getting all the ins and outs of it Bill said he'd like it and explained how we have a plot in Lusaka and so on. Then the farmer said Bill could have the tractor for £130 cash, so he is going to bring it home today. Another man we know very well may go halves with Bill but even if he didn't it is certainly a cheap tractor.

The new Public Works Department man was due to start on 1 May but he has resigned so no one has turned up as yet which suits us. Remember when I was in hospital we were given permission to stay as this man could not get here 'till May. Now I suppose we stay 'till someone else turns up. The Public Works Department is very short of men in all departments. Bill applied to become a superintendent a couple of weeks ago but we've heard nothing yet. He has a good chance. It would be a step up the ladder and a rise in pay too. He has done well here at Mazabuka giving satisfaction to all and then the trip to Livingstone was also a feather in his cap.

Monday. There was so much excitement here yesterday I hadn't a chance to finish this. Our friends from Gwembe Mr and Mrs J and their four year old son, and Jack H who is going halves with the tractor arrived unexpectedly about 11:00am. The men all went off to the farm to bring the tractor home and I wish you could've seen Andrew when he saw his daddy driving home on a tractor. Bill drove it under the trees as a temporary garage and Andrew was calling out, 'Mind tree daddy, oh, oh, oh, tac-ta'. First thing this morning he disappeared and was found on the seat of the tractor. I said to him, 'Are you on daddy's tractor?' and he said, 'No daddy's tractor mummy, Nanoo's tractor'. At least I know where to look for him when I lose him now for he makes all the appropriate noise as well as sitting on it.

Bill and Jack got out spanners and proceeded to look into the tractor after dinner yesterday and couldn't find anything wrong as they tried the engine. They agreed it had a lovely tone. The fact that they had to shout this information to one another over the noise of the engine meant nothing to them. We had a chicken for our midday dinner and as they were still playing with the new toy near tea time I set to and made a huge egg and bacon pie which went down very well.

13 May 1957 Mazabuka. Yes it is quite right bullocks are still used for ploughing over here. The natives of course use nothing else and nearby will be a European farmer with anything up to six tractors like the man who owned the tractor Bill bought. Bill's friends are still popping in to admire his bargain and one even offered him £300 for it. It starts very easily and runs well.

17 May 1957 Mazabuka. Well Lorraine Rose was born yesterday morning. Ten minutes after she was born the phone rang and it was Bill inquiring about me and Sister said she thought he would swallow the phone with excitement when she told him he had a daughter. She said he asked if I was sure so perhaps I'd better have another look. He also asked if he could come and see me right away and she said, 'Oh no, we haven't finished yet she's only just arrived'. Sister said to me yesterday, 'This is a very important baby. The phone has been ringing all morning with nosy parkers asking if Mrs Latimer has had her baby yet'. Apparently news of my arrival in Mazabuka hospital spread like a bushfire. I had no idea we were so well known. Three presents arrived for Lorraine yesterday, two rattles and a blue bunny. Everyone is so good and it means such a lot when one is away from home. Bill brought me a lovely box of chocolates, each one in gold wrap. He tells me he is very proud of us. I'm sure he too is relieved it is all over.

28 May 1957 Mazabuka. The brick makers are doing quite well on our block and the work is straight which does not always happen when a native is left on their own building. We pay the boss brickie eight shillings a day and his labourer three shillings a day. I guess we'll have to raise his wages soon as he informed Bill on Sunday that he has bought a wife. He was hungry too as he had no money left for food after buying his wife. Last night Bill wrote to the immigration about my friend Estelle's proposed visit. They have been rather sticky lately only allowing a certain number in so we thought we had better get in early. Norma's sister and husband were to visit Norma a couple of weeks ago, the husband had a job to go to in Lusaka, but the immigration people refused a permit for them.

10 June 1957 Mazabuka. Lorraine is three and a half weeks old now. She loves to lie and look at things now and if she is looking at me her eyes follow me when I move. People tell me she was two weeks old at least when born. Bill went to Lusaka on Friday with a government truck to take some of his gear to our plot. All the heavy things went such as the engine for pumping water and bits of second hand timber for our roof. He came back with the truck that night. Then after work on Saturday he left in our car taking with him Domino and another native. These two are to break up stones and so forth for the floor.

It will be a cement floor and Bill hopes to put on the roof. Then he wants to start the brick boy on plastering the walls. We hope we can move in by the end of the month. This is a holiday weekend so Bill thought it a good opportunity to get something done on our house. After we've moved in we want to put on a fly screen to the veranda., By the way any mail coming here after we leave Mazabuka will be forwarded to us. The new address will be C/O Public Works Department (PWD) Lusaka.

23 June 1957 Mazabuka. The tractor was put on the train bound for Lusaka last Friday. It is quite an event when Bill starts the engine. Andrew peeps from behind a bush 'till he sees which way it's going and then he comes out of hiding and stands well back out of the way. If he sees me watching he excitedly gives me a commentary of what is happening. The boys at the workshop think Bill can do anything, welding, carpentry, engineering and all sorts and now he has a tractor to make a farm.

1 July 1957 Mazabuka. The Queen Mother is expected here next Monday and we hope to see her. It is a holiday weekend Monday and Tuesday, being holidays for Rhodesia's founder. I guess we'll give the workers the day off. The Public Works Department are busy making 'Standards' and huge elephant tusks to line the route. I think the tusks are to form a kind of arch at the Lusaka airport. The place is a hive of activity. Ed's firm got the contract to make the dais so Ed is making it. (He is foreman there.)

The main street of Lusaka is lined with flower beds but twelve months ago those flower beds were heaps of limestone and rubble from the road and footpath. Now it is a double carriageway and the footpath is finished. When Andrew was a baby it was almost impossible to push a pram from shop to shop. No one wore good clothes for they would be covered in dust and their shoes would be cut with the stones on the dusty footpath. Now the main street (Cairo Road) looks just like any other street in a big prosperous town. The side streets are not finished yet. It is a nice feeling to see a city grow. Even when I came here in 1954 there were not many decent shops but now you wouldn't recognise the place and some women go shopping looking very glamorous. I thought the women especially very dowdy when I first came here but they are not so now.

Tuesday. Bill told me last night that a new Rolls-Royce arrived at the workshops yesterday. A Rolls-Royce employee travelled by boat with it to Cape Town, then he drove it here in time for the Queen Mother's visit and he will stay a week. He has a nice job hasn't he?

Back to Lusaka

1 July 1957 Lusaka Farm. On Thursday we moved from Mazabuka to our farm block near Lusaka. We had a five ton government truck loaded to such an extent that Domino and Poison were literally hanging on it by their toes - there was nothing substantial to hang onto with their hands. On Wednesday we told them to have their gear packed ready for Thursday morning and Domino informed us he wanted to take his other child too. By questioning him I found he had two more wives in another compound. I said I hoped he didn't want to take them all but he didn't want to. He said that would be no good so he borrowed a shilling from me and off he went to get the child.

Next morning there was a hive of activity as we loaded the truck with the help of six natives. Then Domino said there was a man at his hut and he wouldn't let Domino's wife - the one he lives with - go to Lusaka. He was holding her child in his arms knowing she wouldn't go without it. We were finished packing the truck and Domino's things were on board too and this man was still there so Bill rang for the police.

Two native constables came and after talking to Domino, his wife and this other man for awhile they came to Bill and told him that Domino had bought this wife for four cows but had never paid her father anything after he'd given the £1 deposit. Her father has since died and this man is the father's brother and he is now eligible to collect the dowry so he wasn't letting her go until he got it. Bill wanted to know what happens now so the constable said it was a civil case and if they couldn't settle it they would have to go to the Chief of the tribe. Bill told them to be quick and away they all went to the Chief. When they came back the police just dropped them at our entrance and drove off and we were back where we started.

Domino said the Chief said they can go and the uncle said there was a court sitting on Friday and they were to attend. Bill wanted to believe Domino of course so that the truck could start but when the wife went to get into the truck the uncle grabbed the child again. I was the only one who noticed this and when I said, 'Put that child down' Domino turned from what he was doing and grabbed the child too. The mother was crying because she wanted to go with Domino. Then Bill stepped in and put the uncle in the car and drove off to the police station. The others got onto the truck and headed for Lusaka. Domino thought bwana very smart to do that and was all smiles but he doesn't know he'll be getting a summons from the court sometime soon. Bill told the native constable that he thought four cows was a lot to pay for a wife. The usual price is around £6.10 and the constable agreed it was too much to pay for her.

1 July 1957 Lusaka Farm Bill has been busy making shelves for me and he has also made a temporary shelter at the back to put the overflow in. When the rooms are finished we shall put a veranda across the front. We hope to have this all finished before Estelle comes to visit. We are building what is known as a *Rhodesian Boiler* at the back. It is a forty-four gallon drum set in bricks with a recess for a fire under it. This will be our hot water service. It is finished except for the chimney then Bill will pipe the water to the bathroom and kitchen. By then we hope to own a bath.

Last Saturday Bill went to the Lusaka railway station to collect his tractor and he was very thrilled to see it again and all our natives, sixteen of them turned out to see him arrive with the native children peering through the long grass.

10 July 1957 Lusaka Farm. I can hardly believe we've been here on our own place for almost two weeks. On 1 July Bill started work at Lusaka Public Works Department again and I sacked the brick boy's labourer. He was too cheeky for my liking. That threw us into a lovely muddle until today when we were able to start someone new.

A fire, the Queen mother and a missing native

10 July 1957 Lusaka Farm. Saturday. At lunchtime Saturday we noticed a grass fire burning some distance away and by 4:00pm it seemed a bit close for comfort so we filled a drum with water and soaked some bags thinking it might get close to our thousand bricks. Then for the next two hours we fought to save the whole place as the fire encircled us and seemed to spread across bare ground.

Monday. We had a lovely view of the Queen Mother and saw her twice. Near where we stood the African Chiefs were waiting to be presented, all very colourful. One old Chief from Barotseland was just about as well attended as the Queen Mother. He had travelled from Barotseland with three Land Rovers and a truck for cooks and three maid servants and a bodyguard of four. The Queen Mother looked lovely and the town was well decorated. I believe the decorations cost £100,000. The Public Works Department made a lot of the decorations including eight elephant tusks to span the road each way. They each weighed one thousand pounds. The Queen Mother left yesterday morning to go to the Copper Belt and is due back tomorrow. I'm giving Domino the day off tomorrow to go and see her.

I was too tired to finish this last night so I am just another day late. I have very full day nowadays. Domino went to see the Queen Mother and missed her. Bill has been trying out a very old John Deere road grader behind the tractor this evening. It's a real antique.

15 July 1957 Lusaka Farm. We had a nice long letter from you on Saturday the first to be posted to this address. You were hoping it would not get here before we did. We are still living a very busy life here. The only trouble at the moment is Poison. He went off on his bicycle on the 6 July, it was his day off, and he hasn't returned since. His wife expected him back the same day and so did we. However she's been left with no money and no food for herself and the two children so she has been eating with Domino and his wife. Domino is sick of that now. He didn't mind for a day or two but it is now over a week so today Bill will call at the police station and one of the native police should soon pick him up. They are a most irresponsible crowd. I can't make up my mind whether to take him on again if he returns or sack him for apart from anything else he still owes us £3 for his bicycle. I guess I'll make up my mind when I find out what he's been doing. Our house is progressing slowly. Today it is like camping in a dust storm as the workers are knocking out a window in one room to move it to another wall. It opens into a new kitchen at the moment so we want it on the outside wall.

22 July 1957 Lusaka Farm. Bill has been away on a job for a week, he got home yesterday. The job was four hundred miles away. I don't mind staying here on my own but Bill asked if I'd like an Alsatian for company a few days before he left and he brought one home. It is five weeks old and cries half the night. I think someone has made a mistake about its breed but it is a dear little fellow, not boisterous like Chummy and already is a sharp little chap.

29 July 1957 Lusaka Farm. Yesterday Norma and Ed came out and Ed helped Bill put up the rest of the timber for the roof. Then they got a few more sheets of iron on one side. The brick boys are working on the veranda today, the foundations are finished and he is now putting in the half bricks for the floor. This saves cement, then later they are surfaced with cement. Later I hope to have a smooth polished floor. The bedroom floor is coming up nicely now. The finishing layer has red oxide sprinkled in it then my houseboy puts red floor polish on and rubs it with a brush and rag. It gets a lovely shine on it after a while.

When the rains come we hope to make a lawn and a garden in front of the house. At the moment it is a jumble of brick, stone, sand and empty drums and tools. I've started a garden at the side of the house and have peas, onions, cabbages and silver beet sprouting.

6 August 1957 Lusaka Farm. Yesterday being a holiday Bill got busy on his engine before lunch and had it pumping water into the tank. The boys were beaming as it is hard work pumping up the water by hand. Bill said, 'I've put the tap up high out of Andrew's reach', but when Andrew saw it he just pushed his barrow to the pipe and then stood on it. He was then high enough to reach the tap. There is no beating that child. When we first came here I would smack him for playing in the water and I'd say, 'Look at your shoes and socks. They're all wet'. It hasn't stopped him playing in the water but now he takes off his shoes and socks first.

After Bill got the engine going for the water he started ploughing up the cleared land for we are expecting some citrus trees at the end of this month. There is so much to do here before the rain starts. The house is still progressing but very slowly. Bill doesn't get very much time to do anything. It is hard for him to know what to do first. The only time I get to do anything is in the hour or two after Bill goes to work at 7:00am. After that I have so many interruptions I don't seem to get anything done.

Andrew and the dogs have trampled my seeds so goodness knows whether anything will come up. Bill's bad finger healed nicely then he had another sore on his elbow, boils. I think the core is out of it and now there are three or four more small ones around it. The doctor says his blood is in very good condition. Penicillin injections have no effect on Bill at all. I hope they clear up soon as they are very painful.

13 August 1957 Solwezi. Your birthday tomorrow dad and I hope you have a happy day. Once again I'm late with my weekly letter the reason being that Bill had to return to Solwezi to finish the job he started two or three weeks ago. He made all the foundations last time and now has to put in the engines. We decided to go with him this time as there are government rest houses there. Solwezi is four hundred miles from Lusaka and not far from the Belgian Congo border. It is just a small town populated by government employees. There is one store here and eight miles away at a mine there are two stores. Any further shopping needed is done one hundred and twenty miles away at the Copper Belt towns.

14 August. Bill hopes to finish his job today but it is taking longer than he expected so we will be here 'till Friday. We drove up via Mumbwa and through the Kafue National Park supposed to be alive with game. You'll remember a photo of lions I sent you from the newspaper which interested George so much. It was taken in the Kafue Reserve. All we saw was a crowd of baboons. We are going back via the Copper Belt so will have done a complete circle.

Yesterday a girl about twelve years old rode past here on her bike with a monkey clinging to her, Andrew thought that lovely. This morning he has been playing with three children from next door. We had a rather dusty and rough trip up here in the Land Rover but both Lorraine and Andrew were very good. Late in the afternoon Andrew said, 'It's a long, long way daddy' and toward night time he was saying, 'It's a long, long, long, long way daddy'.

I'm hoping work on our plot is running smoothly while we are away. The brick boy is supposed to plaster the kitchen this week. Bill finished the roof before we left.

A thief, a deer for the pot and a poisoning

28 August 1957 Lusaka Farm. Our fruit trees have arrived and must be planted tomorrow. Fortunately two new natives applied for work today so they can dig the holes. Bill has so little time he leaves for work at seven and doesn't get back 'till five or after. Bill went down with Asian flu last Wednesday, it is all over Lusaka.

One night at 10:00pm, while we were both in bed, Domino knocked loudly at the door. Bill went out and Domino told him that Adam, the boy I employed at the beginning of the month but didn't like, (I don't know why I didn't like him and as he worked well I could hardly sack him), had stolen a lot of stuff from one of our neighbours who are away and their houseboy had traced Adam but Adam wouldn't tell them where the stuff was hidden. Bill punched Adam and told him he'd punch him again if he didn't tell where the things were by the time he counted to ten. At number six he said he'd given them to a friend and he didn't know where they were now, so Bill told the other boys to tie Adam to a tree 'till morning and then he could go to the police. Bill came in to lie down on the bed again and Domino was at the door again. He said, 'Adam says please don't tie me to a tree I'll tell you where the things are'.

They had dragged Bill out of bed and all he had on was a bit of blanket around his middle. Bill said, 'Right get it all here and I will go to the police now'. Domino was told to stay in our kitchen 'till Bill got back which was midnight. Next morning when Adam's room was searched Bill's old jacket and his square file came to light among other things, so that is the end of him.

On Monday Domino and the brick boy had to go to court as witnesses of Saturday night's affair and Bill stayed home to look after me. We are quite excited about the arrival of our fruit trees - the beginning of our orchard.

3 September 1957 Lusaka Farm. We had a very busy weekend planting our trees - ten lemons, ten mandarins, ten oranges, twenty grapefruit and one hundred berries. The watering is the trouble, everything is so dry and they need a lot of water. We made a little grass wigwam around each of the trees to protect them from the sun too. The wind here is terrific at times like Helens Plains in Horsham. I don't know why it should be so bad for the ground is undulating and plenty of bush trees. My veggie garden is a complete loss at the moment so I'm putting up a grass fence to protect it from the wind. Sometimes Andrew cries and says, 'Windy mummy in Nanoo's eyes'.

Last week Domino and the brick boy Mateyo had to go to court twice in reference to Adam stealing things from one of our neighbours. After the second trip Bill was annoyed to hear they have to go again Wednesday (tomorrow) so he went to the police and they said they were sorry but there is only one magistrate and that is why things take so long. However today a native constable came out and said they would be grateful if

Domino and Mateyo could go to court again tomorrow. I suppose they thought we may stop them from appearing again. They were both fed up after last Friday's trip. I wish you could've heard Domino telling me all about it. I only understand half of what he says but I get the gist of it. He says they were told, 'Come here, now wait there', then they were put in the witness box, then they must wait somewhere else. They had had nothing to eat all day either.

Thursday. Domino and Mateyo went to court again yesterday and Domino says Adam got nine months jail. We planted two apricot trees and two plum trees as well as our citrus and today Engineer, the new garden boy, wanted to know if he had to put water around those sticks, the sticks being the two plum trees. Not a bad description of them really but I assured him they were good trees.

16 September 1957 Lusaka Farm. Bill is giving Lorraine her 9:00pm bottle while I finish this. Your welcome letter arrived yesterday. No Bill hasn't joined the Lodge over here, too busy for one thing and no spare money for another. Yesterday brought a letter from Estelle too. I owe her a letter already but hoped to have some news from the immigration before writing but we've really been too busy to see about it, however will do something about it this week. I enquired at the chemist about a job for her last Saturday.

2 October Lusaka Farm. Our citrus trees have a small caterpillar feeding on the fresh young leaves so we've purchased some arsenate of lead. I said to Bill, 'We ought to send a snap home of us spraying our orchard with a fly sprayer' (as orchardists you would laugh!).

For the past month native constables have been patrolling the rural districts. Last week I had two visits from them. I have to sign the book to say what time the constables arrived and left and report any trouble. I always put 'no report'. Our natives seem reasonably good especially Domino and Mateyo. We were out of bread the other day and I had some yeast and Domino says he can make bread so we've had home-made bread twice this week.

30 October 1957 Lusaka Farm. Bill is away again this time for two weeks repairing a bridge - a low loader fifteen tons overweight went through the bridge. It is on a main road and must be fixed before the rain sets in properly. Being a rush job he'll be able to make about £30 overtime which is some consolation at Christmas time. Mrs Evans is spending tonight with me as her husband is also away. It is a pity we don't live closer to one another. They are eight miles south of Lusaka and we are nine miles north-west and we have to go into the town and out again to visit one another. However Mrs Evans works in town so it is not such a long trip for her as she will come straight from work.

We were very pleased yesterday when Bill arrived home from his job a week earlier than expected. Andrew and I ran to meet him midday but when he open the Land Rover door to greet us the two dogs bounded in first and climbed all over him When we went into the house Andrew ran in first saying he'd get daddy a drink of water but in his excitement he dropped and broke the cup. All the natives clasped their hands (similar to a clap) and gave a little bobbing type of curtsy and said, 'Morning bwana'. He had a really Royal welcome. Mr Evans has also been away so Mrs Evans has been sleeping here. She came last night too as he is still not home. Tomorrow Bill starts his two weeks leave so will get a lot of jobs done about the place. He hopes to pipe the water to the kitchen and bathroom, finish off the shed he is making, fix up our drive and one hundred and one other jobs.

13 November 1957 Lusaka Farm. Bill arrived home last Tuesday a week earlier than expected and then on Thursday commenced his two weeks leave. It is lovely to have him home all day. He says he'll have to go back to work for a rest. His day starts at 5:30am now and goes on until dark. He has made a shed for our car and tractor and odds and ends with bush poles and cement bags for the walls. He's improved the water system to the garden too. We still haven't got water into the house for the pipe length ran out but it is more important in the garden. Yesterday black clouds gathered and thunder rumbled but there was no rain unfortunately. Bill is also fixing up our drive around what will be our front lawn. We haven't worked out how we will keep the lawn watered. We are now eating our baby lettuces to thin them out and also silver beet. Soon the beans will be ready too. It saves a lot of money to have them growing. My strawberry bushes are doing very well and also the youngberry but the loganberries have been eaten by white ants, also some of our citrus trees. This morning, we mixed up some stuff and put it around each citrus tree to kill any white ants. I did the loganberries last week.

I think I told you I paid eight shillings and six pence from a poultry farm for a setting of eggs. After a troublesome three weeks four chicks came out looking like golden balls. I gave the hen two baby turkeys to look after too and she was doing a good job of mothering her brood, then one evening Domino heard to commotion and on investigating we found a hen in the corner of her pen clucking loudly, her brood hidden in her feathers. Stretched out dead in the centre of the pen still warm was a hen. We blame a snake but couldn't find it. Next morning we found the mother stretched out dead with one baby turkey crouched up close to her dead body his head hidden in her feathers. The others were chirping about the pen. Now I have to bring them inside each night. We didn't find the snake but we found two holes near the run which we filled up. We hope the snake is in one of them.

The plastering will be finished today so things are really looking up. We hope to pay off the brick boy and labourer at the end of this month so that will cost us £15-£20 a month for apart from their wages we have to buy lime and cement each week and sand to keep them going.

17 December 1957 Lusaka Farm. We still haven't got glass in the windows or ceilings and the other night a storm blew up with the wind whistling through the windows and blew our Christmas decorations along the rafters into the next room. Last Sunday evening as I was preparing tea Bill took the gun and said, 'I'll just go for a walk and see if I can find anything for the pot'. Andrew cried and wanted to go too so I started to sing, 'Baby baby bunting, daddy's gonna hunting' and was still singing it when Bill said, 'You want to see it?' and I said, 'See what?' and there were Mateyo, the brickboy and Domino carrying home a dyker (a small type of deer). It appears Bill walked to the end of the land we had cleared and saw the dyker in the trees. He shot it, then thought he'd see if any of the boys were around (it was their day off), but before he could call them he saw Mateyo racing through the trees with an axe (he is a slow moving type as a rule) with Domino, Benny and Alfred in hot pursuit. They had evidently been keeping a close watch on Bill. Usually on a Sunday they are all out visiting. Domino came to the house for a knife and he was beaming. We have the two back legs and they had the rest. Last night we had curried shanks and tonight a meat pie, tomorrow night we'll have one leg roasted. I made soup too and it was lovely. It sounds as if we are real Yankee pioneers doesn't it?

24 December 1957 Lusaka Farm. I have bread set aside to rise and cakes in the oven. I'm cooking a drake to take to the Evans tomorrow. I hated having him killed. The ducks always come to meet me and the little ones nibble my fingers. I have four lovely baby ducks born last Saturday. We have had a few cloudy days after almost continuous rain for ten days. On Saturday Bill finished the ploughing and since then Alfred has been planting mealie maize and peanuts. He hasn't finished yet, it takes a long time one seed at a time.

26 December 1957 Lusaka Farm. Rover is in the dog's hospital at the moment. He was missing for about four hours on Sunday and as he seldom lets me out of his sight I knew something was wrong. When he didn't turn up for his tea we concluded he'd either been bitten by a snake or had eaten grass where we've been spraying arsenate of lead. Just as we were going to bed we found him in his favourite sleeping spot. He could hardly walk and was bleeding badly and next day the vet confirmed our fears he had swallowed a bone. They were going to operate but decided to wait 'till today and see if the castor oil would bring it out naturally. The vet said they usually get blood poisoning and die after the operation. We know the two vets here as they were in Mazabuka. I had the daughter of one of them in my nursery in Mazabuka and he is the one looking after Rover.

Mateyo has just come along to tell me his wife has terrible toothache. She has a big hole in a back tooth, so after looking with the eye of a professional I gave her two disprin. Mateyo and Benny have been bricklaying for our nearest neighbour but are still living here as there is no shelter at the job. They come home when it rains heavily, as it usually does. They have asked our neighbour Mr P for a couple of sheets of iron to make a shelter but he hasn't brought it yet. The other day he told them they shouldn't leave the job when it rains so they left the job altogether then. As usual they came and told Bill their troubles. Benny wants to move on now but then Mateyo wants to stay. So Bill said, 'As you know I've got lots of work for you to do but I've got no money for your wages. If you like I'll make a contract with you to make a 15,000 gallon tank out of stone'. Mateyo was very interested and today started digging out stones. Bill has already done part of the foundations himself. We have stony patches all over the property and as we have no money to make bricks Bill says he can make a stronger, cheaper tank with the stones (I should say rocks, really). The contract means that we will pay for Mateyo's food and subtract that from the contract price when the job is finished.

Evening. Bill was to bring Rover home after work today but he died last night. They said his bowel was badly lacerated and bleeding and it looked like arsenate poisoning. Bill told them we sprayed our trees with arsenate. They are waiting for a report from Mazabuka, having sent his intestines there for an examination. There is grass everywhere, why did he have to eat what had been sprayed? I do miss him as he was always with me. In the morning he used to come in for a piece of toast and was so big he could've rested his face on the table. One day he swept a cup off the table with his tail. He was about six months old and becoming quite a good watchdog.

7 January 1958 Lusaka Farm. We had some good news last week. We applied to the government for the living out allowance, as we no longer occupy government housing. The house must be valued at no less than £2,500 and the valuer said ours was worth £2,750 as it stands unfinished. So we are now eligible for an extra £25 a month. On Bill's pay we will get about £200 back pay too which will be most acceptable. They probably won't get around to paying us for several months yet but at least we know it will come.

Growing tobacco

27 January 1958 Lusaka Farm. Our efforts at tobacco growing are not so picturesque as the film you saw, I'm afraid mum. The film was of Virginia tobacco too. It is transplanted about August when the sun is very hot and the weather dry. It is being cut now and dried in huge brick barns. The fires have to be kept going while the drying is in progress to keep the hot pipes running through the fans at the one temperature. There is a lot of outlay in growing it and sixty to one hundred employees needed on one farm. With Turkish tobacco it is planted during the wet months and dried on sacks in the sun during the dry winter months. Virginia tobacco grows huge leaves but Turkish has small leaves which shouldn't be more than six inches across. That is why they are planted so close together to retard growth. We are now fifteen days without rain and the watering is a problem. The seed beds have to be well watered before the plants will come out, then the rows in the field have to be watered before the holes are made ready for the plants, otherwise the holes can't be seen for dust. Another thing you can't put little plants into such dry soil. The ones we transplanted last week and this week have had no further watering since they were put in and seem to be alright but they would certainly look better if we had a shower. Lusaka had a heavy downpour yesterday but we missed it. However, Alfred is suffering from rheumatics today so that's a good sign. Last time he had it we had rain soon after.

The families we had lined up didn't turn up for the planting this morning. It appears a child died at the neighbouring farm so they went there, but were ready for work again at 3:00pm. They usually do their own chores then get here about 8:30am then work 'till about 1:30pm. Then we knock off 'till three because it is very hot around midday - never as hot as you've been having in Melbourne though - fancy one hundred and eight degrees! I'll get some snaps taken of us at work if you like we haven't taken any so far.

On Friday I stopped at the post office to buy a stamp for your letter and looking across the road I noticed the *Rural*

Engineers Office door was open so on impulse I went across and asked how long it would be before the new telephone line was erected. I told them how sick Andrew had been and how Bill has to go away on jobs sometimes. (I laid it on pretty thick.) I also told him of the time wasted looking for a phone in my efforts to contact the doctor. He was very sympathetic and told me the best thing to do would be to write a letter stating what I have told him and felt sure something would be done. Party lines are a nuisance of course for they ring a lot but they can be handy too. When he counted the pins on the map he found there are fourteen of us waiting for this line and there are only fifteen on the line so another line is definitely needed. However we must wait for a reply.

5 February 1958 Lusaka Farm. Last Friday afternoon Bill arrived home having finished his job on the Copper Belt. Actually he was lucky to be away for those two weeks for everyone living around here was bogged night and morning as they went to and from work. One morning eight cars were lined up waiting for a tractor to pull them out. The road was fixed up but with the now almost continuous rain this week it has been made bad again.

Wonderful news this week, we received a cheque for £150 back pay for housing allowance. Most of it has gone of course but our bills are now behind us. Trying to build on wages with no capital is quite a business but we will be able to get a few extras now such as glass in the windows and fly wire. On Monday Lusaka had a dreadful wind storm which unroofed several buildings. Fortunately it had almost blown itself out when it got here or our roof would've been gone too, for the house is one big draft at the moment.

Bill was on a job about forty miles away today between Lusaka and Mazabuka and on the way got bogged on the tarred road. It had fallen in as there are lots of heavy trucks travelling on it now taking cement to the Kariba Dam where a huge hydro scheme has been constructed. The wind which unroofed buildings in Lusaka also did damage in another district and one school for native children had its roof blown straight up in the air then landed about sixty yards away. Two walls of the building fell in on about seventy children and twelve were admitted to Mazabuka hospital. One native in Lusaka was blown off his bike then along the ground and another boy had his leg broken when the roof of the Public Works Department machine shop fell in on to some trucks.

Too good to go home

12 February 1958 Lusaka Farm. We have decided to come back here for another tour after our leave. It will only be two and a half years next time. Perhaps you could come back with us for a few months. Bill would be very lucky if he got a better job than this anywhere else with the housing allowance. His wage will now be £115 a month (£35 Australian, over £28 a week) and the cost of living is lower than at home. Where else could one build a house on wages in twelve months? We pay no rates on this place and since Andrew was born no taxation and of course there is no hard work. If I decide to make a garden I tell Alfred to dig the selected spot. If I'm too busy to plant the seeds Alfred can do it.

I go to town to do my shopping and native employees carry my parcels to the car and when I get home Domino has the house work, washing and ironing done and the kettle boiling and maybe the meal ready too. Makes you wonder what I find to do doesn't it yet I'm never still. I'd dearly love you to come over and see it all for yourself. Don't worry about us coming back to Australia. When we get enough behind us we will be coming home again permanently. Bill has £100 a year gratuity for each year of service to collect when he does leave here and he wants to build up a bit more yet.

6 March 1958 Lusaka Farm. Wednesday. Remember last year Bill had to go to Livingstone to work in the power station which was eight feet underwater? This year they were ready for the rains, having built a wall fourteen feet high around the station. Flood waters this year are higher than last year and only one foot below the top of the wall. Now Lusaka Public Works Department has trucks loaded ready to answer an emergency at Livingstone. Seven men have volunteered to go there for which Bill is very thankful. He says it is not very nice working eight feet below water level with each surge of water rocking the building. Not one of the volunteers there last year has volunteered this year.

Today Bill came home from work at lunch time. He has another crop of boils and is very miserable with them. After lunch he took three disprin and lay down on the bed. Before going to bed himself Andrew got several of his best toys for daddy to play with before he went to sleep. Andrew always takes an assortment of cars and tractors to bed with him.

Alfred has bought a new wife but she is not living here yet. It appears her mother told Alfred that he must live with them for one month to see if he is a good husband. I'm not sure what qualifications he has to have to be a good husband but I think worldly goods would have something to do with it. Last week he asked me to buy him two new blankets. I bought one plain grey for nineteen shillings and six pence and the other the gaudiest I could find for £1.07. However, he still owes me for them and will be some months paying them off. I couldn't take any of last month's pay for he only had sixteen shillings seven pence left after I deducted all his other expenses during the month. Imagine keeping yourself and wife on three shillings and six pence day. He is quite well paid for a labourer.

New native Petrol lasted one week with me. When he had nothing else to do I told him to cut grass and tidy the yard but he told Alfred he wasn't going to work as a garden boy so he left on Sunday. I bought Domino some new overalls the other day and dog Liza didn't recognise him in them and barked furiously at him. Bill has put on another native to make 25,000 bricks and yesterday he started to make himself a hut. He came to the house here and took an axe to cut the wood for his hut and Liza bit him.

13 March 1958 Lusaka Farm. We have put on a native to make 25,000 bricks and he has just completed making two round huts with sticks and grass for himself and his workmate. This afternoon the two wives made two trips with enormous loads on their heads and the inevitable child on the back. They walked miles and miles from the previous employer's property to here today.

There are so many native men looking for work now. Every day we have one or two call in. The other day a chap asked for work and I said, 'What sort of work, garden boy?' and he said, 'No houseboy'. Next day he turned up again and I told him I still didn't want a houseboy but it appears he was then prepared to work as garden boy. I said I didn't want any more and he walked away. I felt so sorry for him and thought he must be hungry to call twice like that so I called him back and asked if he'd like a bit of piece work and he said, 'Yes, anything'. That means he can do the job in his own time and I said a price for the job I wanted done. He started about 6:30am and about 2:00pm he came and asked if he could go to eat now. Poor thing evidently didn't want to stop in case someone else got the job. There was another native waiting to ask for work when I got home.

21 March 1958 Lusaka Farm. Bill is well again after his poisoned hand. It was like a boil with four cores and a nasty red streak up his arm with lumps at elbow and armpit. Nothing happens singly so Domino has gone to the doctor today to have a tooth extracted and Alfred has been off for two days with dysentery.

28 March 1958 Lusaka Farm. Bill and I have been scraping the old paint off our car ready for Bill to duco it tomorrow - what an awful job too. We've been scraping all day and now the car is just one horrible mess -looks as if it has been to the panel beaters after an extremely bad accident. It is to be done in smoke grey this time which is almost the colour of this writing paper. Andrew of course had to lend a hand with his own piece of sandpaper. One of his many remarks was, 'I just playin' about here'.

7 April 1958 Lusaka Farm. There was great excitement this week end. At the end of the month we bought three hundred feet of two inch piping for £30, and on Friday Bill connected it. We now have water running into the stone tank. We also bought sixty-three feet of three and quarter inch piping which Bill put into the kitchen and bathroom - such a thrill to see water from the tap after continual dripping from a bucket! Even Lorraine tried to turn it on. Andrew of course was running around with taps poking them through imaginary holes all over the place. Today Bill put up a cupboard adjoining the sink. His next job is another cupboard in the kitchen in the corner by the stove. Andrew is never far from any new job and he was hanging up empty flour bags in front of the new cupboard and saying to anyone who'd listen, 'This will be very handy'.

Tomorrow Domino goes off on two weeks holiday so I'll be busy doing the house work on top of everything else. Bill hates getting out in the morning so I'm wondering how he'll get on getting up first to light the fire. We bought Domino and his wife two return tickets to Mazabuka and gave him an advance of £1 to give to his uncle-in-law to help pay off his debt. Domino was supposed to pay four cows for his wife but so far has only paid a £1 deposit. We hope the £1 we've given him will quiet the uncle for a further twelve months and that Domino's family will arrive back safely.

15 April Lusaka. Bill put in a hand basin the other day and also connected the hot water so now we have hot and cold running water over bath, basin and sink! Domino won't know himself when he gets back and finds he doesn't have to fill a bucket for the kitchen. Great excitement!

PART 3: THE LAST YEARS

An Australian visitor

22 May 1958 Lusaka Farm. Yes my friend from Melbourne Estelle Yeaman is with us now! At the moment she is composing a letter to the immigration department for permission to work here. Bill took her to see our local politician and he got her a job as doctor's receptionist and gave her a great build up in a letter she is to send in with her application. We follow one another around talking all the time. So far we haven't missed out on a meal but lots of other jobs are neglected.

30 May 1958 Lusaka Farm. Estelle started work last Tuesday and seems to like it alright.

8 June 1958 Lusaka Farm. Bill is busy today fixing up a car. He is going away on Wednesday for about one month helping to make a steel bridge on a river very near the Congo border (Kalungushwi Bridge). I'm glad Estelle is here she is great company for me.

12 June 1958 Lusaka Farm. Bill was to go away yesterday but word came through that the hundred foot span of the new bridge had fallen in the river so they now have to make up a jib for lifting it out again. He may go tomorrow. It is quite a big job I believe and several men are going. There are lots of Bill's fellow workers away on construction jobs at the moment all in the name of progress - real pioneers.

19 June 1958 Lusaka Farm. Bill finally got away Sunday morning and expects to be away about four weeks. I'm very glad of Estelle's company. Bill will miss Lorraine. She holds up her arms to be lifted every time she sees him and when he kisses me she squeals and holds up her face for a kiss as well.

26 June 1958 Lusaka Farm. Every now and then Andrew packs his little suitcase and tells me he is going to work to build a bridge and won't be back for months. He has heard me say, 'Bill will be away for a month'. I had a letter from Bill written the day after he reached his destination and sent back with a truck which was coming back for supplies. Bill took lessons in bread making before he left and I'd love you to see him at it. He was so energetic with the kneading the bottom of the dish dented in and out with loud bangs. Andrew said, 'Oo makes a lot of noise with that bread Bill.'

10 July 1958 Lusaka Farm. We will be going on our little holiday with Estelle as soon as ever we can after Bill's return, probably the end of August. I'm expecting Bill home any day now. His last letter was full of yearnings for his home so we must put a welcome on the mat. It was a big bridge to build and I guess we'll hear more of it when he returns. Did I tell you he has grown a beard?

24 July 1958 Lusaka Farm. Bill has been home a week now. He took snaps of the job and it certainly was a big bridge. There were two one hundred foot spans and a fifty foot span in the centre. There was a man building it and he dropped one of the hundred foot spans in the river so he wasn't too popular as it had to be raised before anything else could be done. Bill and his four fellow workers fixed it up. Bill was given the job of cook so every evening he left the bridge site at 4:00pm to prepare the evening meal.

Bill looks back in 2001[1]: Four of us Europeans and about fifty Africans travelled about four hundred miles to a remote area to erect a steel bridge across the Kalungwishi River which flows into Lake Mweru. It is near the corner where Zambia, the Congo and Tanzania meet. The Bema tribe there had a bad

---

[1] Interview with son Robert Latimer

health record with malaria, sleeping sickness and bilharzia being endemic. Anyway we took our Paludrine tablets daily, kept out of stagnant water and killed any tsetse flies we saw

Nearly every afternoon I would set myself up with an oxy-acetylene welder and a Bema speaking interpreter and commence trading for bananas, mangoes, chickens, corn etc. etc. There would be a long queue of locals anxious to get pots, pans, bicycles, hoes and various implements including old guns repaired. They weren't going to miss an opportunity as rare as this and we welcomed the change from bully beef and rice, our staple diet. My assistant and our clients would haggle a bit until the price was settled and I could start repairs and I quite enjoyed my task.

Once an historical fifty year-old Martin Henry rifle was produced with a presentation plate from the BSA (Birmingham Small Arms Company) to a Chief. The rifling was worn out as was the breech block which left half the cartridge case showing when cocked. It was an absolutely lethal weapon to the owner and I should guess quite safe to the target. It was a real museum piece. I told the owner in strong terms about the danger and suggested he give it an honourable burial because of old age.

This trade was good for everyone and we were all eating like kings until one day our camp boy Jim came running down to our bridge in a great panic. 'Boss all the chickens are dead!' Shock! Horror! Were we worried! What kind of epidemic had killed all of them so suddenly and how would it affect us who had been eating them nearly every day? Our imaginations worked overtime on the possibility of some exotic African disease unknown to medical science.

What a way to die I thought, Alice won't be very happy. Joe our boss took off at top speed to the camp and sure enough it looked like a battlefield with dead chooks scattered everywhere. But what made them die so suddenly? Some quick detective work revealed that our camp cook boy Jim had not noticed the chickens eating our Paludrine tablets due to the lid not on and the chicken scavenging on our table while he was absent. Joe came back looking very serious and kept us in a suspended, worried state for some time before revealing that we would probably make it back to Lusaka and our wives okay. Jim buried the chooks I think.

The Nile crocodile is at home in all the larger rivers and lakes of central Africa but Africans use canoes everywhere safely. However a Chief was complaining about his people being killed and so the Kalungwishi Bridge came about. The

Chief of this particular tribe pestered, cajoled and whinged making the Governor's life a misery. Anyway the word went out and in the end it was as usual, the Public Works Department's job to carry it out. An old steel bridge had been dismantled at Kaffironde, a place on the Kafue River near the copper town of Mufalira, and just thrown aside on the riverbank. The building department were given the task of transporting these steel trusses to the erection site and placing them on concrete piers which they had to plant in the river bed.

The builders made a good job of the concrete work but unfortunately steel work wasn't their scene and a steel span was dropped into the river while being placed on the piers. This is when the mechanical workshops were called in and we found ourselves erecting *guyed derrick masts* on each bank with a heavy steel cable stretched between. On this ran sheave blocks to complete a flying fox with which, using the chain blocks, we could manoeuvre and move the steel trusses with safety and precision

One day while working high on the bridge with Africans we heard a terrific commotion from the far river bank and native women running away throwing down their head loads of water tins as they went simultaneously out of the reeds. A huge python slipped into the river followed by a canoe load of men who tried to strike the snake with their paddles. The snake ducked underwater heading for the far bank at top speed followed by a bombardment of bolts and nuts from our grandstand. The twenty foot serpent disappeared into the reeds and petrol soaking and flames failed to flush him out. We all counted it as an exciting interlude.

24 July 1958 Lusaka Farm The evening Bill arrived home he complained of a pain in the chest. It hurt most if he took a deep breath. It appears he fell off some of the bridge scaffolding two weeks before so I insisted he see the doctor next morning. After an X-ray he was told he had a rib cracked so they tied him up today. He is in bed with flu and every time he sneezes or coughs he hurt his ribs. The whole town seems to be suffering from flu, even the doctors. Estelle went to work this morning and Bill stayed home.

Yes there are quite a lot of men out of work at the moment mainly in the building trade. For the past six months or more Ed has not had a good word to say for Rhodesia. He was so homesick that New Zealand had become a 'land of milk and honey' to him. He'll find it quite different to buckle down under a boss instead of shouting at natives I'm afraid. I forgot to mention Bill had a beard when he returned and kept it on 'till the Saturday when he shaved it off and took me dancing

Saturday night, while Estelle minded the children. Andrew was greatly taken with the beard but Lorraine was funniest, she put her face up for a kiss with her eyes blinking rapidly as she waited for the beard to touch her. Then she'd draw back and gaze at Bill give a little giggle and ask for more. It is almost 7:00am and Bill is off to work so I must close this and get him to post it.

8 August 1958 Lusaka Farm. Bill has been busy fixing up his windmill. The wheel was broken but he has repaired it and during the weekend hopes to erect it. Andrew said, 'I not want that broken wheel I want one with red on it'. He has evidently seen the new one up the road which has red paint on the tips of the wheel.

Last Sunday we went to the annual Lusaka Show and had a lovely day. We stayed to watch the evening arena program too and it was great. Lorraine screamed and talked with terrific enthusiasm as the band marched on. She loved it and no one sitting near us could hear the announcer.

Taking Estelle to Wankie Reserve

The last day in the Wankie Reserve was the day I'll never forget and I'm glad it is behind us. We saw at least two hundred elephants and had to drive through two herds. One elephant in the second herd let out a squeal and chased us. We also had to pass through a herd of buffalo about two hundred and fifty strong. The road was very sandy and with the trailer on behind some of it was hard going. Once we got stuck and had to unhitch the trailer, and drive the car out then bring the car back along the side of the road and push the trailer up to it. We were all a bit scared I can tell you.

As we got near the main camp the trees thinned out and the land resembled a cattle farm at home. Instead of cattle grazing there were wild animals, then to our surprise, another herd of elephants were at a waterhole only two miles from the camp. Nearer the camp were a herd of cows grazing evidently belonging to the camp. They looked so peaceful and home-like after our exciting day when to our surprise we saw yet another elephant within sight of the cows. It is estimated there about four thousand elephants in Wankie Reserve and we saw more than our share.

At the moment we are staying at a rest hut in the Matopos Hills near Bulawayo. We took Estelle to see Cecil Rhodes grave today. Tomorrow we are going into Bulawayo to do some shopping and Tuesday morning we are heading for the Zimbabwe ruins. The children are very good on the whole. Sometimes they get tired of being cooped up in the car and when we stop do their utmost to pick up all available dirt. This morning I had a real washing day and feel much better for it. I guess there will be letters from you awaiting our return to Lusaka. We've left Alfred and Domino in charge at our home and hope they are managing alright.

3 September 1958 Lusaka Farm. We arrived home yesterday afternoon. The children were thrilled to see all the familiar things (and for the time forgotten things). I told Domino I had a small present for his children so they came to receive them all dressed up in the new dresses their mother had made in our sewing class. They looked very nice and Domino is very proud of them. I intend to get something for Domino and Alfred when I go shopping tomorrow as they looked after the place very well while we were away.

I have to pack up a few tins of food for Bill as he has to go away one hundred and eighteen miles to fix a bore hole. A doctor visited the area they are going to and found the folks sick with dysentery, diphtheria and so forth and blamed the water supply. Bill should be back by Saturday. He received a letter yesterday from the top office thanking him for his part in building the Kalungushwi Bridge, 'A difficult job well done', it said.

10 September 1958 Lusaka Farm. I haven't had my weekly letter from you and I'm blaming the post office as everyone seems to be short of letters this week. They are moving the post office into a new six story building opening on Monday, and not before time. The old one is a dirty old place.

22 October 1958 Lusaka Farm. We've been having quite a working bee this morning. Alfred, Andrew and I have been clearing rubbish from the land we've had grubbed ready for Bill to plough. Bill also works at it each evening. So far we've only got one corner done. We have to gather up all the ash from our fires too as otherwise the crop would be patchy if we left heaps. The native women were also working here this morning. I told them they could have the remaining peanuts if they dug them and cleaned the patch of grass which they have done, so it won't take long to get it ready for more seeds now.

Did I tell you Bill is making a toy garage for Andrew? He drew a sketch of it one evening to show me and next day Andrew found it and played with it all day running his cars up to the pictured bowsers and onto the ramp so I guess the real thing will be appreciated.

22 October 1958 Lusaka Farm. Bill does a bit of ploughing on his tobacco land each evening. I think he should've been a farmer as he looks so happy as he gets his land ready. We have seed beds nearly ready and will start planting next month. The seedlings are planted six to nine inches apart so there is something like 150,000 plants to the acre and we hope to plant about four acres. The native women will help with the planting and reaping as we will need lots of part time workers.

3 November 1958 Lusaka Farm. I'm glad to hear Estelle returned home safely. Today I went along to the government nurseries and got a hundred young gumtrees, twenty-five guava trees and several other plants including a cutting from a double pink hibiscus. If it grows I'll have six different ones. They grow well over here. The nursery man only charged me for the gums and guavas. The rest were a gift because Bill fixed their leaky water tank last week. The day Bill worked there on the tank he was given a lovely Christmas tree, a pine about four feet high, which we will plant after Christmas.

The kiddies are to go to the Public Works Department Christmas party on the 13 November. Andrew said to me, 'I just want a big tipper truck and a meat truck and a nice truck to carry moo cows and a train, a big one I can drive I not want everything just a few'. The train he mentions is a lovely red wooden engine he has seen in one of the shops at £15.15. Needless to say it won't be in his sack. We could buy several windows for that. Bill has planted his second seed bed now.

Someone was telling him that he would do very well if he cleared £60 an acre with the tobacco. I hope it is a success anyway for Bill's sake. It's his first try and he has really worked hard on all the interesting preliminaries.

We have to come back here for a further two and a half years but we are trying to sell out before next September but it would be impossible to give it away at the moment. The long strike on the Copper Belt affected all sales, so it would be foolish for us to leave here without enough behind us to start up again. We've worked hard here and hope the tobacco crop will pay back some of the money we've put into the place. There is still lots to do but spending must stop in December so as to save up for the trip home. We are really looking forward to next September.

18 November 1958 Lusaka Farm. We've had several days of hot dry weather but today we had a good rain so after it was over we hurried out to plant the first tobacco seed bed. The seed is so fine it must be sprayed on with a watering can. Bill said the natives will think I'm mad watering after the downpour we've just had. We also hope the crop is a success for it is to go toward paying for our trip home next year. We've only got £5 saved towards it so far. There is always some unforeseen expense with a property isn't there? We've spent a lot on wages in the past two years, paid for a borehole, bought a tractor, engine and pump and tank for the borehole, bought a disc plough, built native quarters, a house for ourselves, a water storage tank and play area and swimming pool made of stone from the property and cleared three to four acres of land ready for the tobacco. It is more than any of our neighbours have done in the time anyway.

Lusaka Farm, pool area in the background, 1958

26 November 1958 Lusaka Farm. Some of the tobacco seed planted last week is already up. We've had to water it as there's been no rain and the sun is very hot. Today is cloudy which will help the little plants. The journey over here is not so bad mum. There is always something of interest on the ship. Even though Estelle was a bit sick coming over the pleasures far outweighed that bit of discomfort. Talk to her about it when she gets back. Anyway we'd love to have you both stay with us. By the way if there is anything in my letters you don't quite understand it will be handy to have her talk it over with you, she can explain the places I mention over here too.

Lusaka is spending thousands of pounds on improvements and hopes to be a city when the Queen comes in 1960 to open the Kariba Dam. They have closed the gates at Kariba now and are letting only 11,000 gallons of water a minute through as they want to fill up the vast area which will eventually be the dam. The mighty Zambezi River is only a trickle of water at the Chirundu Bridge. Mention this to Estelle and she will show you a photo of the bridge. The dam will take a couple of years to fill up properly and then the river will get back to normal. I'm wondering if the dam will alter the climate a bit as there will be a lot of evaporation from such a large area of water.

Tobacco growing and a theft

2 January 1959 Lusaka Farm. Yesterday we had such a busy day. First Bill decided to transplant the biggest of the tobacco seedlings. We planted the first bed too soon really and some are now over one foot high and they are supposed to be transplanted from four to six inches high. We get heavy rain in

January so we were putting off transplanting however the plants are getting so big and overcrowded in the seed bed we decided to start yesterday. Three mfazis (wives) and an older child, Alfred, Bill and myself all got out at 7:30am. My job was to pick out the plants from the seed bed. Bill marked out the planting rows, the child marked out the places for each plant and Alfred and the mfazis did the planting - all very well organised. By midday we had fourteen rows planted with over two thousand plants but the seed bed looks very little different. We intend putting in more at the weekend. We thought a nice little shower of rain would help the ones transplanted but at the moment (10:30am) we are experiencing a cloud burst. It is pelting down and all drains running very full, each drain is at least one foot deep.

6 January Lusaka Farm. I don't think I told you that we have to be extremely careful with our tobacco seed bed as there are so many diseases they can get. Smoking is not allowed near the seed bed area and Bill told Alfred that if he caught him smoking there he'd fine him a shilling and if Alfred caught Bill smoking he was to tell Bill and then Alfred would receive one shilling. The other day Bill came in and sheepishly asked if I had a shilling as Alfred had caught him smoking near the seed beds.

21 January 1959 Lusaka Farm. We are watering again as we've had ten days of hot sunny days and still no sign of rain. We had good rains but with this hot dry spell everything is drying up and the ground is like concrete. Perhaps you could send a newspaper about the heat wave over there and Bill would also like several Wednesday or Saturday *The Age* newspapers with all the ads for jobs and perhaps a *Weekly Times* or two. He wants to get some idea of how things are over there as regards suitable jobs. He has been very pleased with the variety of stamps you've had on your letters - they always seem to be printing new ones. Over here we have the same old type and poor paper they are too.

At the moment I'm sitting in the shade near the swimming pool with the nips. Last Saturday I got an old wire cot mattress and strung it up as a hammock and Lorraine is now lying on it commanding me to 'push'. If it gets a slight roll on it she calls, 'Oh fall, fall, stop'. She is a great one for giving orders.

10 February 1959 Lusaka Farm. We are very busy still with the tobacco. It is quite a job. Last week we were recruiting more labour and I think I had someone new each day. One old fellow came to work the first morning and leaned on a walking stick watching Alfred feed the fowls. He was supposed to be learning how to do the job so that Alfred could get on with making lines and holes for the tobacco plants. Anyway the old boy told me he didn't want to do the fowls he thought we had a farm with forty boys working on it. No doubt he had ideas of fading in among them and doing nothing. I told him to pick up his things and go.

Another one who was given the job of making holes couldn't even follow a straight line which was marked on the ground for him. Evidently the job really exhausted him for he was sound asleep when Alfred came to work next morning. By the way the holes are two inches deep. Bill made a little frame of five pointy sticks each five inches apart. This has to be pressed into the well ploughed soil until the cross bar rests on the ground (two inches deep). The lines are made before hand I might add.

On Saturday it was Domino's day off so he went to town. On the way back he stopped at the Indian store about three miles from here to recruit labour for our planting. Seven mfazis said they would come on Monday morning. When he left them to come home he found his bicycle had been stolen.

We went to bed about 11:30pm after having had visitors and were sound asleep when Domino pounded on the kitchen door at 12:30am to tell bwana his tale of woe. Bill told him he'd ring the police next morning. However, the police weren't as cooperative as usual for they'd been out all night on nine Lusaka robberies. We had visitors on Sunday afternoon and they were one of the nine who had had their house ransacked. They got home on Saturday afternoon at 5:30pm and evidently disturbed the intruder who had broken the kitchen window to get in. Nothing was taken but the whole place was turned inside out, everything pulled out ready to be taken. The police said if they had got home after dark nothing would've been left in the house. Theirs was the first of the nine cases the police attended that night, so at 7:00am Monday morning Domino went off to the police station to complain about his lost bicycle and I started making beds and so on and then three of Domino's recruits turned up.

After putting them on to planting I started off to get our milk and met a native coming in our road who wanted work. He said he had a wife and two children and no work and no food. He seemed so earnest about it so I put him on and he has proved very helpful. I also put on another. He is a carpenter really but can't get work so applied here. Another two mfazis started this morning making nine mfazis and three boys so we are making progress. All this has put me in a muddle though for I have to be outside almost all the time supervising. The natives soon get confused if left on their own and Domino is away again today. Yesterday the police found out who stole the bike but couldn't locate him so were to try again today. I only hope it turns up today.

It is evening now and the nips are in bed asleep. You will never guess what happened to Domino's bicycle. They charged the truck driver employed by the Indian store up the road who says that he went into town on it and someone stole it from him. Tomorrow Domino has to go in again to the native court and give evidence. I'm pretty fed up I can tell you all this muddling about. The more you have to do with native affairs the more muddling it becomes. Honestly it gets so involved at times you lose track of the original complaint. The Indians are behind a lot of theft. The natives do the stealing and the Indians buy from them then they put up a 'sale' notice and more natives flock in to buy. Some Indian stores have a permanent 'sale' notice on the windows. They don't all buy stolen goods of course. One Indian was buying stolen goods and a native policeman saw the native carry the goods inside. They were caught red-handed. The Indian got two years and appealed against his sentence. He won the appeal and when he got out of jail he opened his store again with a huge 'sale'. The place was crowded with natives.

This week I've had to do my own house work with Domino away each day and the offers of assistance are rather trying at times. This morning Andrew was squatting on the floor polishing a chair with shoe polish, Lorraine was in the sink shoes and all and had sprinkled *Vim* powder everywhere. When she sees me at the stove she cries to be lifted up for every lid has to be lifted so she can see what's in the saucepan. We had a steady rain all last night and it has rained several times today so we started planting for two hours this morning. Domino sat in court all day today and heard fifteen cases and still hasn't heard his own, so has to go tomorrow. I'm very fed up. Bill is going again tomorrow to investigate and see how many more days are to be wasted.

Last year we went with a friend to visit a man who was growing Turkish tobacco, not knowing anything about the work we asked lots of questions and they were very helpful with their answers. We have never seen them since but the friend who took us often visits them and was telling them how good our tobacco looks. Today Bill had a phone call asking if we could sell them some seedlings. It struck me as being rather funny that they should have to ask us 'new chums' for seedlings when they knew so much about it. We have hundreds and hundreds more seedlings then we can use. The piece of land we prepared originally will be filled early tomorrow morning, then we will start on another piece of cleared land about an acre near the house. We have another piece (about half an acre) cleared too which we may use later.

Well this tobacco and Domino's bicycle seems to have taken a lot of explaining. A few minutes ago Bill was standing at the door watching the rain which has started falling again and said, 'Gee, I hope we don't get too much. We've had enough, stop'. He's becoming a real farmer.

18 February 1959 Lusaka Farm. Bill came home early yesterday and was home today. He had a very high temperature yesterday and pains in the tummy but apart from an aching feeling all over hasn't been too bad today. He is going to have a blood test tomorrow as it must've been some sort of fever he had. We have quite a few mosquitoes at the moment and Bill has not taken the Paludrine for quite a few days. Domino puts the tin on the table every morning and the kiddies have half a one each and Bill and I a whole one. If taken regularly they ward off malaria. However with the early morning rush while we were planting our routine was messed up a bit.

We finished the tobacco planting yesterday and paid off the mfazis. They are eager to come again when we start stringing the leaves for drying. I have a young boy hoeing the young seedlings. We have a few to replant where the earth washed away during heavy rain, just after they were planted but the rest look really lovely. In fact we've had lots of folk pop in to see us and I'm sure it is the tobacco they have come to see for they've never bothered before. Three men are after seedlings and we sold one whole seed bed to one man for £4, another man about £2 worth and another who had no seedlings of his own wants enough to plant an acre and will give us four shillings a pound on his ripe crop. The seedlings are nearly done now. They should all be planted by the end of the month. We've finished ours so the rest of the seedlings will go to these men.

I mentioned we have a housing problem at the moment. We've put on four new workers and have no huts for them so one worker has been detailed to build two huts - one for himself and wife and one for an old man. The young lad is sharing Alfred's room as Alfred is once again wife-less. Yesterday I went to look at this new hut and remarked it looked very small and was told the old man has no mfazi (wife) so it would be big enough. It is round with mud put between the upright logs and grass on the roof. One or two logs are left out to make a doorway. I think the old boy will have to curve his body around the inside wall as I'm sure it is not wide enough for him to lie down flat. On fine days he will cook outside but cold or wet days he will cook in his hearth and the smoke will seep through the grass roof as best it can. I wouldn't be surprised if the whole lot blew over either for I noticed the upright logs were only six or nine inches in the ground. I think the author of 'The Three Little Pigs' had these huts in mind when they wrote that little story.

I don't think I told you the end of Domino's troubles. His case was finally heard last Thursday and he came home all smiles with a piece of paper saying the thief was to pay him £11 when he gets out of jail at the end of May. Domino bought the bike for £4 in Mazabuka. All bikes are registered the same as cars so it may be found yet.

We had a terrific amount of rain in half an hour today. Bill and the boys were busy making a tobacco shed from bush poles when Bill heard the rain roaring through the trees as it approached us. He told the boys to grab the tools and they only just got to the house - a matter of fifty yards or so when down it came. A lot of this week's hoeing has been washed away. None of the drains could cope with the sudden rush of water, although they are deep drains – twelve to fifteen inches. We expect to dry the tobacco during April, May and June and will cover it with polythene at night or in case there is a shower. Some of the leaves are ready now so I'm afraid we will have to pick some next month. We won't want too much rain and then we expect to bale it in July. It is then sold and shipped to America where it is mixed with other tobacco, 'blended' is the word I believe.

Alice's mother is worried

I can't understand you not hearing from me for I've written each week as usual. I didn't realise the African situation over here had got into your news so early. I think it was only last week that it began to look serious. They often have little squabbles, however this time they seem to mean business but as Estelle said Nyasaland is miles from us. Everything here seems to be going on just as usual. Anyway Bill says he doesn't want to come back here and we have put the place up for sale now. We are all well and I hope you are too. Don't worry about the reports you hear from here, it always sounds worse and anyway they have rounded up most of the leaders now and they are to get long jail sentences.

11 March 1959 Lusaka Farm. I'm sorry you've been so worried about us. Actually nothing has changed in our lives. We still go on as before and know very little more than you do about the situation for we also have to depend on the wireless news and newspapers for our information on the trouble. I'm sorry I didn't mention it earlier in my letters to you. Maybe had the trouble been nearer to us I'd have mentioned it knowing you'd be worried. I didn't realise at first the news was worldwide. There is often talk of unrest and lately rumours were flying around, however when the government stepped in and openly declared a state of emergency I ceased worry much about it. The rumours were rather worrying but having it all talked about openly is much better and I think more likely to put an end to strife.

I think I told you that we've put our place up for sale. If we don't sell it we will be a bit hard up at first but Bill says he is not coming back. I was saying to Bill this evening that if the place does not sell we could auction all that is on the land and just leave the land as Ed did. Ed had made no improvements on his place so just left it in case he ever wanted to come back. As we are not coming back the government won't be assisting with our passage money so we hope the sale of the property and all the tobacco will pay for that.

No need to mention it to the family or anyone but Bill has applied to the Australian Trade Commission in Salisbury to enter Australia as an immigrant and we've had a letter back saying the application has been forwarded to Canberra. If this is successful the Australian government will pay £75 each toward the fares and we will be able to take a car and used household effects customs free. This would be a great help. I hope you can understand all this. I only mention it to put your minds at rest about our homecoming and to let you know we are doing all we can to get home and have a bit towards setting up house again over there.

12 March 1959 Lusaka Farm. I wrote to you last night saying everything is going on as normal over here and then this morning Sir Arthur Benson, Governor of Northern Rhodesia declared the *Zambia African Congress* an illegal organisation and the leaders were arrested. They have been causing trouble among law abiding Africans and threatening them if they did not follow them and help cause further trouble. When strong enough they had other plans for making more trouble. However the government has now stepped in and put a stop to their activities before their numbers increased any further. There is an election on the 20th and many Africans are eligible to vote. Zambia intended to stop them and had threatened beatings and death to those who tried to vote. The Governor says that now all those eligible to vote may do so without fear of these threats. I thought that you may be hearing this on your wireless today.

I'm thinking you perhaps have not yet received a letter from me saying we are alright so I went into town and sent you a telegram. I do hope it won't startle you but you seemed worried in your letters and it takes a long time for you to get my answers doesn't it? In town everything was as usual, everyone carrying about their normal business and very little discussion going on. Most people are optimistic and have faith in the government. Actually if there is, or was to be any trouble it was to start at official sources so they are not likely to let things get out of hand. The only thing I noticed which was unusual was the numbers of native police constables parading the street. Usually they stroll up and down in twos looking rather bored but today they were in threes and swinging polished wooden batons and looking very efficient. There were lots more of them too so I should imagine any troublemakers would think twice before starting anything this morning.

I know all this sound awful in the news and you naturally think your loved ones are the centre of attraction. It is rather like someone over here reading of the heat wave or fires in Victoria and imagining all their friends and relatives in the middle of it. We know the country so don't get so worried about our folk. It is evening now, and we've just been listening to the news and the Governor's speech again. The police arrested the Zambian leaders without any incidents. No doubt the majority of Africans were glad to see their reign of terror at an end for they caused a lot of trouble in the African suburbs.

Well there is nothing more to tell you on the subject. I hope what I have told you will put your mind at rest. It could've been serious but the Governor has put a stop to it early. No one wants a repetition of the Kenyan trouble. It will soon be September and we will be with you once again.

17 March 1959 Lusaka Farm. Another week gone by and time to write again. I'm very busy as usual with the tobacco at the moment. We have three native men, three young people and six mfazis (wives). The men pick tobacco leaf until about 10:00am, then as it is too hot for picking they go on with other jobs. The mfazis come about 8:00am and they string the tobacco until about midday then it is hung in the shed overnight to wilt before being put outside on the drying racks. The youngsters do odd jobs such as gathering up the boxes the leaf is carried in, light the hot water boiler, feed the fowls and so on. One is only a little fellow about eight to ten years old, but the other two are big enough to do hoeing and grass cutting. They get £2 a month and a hundred pound bag of maize meal between them which is good money for the youngsters. We pay the mfazi three pence a string for their work.

Bill brought home your welcome letter this evening and also a telegram from you. Thank you for the birthday wishes. Glad to know my telegram relieved your mind of worry about us. Life here is just as usual, the only difference being that the trouble is publicly recognised and brought into the open. Here in Lusaka the disturbances have been in the native suburbs but in Nyasaland things have gone a bit far, especially in the northern part where Europeans are few and far between. However, they have troops there and are doing their best to quell the trouble and arrest the leaders.

Thursday afternoon. I did intend finishing this last night but I took a couple of gallons of petrol and some mealie cobs to the neighbour who took me into town and it was a bit late to start letter writing when I got back. Bill brought home another letter from you so that is two for this week. Glad to hear you were pleased with our news of the coming baby number three but I've no doubt it will just add to your worries of us over here. However, everything is quiet here and all our natives seem happy enough and all work happily together chattering all the time.

Domino tells me that the *Zambia African Congress* leaders haven't been here. They have been holding meetings and so on in town and causing trouble but were not strong enough to spread further as yet. Now the leaders are out of the way and the party banned, so all is settling down. I think the British Labour government has had so much to say about the affair that they have caused it to be in the news more than necessary and have worried overseas relatives unnecessarily. Their elections are over there next year and they are grabbing at anything to make themselves heard.

We had a good morning in the tobacco this morning. I did more supervising than usual and the result was forty-two strings of tobacco hanging in the shed instead of the usual twenty-four or so. Bill has two weeks leave due starting on 1 April and with Easter added on it will amount to nearly three weeks. He has so many jobs planned I'm sure three weeks will not be long enough to get it all done. It has been a lot of worry for him really for he doesn't get home 'till at the earliest 5:00pm and it's almost dark at 6:30pm so he has very little time to get things done. For awhile I wasn't too good either and he'd have to attend to the kids as well - bathing them and putting them to bed.

The first *The Age* newspaper from you arrived yesterday. Also some *New Ideas* from Auntie Hilda but they were not the ones containing the Eliza Callahan serial. Bill opened *The Age* at work and it caused quite a stir and so many have asked to see it. It will be travelling for some time to come. It was the same with the ones Bill's mum sent from New Zealand. Folk over here are very interested in Australia and New Zealand.

We've heard nothing about anyone wanting to buy our place yet. There are lots of places for sale at the moment and some of them very cheap too, but no one is buying until things settle down more. It will no doubt pick up.

Afternoon tea by the pool

24 March 1959 Lusaka Farm. Some of our tobacco is dry now and hanging in the shed waiting to be baled. Bill has two weeks leave starting on 1 April and has great plans afoot. I doubt whether he'll get it all done. Life is settling down again over here - troops are being released from Nyasaland as peace is restored there. Glad to hear the telegram was acceptable. Bill thought I was silly to send it.

9 May 1959 From Alice's mother, Springvale Road, Donvale. Dear Alice, Bill, Andrew and Lorraine, We were very pleased to receive another letter from you. You must've known I wasn't feeling too good. I have some pills and some medicine to encourage my appetite a bit and I do feel better but every other person has had the flu or feels they are getting it - Auntie Nellie had it for about a fortnight. Fancy Lorraine remembering all the naughty things she did. Usually they want to forget it.

16 May 1959 From Alice's mother, Springvale Donvale. Dear Alice, Bill, Andrew and Lorraine, I haven't been the best lately and I missed out on your letters. There has been a lot of Asian Flu about. Thanks a lot for the nice photos. Oh my goodness Lorraine looks as if she would try anything once. Haven't they both grown and the property has come on the map with the tobacco. There is quite a lot in what you and Andrew are holding, it looks very nice. It must be on town day.

I'm glad you are busy in preparation for coming home now. I will miss the mail if I don't close. I haven't much news this time as I haven't been out to hear any. Auntie Effie and Uncle

Gus and young Margaret and her boy friend are down doing shopping for their glory box. Ian and Gay have a little son. There is a lot of flu about but the weather is sunny and warm. We are all looking forward to your homecoming and our two new babies. Lots of love and best wishes to you all from mum and dad.

1 June 1959 Letter from Alice's sister-in-law Nell. Dear Alice and Bill, I expect you are waiting anxiously for more news from mum. There is to be an operation but so far they haven't said when it's to be. Lin flew home from Brisbane as soon as he got word that mum was in hospital and now he has gone back to bring his family home as their holiday is nearly up anyway, and of course as soon as they arrive home I will go home. I'm with dad at the moment making sure he has his meals.

10 June 1959 Lusaka Farm from Alice to her father. Dear dad, I have sent a telegram to you saying I am leaving here on Monday the 15th. The kids are very excited about going on an aeroplane. It is lovely to be young and free from worry isn't it, everything is just a new adventure to them. The doctor told me it would be far better for me to fly home than to stay here worrying, so tell mum I'll be there to look after her.

Lusaka Airport bound for Australia. Seven months pregnant.

Bill is solo again

15 June 1959 Lusaka Farm. From Bill to Alice. Dearest Alice, By the time this arrives today I will have faded in your memory with all the excitement of your arrival home in Melbourne. I will have received a telegram from you telling how things are with your mum. I hope you find her back at home by the time you arrive and excited to see you and our two hopefuls. I'm glad you made the plane, there wasn't any time to spare with all the difficulties about the luggage. I saw you waving from the window and the children too and felt a little lonely wishing I was on board as well. I said to Dennis

Tilly, 'Well that is stage one over, all I've got to do is get myself over now.'

After seeing you off and saying goodbye to the people who came to the airport I went with Dennis and Mrs Teese for lunch at their place. In the afternoon I came into town and bought some hessian after cashing a cheque at the Indian store. He said £5, £10 all the same, cash a cheque any time. I said £2 will do thanks knowing there's just £7 in the bank. I went along to Cooks and saw Peter and Irene. She said their Land Rover had broken down and the car is getting serviced so they hadn't been able to get up to see you. I collected the engine parts and milk and came home. What do you think about Mrs Smart saying that their place had been put up for sale that morning?

Anyway the last of the tobacco has already been baled making fifty-one bales for sale tomorrow. It is all ready, hessian on, scales up in the big shed with a rope sling to put the bales on and the scale set to zero. I organised a truck from 'Todd' and it will be here at 11:00am tomorrow. All we can do now is sit back and wait for the judge to learn what it means in pounds, shillings and pence.

Domino was ironing when I got home so he finished and made the bed in the small room, then I told him not to worry about tea so he has gone home. Martin De Goede came at 5:45pm with news that there was no mail. He also bought a small parcel of tobacco, about fourteen pounds for Tony Roakes to price. Good night dear Alice. I'm thinking of you all the time and wishing the days away until I step ashore in mid October.

16 June 1959 Tuesday. Dear Alice, Another day passed and it is evening again, 6:30pm and tea just finished. The cats are howling for theirs but they can wait a bit longer I guess. Well Cogan came and the tobacco is sold and on its way to Salisbury. I was disappointed with the price we got really, £244.16.7 for the fifty-one bales weighing 2,064 pounds. That's an average of 28.5 shillings per pound. We got £202.08 clear and I have a cheque for this amount. £2.17 came off for the government levy. I will clear the loan at the bank tomorrow for the new van and that will be over. The last bales done were the best ones bought for £12.18. The earlier bales let us down badly. He said we had picked too ripe on the earlier bales and also not spread them out far enough on the racks causing a lot of condensation between leaves. Some had been over conditioned and also he further said it was very good tobacco but spoilt from wrong handling.

I told him what Mr Bland, had said about picking them when they were just turning yellow, then later telling me to pick them when they were changing to light green. He didn't say much. Anyway I've started baling the small stuff today. It is tedious but it can be done. I have the youngsters cutting the tops as fast as they can and I'm placing the leaves between layers of grass.

I did a bit on the boxes this afternoon, also making lids and finalising packing the box with the sewing machine in. Well I'm just thinking you'll be in Mauritius tonight. Hope everything is going well and Andrew and Lorraine are good, considerate travellers. Well dear I suppose I have to get back to work tomorrow, not very keen but I suppose I'll see it out somehow or other. I want to have as much of these tobacco tops baled as I can in the next two weeks.

It is very quiet here in the house without you. It's not so good being on your own really. Anyway I have something to look forward to in October. Lots of love and kisses and a safe journey home dear. Bill XXXX

21 June 1959 Lusaka. Dearest Alice. I received your telegram yesterday morning at 11:00am and am relieved you arrived safely. I am now waiting eagerly for your first letter when you get a spare moment to write. Glad to hear mum is improving. I hope your arrival will help her to recover. What does she think of Andrew and Lorraine? I hope Andrew behaves with his pa, not cheeky or anything and that Lorraine isn't made too much the centre of attraction. I will be waiting to hear how they stood up to the flight and all your adventures on the way over. I remember Andrew could hardly spare time to say goodbye to me he was in such a hurry to get on the plane.

I have the boxes ready for dispatch now. Jimmy Hall came yesterday and while I finished strengthening them with timber he painted on our name and destination. I got stencils from work and I had Domino paint them in during the week. Jimmy and I had tea then we worked on the boxes until 11:00pm and finished them. They look very smart painted black, the lettering in white and each box numbered. I will get them away during the week. Tomorrow I sign the land sale agreement at Beaton's. I am getting the deposit and the balance in about three week's time when the building society has finished the paperwork.

I will move out of our place at the end of the week and to Dennis Tilly's. I'm still on the tobacco, nearly finished all the tops on the fourth bale now. I will take the bales away with me of course. I have been extremely busy today. Made a crate up for the pram and then did a little strengthening job on the big black box, folded some hessian and papers for baling, told the boys what to do, put the carburettor back on the van and a few adjustments. The pumping engine wouldn't start so had to grind the valves on that. It was dark by then so I came in and had some ham and macaroni and cheese sandwiches for tea.

I have decided to send Domino off on Friday with his family to Mazabuka. I will take them in with the van and their mountain of gear, beds included. I've told him to take two weeks off then come back alone and report to me at the Public Works Department once he's got his family out to their village. He can potter about in Mrs Leese's garden to fill in the time until we leave. I am getting along alright more or less. It's deadly quiet at night though just the lamp hissing and I'll be glad to move out next week. This place is just a memory when I look around and remember us all in here together. I don't want us to be parted ever again Alice and I wish I was sailing tomorrow.

23 June 1959 Lusaka Farm. Darling Alice, I was so pleased when your letter arrived yesterday morning from Mauritius. I hadn't thought that you might write along the way so it was a complete surprise. Well dear I am so glad everything went smoothly after the hectic getaway here and that I have reason to be proud of Andrew and Lorraine. So you did see Kariba Dam after all, by the most comfortable way. So you did have sumptuous quarters in Johannesburg. I didn't think they called it the best hotel for nothing. I'd like to have been there when Lorraine pressed the service buttons.

29 June 1959 Monday. Hello darling, Sorry I haven't finished this and posted it but I have been pretty busy the last week with one thing and another. I have sent off two letters since you left and I'm really waiting most impatiently to hear how things are with you all over there. It is 7:00pm now and I am sitting by the fire writing with the pad on my knee. Dennis is reading the papers and Mrs L is just bringing the tea. We have dinner early about 6:00pm and it's a home from home really. It's nice after sitting out at our place alone in the evenings.

I got our boxes away on Thursday and insured them for £300. They are on their way to the Cape now. On Friday morning I took my gear up to Kabulonga and in the evening took Domino and his family to the rail station for their trip home to Mazabuka. He had a mountain of luggage. The new owner Rex was busy moving in to our old place on Friday and Saturday. On Saturday afternoon I showed him how to use the tractor and the engine etc and then loaded up the balance of the tobacco (six and a half bales of top leaf) which I have here with me for the sale about mid July.

I called on Jimmy Hall on the way into town. He sprained his ankle that Sunday afternoon before you left so didn't come down. He was sorry he didn't say goodbye. I also called at Hallam's and saw Joe Puckett and Beaton and the Building Society are sorting out the sale. We have signed an agreement and the lot should be fixed in about a fortnight. I'm glad it's all over but will be happier when the money is in the bank and on its way to Australia. There is a possibility that Dennis will come down to the Cape with me if he can get a month's leave. It will be grand if he can. He will come back by train. I'm not looking forward to the trip on my own and it will be a change for him as he has never been further south than Livingstone.

30 June. Well as forecast your long awaited letter arrived this morning and I have since read it several times in case I missed something. I'm sitting as last evening, just finished dinner with the pad on my knee. You certainly didn't waste much time ringing up mum and dad in New Zealand. I'll bet they were surprised. Mum will be talking about you phoning for weeks to come telling them about her lovely daughter-in-law. I'm glad to hear your mum is somewhat improved. It must've been heartening for her to see you and the children.

Give mum my love and tell her I'm waiting for her to greet me when I arrive in fourteen weeks time.

It's July tomorrow and twenty-eight days to go before I finish up. Our boxes are on the way to the Cape. I had to pay £52 freight and insurance charges today. I also paid the grocer £22 and told him to close our account explaining everything. He asked me to call in before I finally left Lusaka. Perhaps I'll get a bonsella (present). I'll send money over just as soon as I can Alice to the State Savings Bank, Box Hill. I presume you have altered your name there from White to Latimer. There will be no trouble about the van.

I had to smile about the biltong. It's too late to retrieve it now because the pram is on its way to the Cape all crated up. The agent said that if everyone boxed things up as strongly as we had they would have no trouble at all. All my love darling as you know and look after our expected newcomer by relaxing. Sweet dreams from your loving Bill.

6 July. Hello Darling, I've just had a bath and I'm in ved finishing off this letter. A letter came today from my mum sympathising with us for your mum's illness and saying about the telephone call and Andrew and Lorraine saying hello to her as well. I do hope there has ben more improvement in your mum.

7 July 1959 Lusaka Farm. Yes Cazan took the seed and said when it had been tested and treated I would hear from them. He is buying again in Lusaka on 23 July so I'll see him then as I have six and a half bales of top leaves here to sell yet. Anyway it has more than paid for the van. I met Dennis Larkin today. You know the man who planted twenty acres of Turkish, do you remember? He told me it was a colossal headache and that even ten acres was more than enough. Labour has been his trouble - mfazis one day and none the next. You know the sort of thing. He said only about half of his was cured so far and a lot of it is not so good anyway. For us it was an experience and something to look back on. I know one thing and that is they will never do anything in tobacco, they're not the type. You were the main reason things went as well as they did for us. Even if she stayed home, his wife just couldn't organise or cope with it. Rick said so to me, and if anything he is even more useless - commonly called 'the clueless type'. I couldn't care if he grows nothing -we're not there now. Remember we had some good times there really - Africa has been good to us looking back over everything we've done.

I will go into Beaton's this week and see how the conveyancing is going, be glad when it's finalised. I felt sad myself reading of Andrew and Lorraine and wondering when are they coming back to our house and daddy, it must be an upheaval in their lives and I hope they soon forget about Africa - but not about me darling.

8 July 1959 Lusaka Farm. This coming weekend is Rhodes Founders' Day. On Saturday afternoon I will be working on the van. I have the oil cooler off now fixing the oil leaks on the engine so I am going into work with Dennis for a few days. On Sunday we will be out most of the day on this picnic and on Monday plan to go down to Kariba for the day, just Dennis, Mrs Leese and myself. On Tuesday I will be all day working on the van. I have got the windows (quite costly) and will now get them put in. Everyone I see asks how you are and your mum and I tell them as best I can. I do miss you so Alice, more than ever I did. (A case of absence makes the heart grow fonder.)

How is the new one coming along? I noticed he or she will be here about the end of August when I will be halfway to Cape Town. It's rather trying not being part of that this time but it's worth it for your mother and your own peace of mind. I've had no letters at all from Australia from you. I guess everyone knows that you are back by 'Bush Telegraph' or 'Mulga Wire'. It certainly is galling to have to wait so long to get on the ship. I suppose we will wish we were coming back to Africa once we've arrived in Australia. You sound as though you miss our home together here as well as the children.

9 July Thursday. Well my dear Alice another day has gone and here I am finishing off your letter. I took this afternoon off and put the engine in order again so no oil leaks now. Also put a tire on that I have retreaded. I look every day in case there is an extra letter from you but no luck so far. I can count on one on Tuesdays. I was told today that there is a job putting in generating sets at *Chickuni Mission* near Chisekesi. Do you know where you take the main road for Gwembe-Boma? I will probably leave on Thursday next week so will be back in plenty of time for your letter the following Tuesday.

Things are much the same in Lusaka except that the congress are boycotting the shops again and have pickets trying to stop Africans from buying. Ed Beckford was telling us this morning that one of the police in plain clothes saw a congress boy snatch a loaf of bread from a mfazi and trample on it. She had just bought it. The policeman saw the boy and took two shillings and six pence off him which he gave to the mfazi to buy another loaf. Then when he saw this congress hooligan again he pushed the small change into his mouth. The boy complained to the charging office and received short thrift after swallowing a couple of 'tickies'. About twelve have been charged with molesting Africans at the shops. This will soon be a thing of the past all this nonsense about the rising generation. I still say taking everything into consideration that we are doing the wise thing to leave, though it will be sometime before we become accustomed to a new way of life in Australia. I'll feel like a foreigner coming back.

15 July 1959 Lusaka Farm. Dear Alice, Your awaited letter reached me this morning after the Rhodes Founders holiday. I couldn't wait until 10:00am when mail is brought across to the workshop so I went across to the registry myself at 8:30am and asked for my mail which the lady there was sorting out for the different workshops.

We had a busy weekend and holiday here. We didn't go out Sunday as Dennis was at work most of the day. I worked on the van which is progressing nicely. By the way I went to the Automobile Association this morning about bringing the van over and everything will be alright. I am writing to the customs in Melbourne about an import.

Well on Monday we got away early for Kariba and had a big day travelling three hundred miles altogether. We went in by the Southern Rhodesian side and saw the township and lake from various points, then went around to the dam wall itself. It is a mighty job alright. We drove on down the gorge until we came to a barrier across the road. Here the native on duty asked us for our permit from the authorities to let us pass through the workings and across the temporary bridge to the north bank. We had no pass at all but when the guard said, 'Think of the poor African bwana' I knew what he meant and crossed his palm with silver, where upon the barrier was swung open. Being able to return by the north bank saves a hundred miles of travelling to Lusaka. It won't be long now before the road across the dam is finished when everyone can pass back-and-forth.

We were only a mile from Chirandu when we came across a motor car crashed off the road about ten minutes before our arrival. We were first on the scene and took a woman passenger and her child on to Kafue. She was covered in blood having her face damaged by her glasses. When they crashed the children were bruised and shocked. The car had turned over and was facing the way it had come from. Anyway I handed them over to the police at Kafue who took them to a doctor. Mrs Leese didn't sleep that night she said from seeing the car and the woman lying beside it. It certainly makes one slow down on the road alright. During the day we saw about six cars that had come to a sticky end at various times.

It is a month today dear since you left so the time is moving toward our reunion and it will be all past history in six months. I had a letter from mum today. She is worried about us, or rather about you having a new baby and being upset about your mum. The New Zealand maps came. Do you think you could get hold of some decent large-scale maps of Australia for Dennis? Your dad is in the Royal Automobile Club isn't he so perhaps he could help? One of each state would be ideal. Dennis says he will definitely be in Australia next year. He's got the Northern Territory and Queensland in particular in mind. He's scared of the winter climate in the southern states, so am I. I suppose we will sort out where we are going to settle eventually. What are your views now you're experiencing a typical winter again after five years of near perfect weather? Out in the Murray Valley it must be milder surely?

I called into Beaton's this morning and he said not to worry everything is in hand. The building society solicitors are doing the documents now and it will be through before the month's end. How is the money situation? I think I had better send a money order shortly in case you are short pending receipt of the land money which I will get the bank to transfer. Could you find out if a bank there will cash £5 in Rhodesian notes? If so I could send some in letters registered.

I picked up all the odds and ends at our place you mentioned Alice, even the secateurs still covered in tobacco tar. I was interested to hear about Lorraine and Andrew and Pa. It's inevitable for something like that to happen really knowing our pair and their strong willed characters and I'm glad to hear they're coming to a working agreement anyway. Well darling I don't really know how to finish up. I feel so much for you over there as the time nears for our new arrival especially. I do know you will be looked after anyway even if I can't be with you. Please give me the right dates so I can work out a plan of communication while on the road. It is nice to hear the children ask for me and I smile to think of him saying the kisses on my letters aren't big enough. Again my dearest Alice with never-ending love for you and often in my thoughts, I say good night with endless love and kisses in the future. Bill.

20 July 1959 Chikuni Mission near Chisekesi. My dearest Alice, As you will see by the above I'm away on a job and will be down here until next Monday or Tuesday. I'll miss your letter that I know will be arriving in Lusaka tomorrow but will get it on Thursday as the electrical engineer will be down then and I have asked him to bring any mail along. This is my last job with the Northern Rhodesia group and I will arrive back in Lusaka on the 27 or 28 July when my notice is expired.

We called on Sutton's at Mazabuka having lunch there today. They were surprised to hear that you were in Australia already and send their regards too. The electrician and I have a job of installing two generating sets at this Catholic Mission and *African Teacher Training Centre*. The priests here are all Irish and a very jolly crowd. We have a nice new house to live in and Domino is here with us as general factotum. This is the mission he is actually from. The government is advancing a lot of money to this place, I heard £200,000, and also to an Anglican Mission at Livingstone for training African teachers.

And how are you keeping darling? Still looking forward to my arrival as I am longing to be with you again? I try and remember what it's going to be to cuddle into you again. I think of you especially as I am getting into bed and think how lovely it will be to see your head on the pillow again. The time can go as quickly as it likes now. How is your mum now, still improving as you wrote last time?

Dennis, Mrs Leese and I went out and saw Mr Hallam yesterday and Helen Hallam said she had had a letter from you and was sounding thrilled at having received it. I showed Rex how to connect up the windmill. The new rooms are up to roof height at the back of the house but I didn't show much interest in it. I showed him about the windmill and we left straight away again. The old place has too many memories for me to want to stay around long with strangers in it.

Yesterday morning Dennis and I went out and saw Mr and Mrs Evans. They have been back a week now. Son Harold was full of what he had seen in England. They had a wonderful time despite the fact of having to stay in a lot when Mrs Evans's mother broke her hip. Do you remember how Mrs Evans wasn't keen on going? Well now I guess she'll be talking about it for the next year. They're talking of going again on the next leave already. I gave Mrs Evans your address and she will be writing soon. I explained why you couldn't write before you left.

I have left the van with a panel beater from work and he is putting in the windows for me while I am down here on this job. Dennis won't be coming down with me. He is finishing up in December and will be due three months leave. If he takes a month now he won't get leave until later next year and if he tells them he's leaving he won't get any leave from them at all so will take his paid leave and just not come back. He says he will be in Australia next April or May sailing from England which he wants to see again first. How are Andrew and Lorraine these days? I do hope they're not suffering from the cold too much. It will soon be spring and getting warmer. You couldn't have gone back home at a worse time for weather. It is warming up here now during the day so our winter is finished. I wish we could find a place with a climate like this, perhaps with the rain spread over the year a little more.

24 July 1959 Chikuni Mission. Guess what? The two chaps who came down here today to see the job forgot to bring your mail with them. They say there are two letters from Australia but they are in his desk at the workshops. Well he was most apologetic and will give them to one of the catholic fathers who is in Lusaka who will be back tomorrow from there. We will be here until Monday afternoon. At least the generator's running now and there is the odd father and brother dropping in at all times during the day to see us working. It is something for them as it is pretty quiet here usually.

Well dear and how are you keeping over there? I hope your mum is still improving. The last of our tobacco should've been sold yesterday. It will be interesting to hear what we got for the last six and a half bales, also the seed. I think I told you about visiting Evans last Sunday. You should be getting a letter from Mrs Evans - probably before you read this. I am doing alright, as well as can be expected. Anyway I do miss you and we'll make sure it'll be a long time before we are parted for such a length again.

Just shows you how I miss you - I came away from Lusaka and forgot to bring my blankets, sheets, pillow and a few other odds and ends. Usually everything would've been ready for me to throw on the truck. I borrowed sheets and a blanket from Suttons in Mazabuka and just roll up my overalls for a pillow.

25 July 1959 Lusaka. Don't forget to let me know as nearly exactly as you can when the new arrival is due so that I can sit down in one place to await a telegram - maybe Tuesday's letter will inform me. There was quite a bit of tobacco left Alice though very patchy picking, you know two days picking then a week's wait for more. I got in all there was and baled it before I moved out. Don't worry it takes a lot of tops to fill a bale. I should know on Tuesday how much we got. I took the bales to the depot and left a letter for Mr Cazan with Harry Beelders who had a small lot to sell.

I am still taking Domino down with me and intend to leave about 20 August from Lusaka. I think I explained that Dennis won't be coming because of it interfering with his resigning in November. I'll pass on your thanks to Mrs Leese, you could drop her a line some time. It's Mrs J. Leese, c/o Curray and Co. Ltd. Woodgate House, Lusaka if you like. She would appreciate it very much. I had a letter from the Automobile Association today with a lot of forms to fill in and the price to bring a vehicle over is £162, plus what the Australian customs clearance robbers charge in Melbourne. The letter from Anderson's says they have cancelled your berth as requested by me and that my fare to Melbourne is now £154 this end. They want to know also if we still want our return booking for April next year.

Fancy meeting someone in Melbourne who was in Lusaka back in 1927, it would have been just a few shacks back then. Building is going on all over again now - the Civic Centre is underway, a new library etc. I'll take quite a few photos before I leave you can be sure dear. Now the time is getting near and apart from the fact that you are in Melbourne I'm not that happy about leaving Lusaka. It's been a good place to us really and I am just a bit frightened that we won't be able to live as happily as we did here, but one is always frightened of what is ahead so we've just got to put Rhodesia behind us and concentrate on Australia - the warmer parts I hope.

Before I forget dear, Mr and Mrs Evans say that the movie they took at our place over Christmas came out wonderfully. I am hiring a projector and we are having a film evening on 1 August at Mrs Leese's - all the films they took overseas as well. I will bring this one film with me. Their friends in England marvelled at Domino in his uniform bringing tea to us in the play area etc. Did I tell you that Domino is down here on the job looking after us? Have to make the most of it now - he'll soon be just a memory. I welded up a couple of bicycles today and made two cuckoos. Domino cooked for fourteen at dinner tonight and it went down well with roast potatoes, cabbage, rice and pumpkin. I did a pot too and got some eggs which the boys got for tea. I guess I'll miss these affable natives. It's about bedtime now darling so I'll leave off for now. I'm sending all my love and thoughts to you, and a big hug and kisses for dear Andrew and Lorraine.

29 July 1959 c/o Mrs Leese. Woodlands, Lusaka. I went into work this morning after being away eight days at Chisekesi. I officially finished here yesterday and I've spent all today doing something or other. You will note the address to write to now dear, it is Mrs Leese's post box and will be easier than running down to the workshops all the time. I will be leaving here on 20 August so you can write to me here or a telegram if the new baby arrives. I will leave the naming in your competent hands. I promise no recriminations about it but make sure the initials aren't A.W.O.L. or W.C. or some other such burden. And if you write to me here before 10 August I will get it alright. If the baby comes before the eighth I will get the cable here. I am enclosing a timetable for posting out and if you follow it closely I will get all your letters, post office delays excepted, also telegrams. I have a copy of the timetable on the back of this pad and will be waiting around at the places mentioned to check up if you wrote within the enclosed dates. Enough instructions and directions, tell me darling are you still missing me these cold nights? I will let you warm your feet without moaning too much.

I'm enclosing a money order Alice, should be about £50 Australian when you get it. Don't forget the exchange. That is all I have just now but next week I should be transferring over the money from the land. I saw Beaton this morning - one of my first jobs. I will be taking out my fare, the van expenses and trip down expenses so I will send £1,500 through to the bank. They tell me it will only cost £4 for this amount. I will make it out to you and you will have to produce your passport to claim it. It will be sent to one of the Commonwealth Bank in Melbourne. It will be worth about £2,000 Australian. I suggest you put £500 in your State Savings Bank and the balance on a fixed deposit somewhere at the highest rate of interest you can get. Maybe there is something like a Building Society there, but there's no need to say be careful. Your dad would be able to help there I think. I will have my leave pay coming and about £1,000 in gratuity at the end of it so if I start work pretty soon after I arrive in Australia we should be comfortable enough to kick off.

Poor little Andrew, I told Domino that Andrew was wanting him and asking where he was and he said, 'Oh thank you bwana.' Well darling I will close now sending all my love to you and our family. Bye-bye sweetheart for the moment.

4 August Tuesday. Yesterday morning - a holiday - Dennis and I went and called on Avis. She showed us the photos taken at the airport. They are extremely good. I was given a couple, one of you and me and the children and another of Andrew and Lorraine by themselves. They are a smart looking pair. Andrew looks school-age in his blazer. You look very nice and I have the photo before me as I write. They are beside my bed. Avis said she had sent some to you so you know how good they are for yourself.

I can't wait for the time to go now until we meet at Melbourne. At least I can say that I get on the ship next month, even if it is the end of the month. Dennis and I went to the Lusaka Annual Show Sunday morning but I wasn't very interested. Remember us there last year when Estelle was over? We came away about 1:00pm when it appeared that we were likely to get involved at the bar and didn't bother to go back in the evening. Well the holiday is over now and everyone went back to work today. I have been working on the van today and will be over the next two weeks. It is quite pleasant not having to get up at a set time. This morning it was 6:15am

Dennis and I went in and saw a film *Carry on Sergeant* and quite enjoyed it. We have been back an hour and I see the time is midnight. I thought it would be nice to write a few more lines to you Alice. If I don't hear from you tomorrow I will post this and start another one. I do miss you so, perhaps you've got some idea darling the feeling is mutual. I am sleeping very restlessly, something that usually doesn't worry me and I've heard that people say I'm getting thin but I don't think so. I do know that I won't be the same until we are all together again we're not meant to be separated for more than a week. Well dear I will say good night dreaming how we used to whisper in the past when our net was tucked in.

5 August Your welcome letter to hand. Things are pretty much as I thought they would be. Grandparents are alright if they can visit the children but twenty-four hours a day is too much. I suppose we'll feel the same in thirty year's time but it must be irritating for you to have to watch things happening that you can't do much about. As you say you are the intruder - my responsibility too. Well we agreed on the sacrifice of being separated because of the circumstances, so there's not much to be done except try and be patient until I arrive. You are not helped of course by your condition dear and it must be a great trial for you not to have me to talk to you about things. Also you are virtually marooned except for visits to the hospital. I guess time is still life's major problem to your dad even though there's twenty-four hours a day to play with.

Now one thing darling, I would rather have you at home safe, than going anywhere to visit in a hurry and arriving 'dead on time'. Have you had many visitors out to see you, you don't say whether or not. Well dear I don't look on your letter as a moan it is a plain statement of fact and nothing is surer than that we will have to find a home of our own as quickly as possible. Many marriages are rocked because of the parties living at the old folks place. I know our circumstances are not like that but once I arrive we will get organised with a roof of our own. I know your father has said we can stay there and that everything is taken care of as far as accommodation goes but he didn't really realise what it would be like - not with a pair of kids with the initiative ours have got. No he'll be pleased when we move into a corner of our own though he mightn't say it.

6 August 1959 c/o Mrs L, Woodlands, Lusaka. Dear Alice, What a lovely surprise to receive two letters from you this morning. I was thinking this must be the result of a burst of energy before the baby is born, you usually have an urge to do things then don't you and the baby was born not more than three days after. I feel so sad and wanted, especially with Lorraine asking for her daddy and you having to explain about my ship having to come in so that they can meet me. I told Domino that he was being asked for and his daughter Messia. He said, 'Thank you Bwana' He is in the house now as Mrs Leese's boy is having a holiday at his village.

Fancy a letter of mine going to New York first, some idiot here must've put it in the wrong bag I guess. Yes Alf and his brother Campbell are planning to open up in Charter House in the old Netherlands Bank shop.

I think of you plenty when people say how cold it was today and for Rhodesia it was cold. Today started well with an earthquake at 6:05am, the first I've felt since 1942 in New Zealand. It shook enough to wake Dennis and me up. Mrs Teese was walking about and didn't notice it. It was in the paper this afternoon and a window was broken on Prospect Hill. I have been busy all day on the van. It is coming along nicely now and will be a real mobile home or as near as without spending too much money. Talking about money I'm going in on Friday. Beaton is confident the Building Society will be finished by then.

10 August 1959 c/o Post Restante Bulawayo. I hope this finds you and the new one, name unknown, well and just about ready to come out of hospital. Try and stop in as long as you can for the rest as you know well enough the work you'll have once you get home. The telegram came this morning at midday. I was in the middle of welding the roof rack together when Mrs Leese gave it to me. I thought before I opened it that maybe it was bad news but it was the big news saying, 'Our baby boy born on 9th love Alice.' I was a bit surprised as I thought it would be near the end of the month but then I'm out of touch. I knocked off working, had lunch then went to town and got a return telegram away at 2:00pm. You should have it about midday tomorrow. This is old news as you read it now. I wish I were there with you dear it would be so much easier wouldn't it?

Well dear you must be relieved it's all over and that you are no longer five feet by five feet. I will feel better when I've had an account of it all by letter. You will know to write to Bulawayo in answer as per the writing schedule sent earlier. You should get this by the 20th for sure. Anyway, I won't move from Bulawayo until I get a letter. I intend to leave here on 20 August. I saw Beaton again today and the money will be fixed by Friday. He says the Building Society is the hold-up though they have been told I am leaving the country. It is all alright and just as soon as I get it I will send it over, the delay is rather annoying though.

*11 August. W*ell dear your letter received this afternoon dated 29 July as I hoped it would. It seems old to read it now. The baby has arrived and the doctor saying it would be 27 August makes you the better judge doesn't it. I rang Mrs Evans this morning and told her the news. She was pleased and said she would write to you from Barrow. You may have written her already but if she doesn't get it before Wednesday she won't for another three weeks on account of being away.

I forgot to mention I think the balance of the tobacco was sold while I was away the other week at Chikami mission. I was disappointed to say the least of it. What we got for the six and a half bales will be £22 only. He said the tobacco had been left on the rack too long and had lost its oil. It was too dried out in other words. Anyway, as old Mrs Mel said about the bore hole test fee, 'We must pay for our experience'. I am still waiting to hear about the seed though I have sent a telegram requesting payment as I am leaving the country, so there you are dear. Glad to hear your mum is so much better and no doubt will be all a twitter to see you and the baby.

18 August Dear Alice, I have just been into the hospital and got vaccinated by Sister Wheeler. She was surprised the baby had arrived already and wished us all the best for the future in Australia. I saw Mrs Puckett last Friday as I passed by on my way to visit Jimmy Hall who has resigned from Chilanga and is now unemployed and living out on his place. Mrs Puckett's address that you wanted is Mrs D. Puckett, PO Box 1744, Lusaka.

The van to be shipped to Australia

Well dear I am pushing off from here on Monday next (24 August) with Domino. Jimmy H is coming with me in his van as far as Beit Bridge at the South African border so at least I'll have his company part of the way. I was in at the Automobile Association this morning and paid them for the van freight. I just have to pay the ship for myself now. The A.A. secretary said he advised me not to take Domino into the Union as it could become very complicated, so I've decided to take him only as far as the border and he can come back with Jimmy Hall. It's probably the best way and I've explained how there might be trouble for him in South Africa so he agrees.

You will be relieved like I am that we have the money for our place at last, less expenses. Do you know that that Power-of-Attorney we did on the morning you left came to £16.16 shillings (quaint old guineas to make legalised robbery appear genteel). I hope our imps escaped the measles, though as you say I don't see how they can, never having had them yet. Remember how I got them just before we came back last time? It'll mean a lot of work for your dad and mum and Auntie Alice though they have a better understanding of each other now according to your last letter.

Well dear I am sitting in our van outside the hospital writing this. At 4:00pm. I am going down to a friend of Denise's who is going to help me line the inside roof of the van with a stick-on washable oil cloth. It is a pretty Mediterranean blue colour and this chap is an expert interior decorator so I will be his boy helping. The inside bunks and cupboard I'm painting cream and I do hope you like it all when it arrives. Whenever I do something on it I think of you. I have at least got you a travelling home as practice for finding a permanent one in Australia somewhere. The windows make a world of difference but I haven't tried my hand at the curtains yet. I will probably do that on my way down to the Cape. It will be something to fill in the time.

I went into the Netherland Bank this morning and got them to draft £1,000 out of Rhodesia to you. It will be converted they say in Australia and will be about £1,250, something towards our new home. The rest I will send later in the week by another letter after I have paid the passage money and taken out expenses for the journey. I have enclosed the draft copy to you. Please don't lose it as it is our proof that the bank has sent it from here. The money will be sent to the Australia and New Zealand Bank who will credit it to your account at the Box Hill Savings Bank. You could go over in two weeks just to check whether it has arrived. Paul Dennis and his family were up for a visit on Sunday night. They wish to be remembered to you. Burt Barrett and family were there also.

Dennis, Fred Leese and myself went out to a dinner dance at the *Moth Club* on Saturday night and had a gay time. I do miss you though Alice I would like to take you out for a bit when I get over there. We should be able to organise it as long as you don't go dropping irons on your toes again or I catch measles or something silly.

Good-bye Lusaka

24 August 1959 C/O Post Restante Cape Town. Darling Alice, This is it the big day of leaving Lusaka. I am sitting in the van in the car park opposite Patels waiting for Jimmy Hall and thought a profitable way to fill in time would be to start a letter to you. Well Jimmy arrived 11:15pm and is just away to get a few odd things. I have been to the workshop this morning for the last time and returned some gear I had out of the store and to say goodbye to the plant shop for the last time. Sitting here now watching the traffic go by it seems unreal that I'll never see Lusaka again - at least not in the foreseeable future. It would be nice though to come back for a visit in fifteen or twenty years hence. As I say to the blokes, I've had seven good years here and the seven years ahead are going to be tough years for central Africa. Anyway we will follow its fortunes from afar.

I can't get down to Livingstone quick enough now as I know there's a letter from you waiting for me there. I saw Avis on Saturday afternoon – went around to say good-bye and I was a bit put out to find she had just received a letter from you.

I read it and was glad to see everything was well with you dear. Robert Oliver is quite a good name and I suppose your dad would be pleased about it. At eight pounds twelve ounces he's pretty hefty, something like Andrew was. Avis flew down to Durban this morning. She has the chance to adopt another child there so she and David have gone down. I will be seeing her there on my way through.

And so darling how are you feeling? Our new baby is sixteen days old and you will be well home from hospital by now. I wish I was on the ship just a day out of Melbourne but the time will come as it always does sooner or later. Jimmy is away getting a haircut now so we will push off in a few minutes when he gets back. We won't make Livingstone today - probably stop at Mazabuka as Jack Sutton has asked me to stay there. Doug Mc Kell is there at the creameries and I might go out and see Smith's too, or are they on leave yet, I will soon find out anyway. I have over a month to get to the Cape so what's the hurry? I just want to get that letter of yours from the post office at Livingstone.

It's nice having Jimmy Hall come as far as the South African border. Domino is sitting here waiting for us to push off too. I will take it steady on the way down as I mean to arrive in one piece, van and all. Everything is fixed. I have paid my ship fare and Anderson's are holding my ticket. Also the van fare is fixed. I've just got to arrive at Cape Town. Oh one thing Alice the car has been in your possession since January this year remember. I have a properly stamped receipt to this affect from Pretoria on the advice of the Automobile Association - just in case of trouble with those bandits in the customs. I will fix everything in Melbourne. Just remember you paid for the van in January.

25 August, 1959 Livingstone 3:30pm. Hello darling, I just arrived here ten minutes ago and have read your two letters already. I came on ahead of Jimmy's vehicle to catch the post office before it closed and I'm sitting outside the place in the sun starting to reply. It seems a long time to me since I last wrote, also since I received a letter from you. Well darling I am as pleased as anything at Robert Oliver and I'm happy to hear that everything went off without a hitch. It's nice to know Andrew and Lorraine are being well looked after.

We left Lusaka at midnight yesterday and stayed the night at Sutton's in Mazabuka. Of course we had dinner and a talk after, then Jimmy and I slept in our vans parked outside. I left there this morning at 8:00am as I did want to get here in time for your letter. Jimmy is still coming but may be a bit behind me especially if he stopped for lunch. I haven't had lunch but will make up tonight. Domino is away buying himself some food. Yes dear you must want me around at a time like this but I feel as if it won't be too much longer. It's nearly September already.

When Jimmy arrives we will go over to the Southern Rhodesian side and make camp about where we parked this time last year. I kept thinking about us all last year as I was driving along today. Remember when we went away last year? The school holidays are on the same as well. Well darling I'll get this on its way now. Happy to have got your letters at last and will start another tomorrow.

26 August 1959 Northern Rhodesia Rest Camp, Livingstone Wednesday 10:00am. Dearest Alice, Here I am again seated in our camp about a hundred yards from the river just behind the Northern Rhodesia police post. I posted your letter yesterday afternoon and then had time to look round the curios before Jimmy rolled up. We went across the Southern Rhodesia side to the rest camp, then discovered one big snag - Bruce the dog. To take a dog into Southern Rhodesia you need a movement order from Northern Rhodesian Veterinary Department which we haven't got. They wouldn't let us stop on the south side so we had to come back and camp here. We are going into town in a short while to try and organise a paper for Bruce. We were told yesterday that the road between Wankie town and Van Niekerk's Hotel is one shocking deviation so it would be sensible to go through the game reserve in order to miss the chance of damaging the van. Will continue later dear as we are off now.

4:10pm. Well dear we are back from town again having had to wait until 2:00pm to see the vet. He gave the dog an inoculation and Jimmy a movement order. It appears you shouldn't take a dog even from one town to another without one. We still haven't decided what to do about the route down. We know dogs are definitely not allowed in the game reserve. We looked around the museum this morning. They have a lot of David Livingstone's relics there since we saw it last year. There are a lot of tourists here just now I think a lot come to dodge the winter down south. The Falls are just the same as when we were here last year. I suppose they were the same one million years ago though a few miles downstream. I can hear the falls roaring as I sit here writing. Strange I might never be here again.

I called in at the creameries in Mazabuka and saw Doug Mc Kell who was transferred from Lusaka recently. Smiths from the research are on leave at the moment so I didn't see them. It is afternoon now 5:40pm and the sun is low down across the river. I walked over to the tea room just now for some cigarettes. I had a drink while I was there and sat not far from where we were this time last year. You'll remember the afternoon - we met Smiths there. I had a look at the curios in the shop but they're not as good as in town.

28 August 7:00am at the Matetsi River. Hello darling, It is morning again and I am sitting by the fire on the banks of a river in Rhodesia. You know the river where we stopped last year for lunch on our way to the game reserve and where we cut some stooks for our tent. Jimmy Hall has just left with Domino to go through the Wankie Reserve and I will go with dog Bruce down the main road through Wankie to Van Niekerk's Hotel where we'll meet this afternoon about 5:00pm. We will camp on the Gwayi River there tonight and go on to Bulawayo tomorrow.

Saturday. It was cold last night and this morning about thirty-eight degrees and my feet and hands said it must be right. Anyway the sun is just coming up behind me and the fire is hot in front of me so we'll soon be thawed out though my toes are tingling at the moment. Bruce is tied up behind the van and whining and looking in the direction Jimmy has gone. I wish you were here with me it is very snug in the van at night.

I think you would enjoy it out here in the bush too if I were with you.

I went into the post office yesterday but there were no more letters. I didn't expect any really but you never know. You must be writing correctly according to the timetable, there were the two letters at Livingstone. The last one of seven pages had arrived on the Monday and I arrived there on the following afternoon. Yes Dennis didn't want me to leave. He said the two months I was there seemed like two weeks. I'm pretty certain he'll be in Australia for a look around next year. No dear the stamps I am putting on are not the new issue, I will put some new issue on this letter and enclose some unused ones of the old issue.

So you reckon baby Robert is a little Latimer? Well I had a little to do with it so I'm glad he turned out with a similarity to one or the other of us. The appetite is a Latimer trademark of course and I guess I make a row for it as well. I'm glad to hear your dad's getting on alright with Andrew and Lorraine. It's something to get decent attention in hospital regardless of what it costs, though the government child allowance sounds like money for jam to me. Talking about money Alice, I have sent another £500 so there should be £1,500 British paid into your account. I have mislaid the ticket among my gear somewhere so I can't enclose it as I did for the last lot.

I guess it would be better to leave the question of our future until after I'm over there dear. Well my dear wife, I look forward to a letter at Bulawayo that will be on Monday morning. I will post this at Wankie this morning as I pass through, a few miles nearer to you. The time will soon go now and I'll be looking down from the *Monarch.*

29 August 1959 On the banks of the Gwayi River Southern Rhodesia, 12:30pm Saturday. Hello there Alice darling, Here we are again and I send my love across the distance separating. I am slowly closing the gap and it is nearly September. Well dear I arrived here yesterday afternoon at 1:00pm and picked out a place to camp. Jimmy and Domino arrived at 3:30pm and had driven through the Wankie park where they saw everything except lions. He moaned about the road a lot which he said was badly corrugated but was worth seeing, though he wouldn't go in again.

Anyway I went to VanNiekerks Hotel and asked where a good camping site was as soon as I arrived. We are only five hundred yards from the hotel towards Livingstone and twenty-five yards from the river. The main road is sixty yards away and we can watch the traffic go by. It is a nice spot so we decided to stay here for the day going on to Bulawayo tomorrow. Monday morning I will present myself at the post office when it opens. It is nice here under the trees lining the river. I am lying down in the van with both side doors open to catch the breeze. I can see the river on one side and Jimmy's van on the other parked about eight feet away. Lunch is ready pork chops and baked beans - Domino is handy, will continue later.

4:30pm Well dear the sun is going down now and it is cooler, temperature eighty-five degrees. We have been talking about the properties for sale in *The Age* which Jimmy has just seen for the first time. He is just cleaning his van down now, worrying about scratches it got in the park when he had to go around trees knocked on the road by elephants. We went along to the hotel this morning and bought some meat, bread, butter and bacon. It has been a really lazy day today and I have been lying down most of the time reading. For dinner we have a big stew on which has been cooking since 1:00pm and we seem to be eating well, despite having nothing much to do except loaf. Well darling I can't think of a great deal to write about at this moment except that I love you still and wish you were here with me on a leisurely trip south. I suppose it wouldn't have been the best with such a young baby but we would have waited until another week before leaving Lusaka.

31 August 1959 Bulawayo Monday 7:00 pm. Well darling at Bulawayo now and a bit further on the journey to you and family and a nice letter waiting for me this morning written the day before you came out of hospital. Pleased to hear you feel well and look like Jane Mansfield. I'll be the judge of that in about six weeks from now so have the tape measure handy. Now the thought of you there makes my tummy excited, that sinking feeling you know.

Well dear I have thought it over and have decided to go straight from Beit Bridge to Durban by-passing Johannesburg. Going into the *Kruger National Park* won't be any novelty and no fun without you to share it. Maybe we can come back one day twenty years on. If I can get into the right business in Australia we should be able to do it. Do you know it has taken us a week to travel the six hundred miles from Lusaka. Not bad going is it?

We left van Neirkerk's at 9:00am yesterday and got into the camping site here at 3:30pm to find the biggest most luxurious collection of caravans I'm ever likely to see. There are over forty American caravans drawn by big four-wheel-drive power wagon utilities. Every caravan is built of aluminium about twenty-feet long and fitted with every conceivable device. The outfit is called the *Wally Byam Caravan Club* and they are going from the Cape to Cairo, the holy land and Europe. I am told the holiday is costing £4,000 each, without the caravan and vehicle about another £3,000. What a life! and it's well organised American fashion. The caravans park on a large circle about fifty yards in diameter. Plastic pipes run around the perimeter and each unit couples into this for their water. They have doctors with them, a workshop repair truck and a mobile film unit, water softeners even, and super folding camp gear.

Jimmy and I went over last night and saw a film show, everybody being invited to see the colour movies of game taken by a game photographer. It was really good, mostly taken in the *Wankie National Park*, elephants close-up and buck of all descriptions taken with a telephoto lens, but taking weeks to obtain. Some marvellous lion shots taken in Mozambique at the *Gorongoza Reserve* were shown also. As I said to Jimmy, 'People who can afford a tour like this expect to see decent films.' There would be over a hundred people in the convoy men, women and children. Most of them appear to be middle-aged about forty-five to sixty years old and must be extremely wealthy. One woman called out to the film operator in a raucous accent, 'Do those lions ever bite the tyres on autos?'

They are real tourists, and Jimmy and I have been imitating them talking ever since. Domino is amazed at it all just says, 'mushi stelek' (very nice) and can't understand why they haven't any African servants with them. We passed one of their trucks going into town this morning and he said translated, 'Bwana Bill no way. Very, very nice. A serious matter steering wheel other side'. I tried to explain that in their country they drive on the other side of the road where they can see alright but I don't think it sunk in. I took Domino to the museum and he was quite amazed I think. Saw all the stuffed animals, birds and snakes. Also a collection of African tribal gear, weapons, drums, tools, dress and witch doctor relics, also a lot of things from old Zimbabwe. He thinks the city is great and comments on how few Indians there are. Reckons that's 'mushi' (very nice). He talks to the other Africans in kitchen kaffir - the good old esperanto of this queer continent.

Well darling, it looks like I found something to write about. I am propped up in the van on the bed cushions at my back and rug is on the legs writing. Jimmy is away with Bruce for a walk and Domino is crouched over the fire and was singing 'till a moment ago. The tent is very handy and a nice size too not too big, not too small and of good material. I think we should have some good holidays away in Australia with the van. It is ideally suited. Tomorrow we leave here and will go across to Fort Victoria stopping out at Zimbabwe of course.

I will most likely leave there on Thursday morning 3 September and arrive in Durban on the 5th staying at the same small town campsites, near Johannesburg. I see that the 5th is the last date I can expect any mail there by the writing chart. I have left Cape Town as the address to forward anything on from here but I don't expect any more as you are writing according to the timetable.

Look after yourself now you're home, don't be too energetic or Robert will be getting hiccups caused by malted milk shakes. I'm just longing to cuddle into you like the little fellow is doing - remember dear? So another letter has been written, another one nearer. I don't suppose I'll ever write so much to you, or you to me again. I hope not. Give my regards to your mum and dad.

Farewell Domino

2 September 1959 At the Zimbabwe Ruins. Darling Alice, Hope this finds you well and happy, also the children and your mum and dad. Thought I would write a very last letter from Rhodesia before I cross the border tomorrow into the Union. We came across from Bulawayo yesterday no trouble and arrived out here about 4:00pm. Our camp is about five yards further along from ours last year you'll remember. It was cold all yesterday. At 8:00pm the thermometer said thirty-nine degrees outside so you can tell it's about the coldest I remember it in Rhodesia. Anyway I slept in my shirt with my old blue jersey on and was not too warm. It was a night you would have been really appreciated Alice, believe me dear.

This morning was fine and the sun shone brightly in contrast with yesterday's overcast. After breakfast Jimmy and I climbed up to the top and wandered about the ruins sitting in the sun for awhile. We came down and went across to the temple, then had a drink at the tearooms before lunch. I lay down under a tree after lunch for a snooze then woke up about 2:30pm because it was becoming cool. We had some tea then climbed up the hill again by the modern ascent taking some photos on top. I picked up a piece of pottery lying between a pile of stones. I may show it to the curator in the morning for an opinion. It is only about two inches square with a line etched on it, nothing much really. Jimmy likes it here and says he knows the place to come for a quiet holiday now. It is peaceful alright. It would be nice to be camped here all together.

Tomorrow morning we will go into Fort Victoria and find out about getting Domino onto a bus. Jimmy is going to start looking around for work trying a dam being built near here and also Shabanie Mine. He doesn't seem very happy about it all and wished he was coming through to Australia with me. Well darling I will probably camp at Beit Bridge tomorrow night then cross over on Friday morning and should get into Durban all going well on Saturday afternoon. I will be at the post office early on Monday. I think Avis flies back on Monday 7th so I will see her on Sunday afternoon the day before she leaves - probably got her baby by now. The weather should be nice in Durban. I hope it's bearable in the Cape too.

It has been alright having Jimmy Hall for company and Domino too but after tomorrow I'm on my own. I guess I'm not cut out to live by myself and I can't get over to you soon enough for my liking. Well darling I can't say much more at the moment except that I love you and look forward to our starting off together again. I suppose there will be problems ahead, there always are but if they're no bigger than the ones we had in Rhodesia we will be getting it easy.

6 September 1959 c/o Post Restante Cape Town, Dearest Alice, Here I am again sitting in the van on the Marine Parade in Durban with the Indian Ocean rolling up the beach less than fifty yards away. The sun is hot with a slight breeze. All it lacks is you dear and the children playing in the sand. Surely there can't be better than Durban for a holiday anywhere in the world but it's not much good by oneself. I arrived at Durban post office at 11:45am yesterday. Just fifteen minutes to spare until closing time and collected two nice letters from you and one from mum. I was hurrying along to make it in time safely and just as well because Monday is a public holiday here so I wouldn't have got mail until Tuesday. I sat by the War Memorial in the square by the post office and read through them and felt quite proud of Andrew's drawing. The stamp fell out first and for a moment I wondered what had been sent.

Well I left Jimmy Hall at Fort Victoria last Thursday morning at 11:15am. He was going over to Umtali to do job hunting, then on to Salisbury if unsuccessful.

I took Domino to the railway station and got him a ticket for Lusaka. I paid him up for the September, then said goodbye and shook hands with him. I'm sure he was sorry to see me go. I left Fort Victoria then and headed for Beit Bridge arriving at 5:00pm. The customs and immigration were no bother and I went on a few miles toward Messina stopping under the baobab tree to cook up as I was hungry. Then I drove on south until 11:00pm to Petersburg where I pulled up behind a garage and slept until 5:00am and carried on down the old Transvaal. It's nice driving in the early morning, watching the new day starting and the glow becoming sunrise over the great plains. I stopped for breakfast at 8:00am and thought I would do it in style so went to the hotel at Nylstroom.

I filled up with petrol at Warmbaths then carried on to Pretoria and beyond bypassing Johannesburg by way of Delmas, coming out at Standerton on the Johannesburg-Durban Road. I had lunch on the road and kept going toward the coast.

Twenty-four miles north of Ladysmith I was stopped by a man and his wife standing by their car on the verge. He had just run into a buck which had damaged the radiator. The water poured out of it. A nice fat reed buck lay on the other side of the road which he said he hit at seventy miles an hour. It turned out he was a policeman and gave me a note to give the police at Ladysmith, which I did. As it was 10:00pm then and I was feeling tired I stayed the night at the camping grounds in Ladysmith.

The traffic along the Johannesburg-Durban Road was very heavy and travelling at speed too. I kept at a steady forty to forty-five miles an hour, slower on hills of course. Cars were never out of sight streaking past. The only thing I am faster than are donkeys and bullock carts, but I get there in the long run. I saw one car near Mooi River smashed up and standing vertical in the air against a bank at the foot of a hill with a crowd gathered viewing it morbidly. I left Ladysmith at 6:30am and carried on realising I would only just make the post office at Durban by 12:00pm. I had breakfast near Estcourt then carried on through lovely scenery to arrive as I said just in time.

Well darling, so much for my homeward journey today. We are getting nearer to each other all the time. Looking out over the ocean here I wish I were on the ship already and rolling across to Australia. I called on Avis yesterday and saw the new baby, now nine days old. Young David is talking very well now. I was going to take them for a drive out today but Avis said this morning that she had been up all night with the baby so she was resting today. She leaves in the morning to return to Lusaka and isn't looking forward to the plane trip as she was sick on the trip down. I'll call on her again about 5:00pm to say goodbye as I only spoke to her on the phone this morning from the hotel office.

I was pleased to read that the flowers were presentable dear. I wish I could have given them to you myself. Maybe I should cultivate the habit. It's nice to read about how Andrew and

Lorraine have taken to the new baby. They'll be happy to show him off to me when I arrive after the stories you've told them about coming to the ship to fetch me home. Don't forget to find out about passes to get on board, or are they not required, it wouldn't worry us much. Was amused to read about Andrew telling Lorraine how to dress, must sound comical to overhear. The holiday flat sounds alright to me Alice. You go through Rosebud on the way to Sorrento don't you, along from Frankston?

I'll stay in Durban until Tuesday Alice, that is if I can get the VW van serviced tomorrow. Durban at the moment is the same as it always is. There are hundreds of people here along the beach and parking is the problem rather than the natives. The trouble is out at Cato Manor and a few other places, mainly to do with not being allowed to brew beer. There were a couple shot yesterday when the police were attacked. Africa is still marching and maybe 10,000 will die here one day, who knows.

I am camped at a caravan park at Brighton eight miles from town near the bluff. I have the tent pitched and my boxes and loose gear there, it is quite safe in a nice area. I will say adieu for the moment darling, longing to be with you again.

An old friend in Durban

8 September 1959 Durban. Dearest Alice, I will leave this sunny city tomorrow and start on down the coast. Thought I would start another letter meanwhile to post along the way. First a couple of things to relate - coincidence I think is the word. I think in my last letter I finished up saying that Avis had been up all night with the baby so was resting up that day (Sunday last) instead of coming out for a drive. After talking to her on the phone I went along to the beach but it not being any holiday by myself watching everyone else's families.

I got an idea to go along to the berthed ship *Australia Star*. I had noticed it in port driving along the esplanade and thought perhaps there might be a few New Zealanders or Australians on board to talk to - for something to do. Anyway I climbed briskly up the ladder alongside and spoke to the quarter master on deck asking if there was a New Zealander among the engine room officers who was off duty. He said there was only one, the second engineer and that he thought he was about to go ashore with some others to the swimming baths. As he finish speaking a group came on deck with towels under their arms and the quarter master pointed out the second officer to me. I could hardly believe my eyes when I saw it was Reg Gilbert - the chap I was in my apprenticeship with in New Zealand and who used to go about with George and myself before I left home in 1948!

I called out, 'Hi Reg' and he looked at me in astonishment before he recognised me. We got talking then after our surprise, the others going ashore to the baths and leaving us to it. The last time I saw Reg was in London in 1951 when George and I visited the ship he was then on and we were coming back to New Zealand then, so Africa was the last place he expected to see me and wanting to know what I was doing here etc. etc. He was surprised to hear I was married so I had to tell him the story of my life since 1951.

Asking about George I told him how he was more or less a morally fanatical Catholic now through marrying that way and that I hadn't seen him since we were on leave in 1955. Reg said he was more or less in the same boat as he was engaged to a nursing sister in England who was Catholic. When he was ashore on leave he'd just think he was getting her into his way of thinking then go away to sea for a trip, to return and find that the priest had undone his good work for him.

I must say that Reg is quite a quiet character now, unlike in New Zealand ten or twelve years ago when he went about with us. Perhaps it's his responsible job now in charge of a 30,000 horse power ship. He is second out of the fifteen engineers on board and runs the works. The Chief, a Scot, visits the engine room about once a week keeping out of the way the rest of the time on the ship where everyone is competent. That's how it should be and Reg says he's the best chief he's ever sailed with. Says he should be chief on the ship within two years himself. We went ashore after awhile and I drove him around Durban for an outing. He said we should go back to the ship for dinner but as I had bought food for the intended outing with Avis and David suggested we have a picnic tea on the beach which we did. Afterwards we walked along the Marine Parade.

Returning later to the ship he showed me over the massive engines, twenty-four years old and requiring plenty of work to keep them running. Two men were at work down below and had been for twenty-four hours running getting an evaporator right before sailing. Both were absolutely covered in black oil. The engines leak oil through the wrong seals having been fitted. Two hundred gallons of lubricating oil a day is used, most of it thrown out of the engines from leaks. Reg said his predecessor had got the sack through neglect and that it would take another couple of trips before things were right. Anyway unfortunately the ship was sailing the following morning, Monday, so I said goodbye and drove back to my home here at Brighton. I saw the *Australia Star* leaving harbour the next morning on her way to England after unloading a large load of butter for Natal.

Yesterday was a public holiday so I was unable to get the van serviced. I spent the day on the beach in perfect weather and even got a bit sunburnt, was careful though. This morning I was in town by 7:30am and took the van into the Volkswagen agents. As I was talking to the receptionist there, who should walk in but Jock Patterson on his way back to Lusaka from long service leave where he had taken delivery of a van from the factory in Germany. You'll remember dear he was to come out and visit us one Sunday but didn't arrive due to being called out on a breakdown. He is staying in Durban for the next two or three weeks as his wife's family live here. I spent the rest of the day with them which made a nice change. They have two children a girl about three and a half and a boy nearly two. The boy has no fear of the water and runs into the sea with the waves breaking over him making him come up spluttering. If not watched he'd be on his way to Australia swimming.

Well darling it's getting late now so will continue tomorrow night where ever I am as I intend leaving here in the morning and moving slowly south at leisurely speed. Good night Alice,

I do feel so lonely for you just now XXXX. PS no use writing to Africa any more (hurray!), Fremantle will do.

9 September 1959 Wednesday 8:30pm. Hello again my own little cuddlesome girl, another day nearer and this evening finds me camped by a stream near a village called Izingolweni about thirty miles inland from Port Shepstone. Remember the road? I was up bright and early this morning and after breakfast washed up all the dishes from the last few days before folding the tent and picking up the van. It has been a rough day blowing a gale of wind which rocked the van this way and that as I drove along.

Before I left the caravan park an old chap came up and talked to me - father-in-law of the proprietor. He is seventy-one but looks sixty and says he's been out here forty years from London and was in Northern Rhodesia when Livingstone was still the capital. He and his wife live six miles south of Kakena where they are retired and he invited me to bring the van to their house on my way through, said he would be back there on Tuesday but if I arrive before to just tell his Zulu boy whatever I wanted, and to stay as long as I liked. I may stop there, we'll see in a few days.

Well I paid my rent at the park and got off into Durban about 10:30am. I went to the Automobile Association and got some maps of the 'garden route' then after a visit to the Indian market where I bought a couple of souvenirs, I went along to say goodbye to Jock Patterson. I left there at 12:30pm going down the coast and getting blown about by the wind - half a gale. I stopped for lunch at a cafe then apart from a halt at Port Shepstone for some groceries, drove on until 5:30pm doing a hundred and eight miles. In the afternoon I made a tasty dinner by browning onions in the frying pan then the sausages. I made some bisto up [gravy], removed the sausages and mixed the bisto and onions together. After stirring for awhile I replaced the sausages put a lid on the frying pan and sat back patiently for it to cook. It went down well with new bread and butter, a few dates for dessert, and tea. After that I made up my bunk and here I am propped up cosily with the wind whistling around outside. It's cold tonight. The temperature is fifty degrees. I suppose being 2,000 feet up now is the reason. Durban has been warm, only needing one blanket on at night.

14 September 1959 Jeffreys Bay, fifty miles south of Port Elizabeth, Cape Province. Hello again darling. I do miss you very much these days and consoled myself with the thought that I'll soon be over there. In exactly a fortnight from today I'll be on the *Dominion Monarch* leaving the Cape and another fortnight I'll have you to hold again. It seems such a long time and it will be wonderful to be together again. I'm just not meant to be left alone for so long and the thought of you waiting there makes the time go so slowly.

Well dear I left East London this morning and I'm now some two hundred miles further down the coast. I called in on Mr and Mrs McNally on Saturday morning. They are living in a nice house which Peggy (the eldest daughter) is buying with her husband. They all seemed quite happy and pleased to see me and I stayed 'till about 10:00pm. They wanted me to stay there but I explained that I was at the campsite. It turned out a miserable day raining in the afternoon and all night long, cold as charity too. I slept well though despite the low temperatures. Yesterday was clear from mid morning when the rain stopped and after lunch at the McNally house we went out for a short drive around. I called at the house this morning early (6:45am) and said goodbye.

I was up at 4:00am, lit the Primus stove, had cornflakes and coffee and packed the camp up at 6:00am. As the sun rose from the sea a Union Castle ship came into the harbour. It was a fine sight though I wished it was the *Dominion Monarch* coming into Melbourne with me on it.

I found out this morning why it was so cold on Saturday and Sunday and today for that matter, my feet didn't get warm until mid-day. As I left East London ten miles or so out the hills in the distance were gleaming white and snow capped and all the way down the road from King William town to Grahamstown the same. Really it was a fine sight despite the chill in the air. The temperature was forty degrees at 4:00am this morning and it was cold turning out in shorts but the old overcoat is handy and the beret keeps the chill off the head (just had a haircut). I must look elegant in my rig as people give me a second look - usually reserved for foreigners.

I camped this evening in a nice spot - a camping ground with me the only occupant. The ocean is a hundred yards away but the sand dunes give some shelter from the chill breeze blowing. Propped up in bed in the van writing this it is very cosy really but rather lonely. Humansdorp is about ten miles away.

Do you remember getting a telegram from here on the *Arawa* when you arrived in Durban? I was on my way to the Cape then. I was thinking about it all and how it was as I drove along this afternoon. Then it was me waiting for a ship. Now it is you waiting for one. It has been anything but a monotonous life for us really. Well dear I am looking forward to a few letters in Cape Town. I should be there on Wednesday or Thursday. I will finish this in the morning. Good night darling. Happy dreams of our future, all my love, Bill.

15 September 1959 Tuesday 10:45am. Well another day started, one less to go. I was up late this morning 7:30am, a lovely spring day with a breeze blowing hot in the sun after breakfast. I washed some socks out and spread out a few things today that had got wet in camp at East London the other day. While they were drying I went for a walk on the beach - miles of nothing. I met an elderly lady collecting shells and got talking to her. She was on her way to East London from Cape Town driving by herself and collecting shells along the coast which she sends overseas to collectors in a lot of countries, including Australia. There is evidently pocket money in it and she says it is her big hobby, especially since her husband died last year. Jeffreys Bay is evidently known throughout the shell collection world.

I got back eventually and packed the van up and I'm away to a late start. Knysna will do me for today a hundred and twenty-eight miles away. I am parked off the road now above Jeffreys Bay and thought I would finish this and post it in Humansdorp for old time's sake. It is lovely looking out along the coast from here. The bay sweeps around into the far distance with a white border of surf. On the sand on the slope to the beach below me for half a mile are cattle grazing and sheep with lambs. If I don't start moving soon I won't even get to Knysna today, it is nearly lunchtime. I will just cook tonight and have some fruit along the way for lunch.

Marking time in Cape Town

17 September 1959 Pelican Park, Zeekoevlei. Darling Alice, I have at last arrived in the Cape twenty-four days out from Lusaka, which makes it seem a long way taking so long. It is 2,500 miles so I only averaged a hundred miles a day, like a tortoise. Anyway I am at least here safely with no trouble to the van along the way, not even a puncture in that distance. There were four lovely letters from you at the post office (one only had that paper to sign though). I parked outside the post office in the ten minute area with a policeman patrolling up and down. Parking is terrible and the traffic heavy so I went up to Queen Victoria Street, near the Automobile Association where I could read your letters in peace. I am glad to hear everything is alright with you all over there and that you still love me Alice.

Having read your letters I thought it better to find a place to camp so I went along to the Automobile Association who said this place *Pelican Park* near Strandfontein along the bay from Muizenburg was alright and had bathrooms etc. It's the nearest place to Cape Town one can camp at and is a caravan park really. I am the only one in it - in fact first - as it doesn't open until the end of the month. The builders are still working on it but everything is in working order bath, showers, laundry etc. The proprietor is Herb Taylor ex South African cricketer and he has been in Australia and New Zealand years ago when he played for South Africa. Your dad will probably remember his name. Well darling I will continue tomorrow when I will have visited the shipping company, Automobile Association etc and will be able to tell you more. Good night dear, another day nearer, your loving husband, Bill.

18 September Friday. I note your last letter written on the 8th was stamped 14th here in Cape Town making it only six days since you wrote. It must take another four days to get to Rhodesia then.

Everything is organised really. I called into the bank and collected the money I sent down by letter of credit. I went to Anderson's where I collected my ticket after filling in various forms, also having to show my inoculation certificate and passport. We are to be on board from 9:00am onwards on Monday the 28th, sailing at mid-day. I forgot to ask when we arrive but taking the usual fourteen days I should be in Melbourne on the 12th making it just right to see Andrew as a tree in the church play. The little man will be so happy, and his dad.

I went to the Automobile Association next to find I had to pay an extra £14 for freight. It's costing quite a lot all told. I have to be alongside the ship on Sunday morning 27th at 10:00am, meeting the Automobile Association chap who checks that the petrol is drained and the van will then be loaded on board. I will come into town on Saturday and stay at the Helmsley Hotel, Saturday and Sunday nights. The Royal Automobile Club of Victoria will see to the unloading and clearing in Melbourne. They have a letter to that affect already of which I was sent a copy - more fees I suppose but roll on to Melbourne at all cost.

I went around about the boxes next and everything is alright except that I can't extract the two tin trunks from the baggage room. They are on a cargo manifest and through customs etc and unless eight articles appear at the other end - six boxes and two trunks - there will undoubtedly be an 'indaba' as they say. The agent was very helpful really and I have to find out next week what the storage charges and handling will be. Fingers crossed.

I went to Singers and was shown that pleating gadget you want but the price was £18.06. You said £12 so I have got your letter out explaining it and will show it to them on Monday. The lady there said you would have got this with the machine if you had bought it new. Anyway I will pursue the matter next week. I made an appointment to get some paint work done on the van for Monday so will be in town early. I have bought four large bottles of the Vaseline bath oil lavender you wanted and the chemist has packed them professionally for me against breakage. As you can see I had a busy day and feel it on my feet not having a great liking for walking about cities.

The weather is nice here at the moment but likely to be changeable being spring. I feel safer driving in the city than walking, having become accustomed to heavy traffic again. I should imagine it is even worse in Melbourne than here if that's possible. The streets are so narrow in Cape Town and a lot are one-way which have to be watched for. I will be watching for another letter from you Alice perhaps Monday, not many more to go now.

20 September 1959 Cape Town, Muizenburg Beach. Dearest Alice, I can now definitely say this is the second from last letter I will ever write to you from Africa. In a week from now I will be getting ready to go on board the *Dominion Monarch* and when you are reading this I will be on my way across the ocean. It is most tiring having to wait about now but every day brings the ship four hundred miles nearer. She will be up by the Canary Islands Teneriffe way and it is some consolation that each day brings it closer. I am lucky having a quiet place to camp, though on my own it is deadly tiring, like solitary confinement - no one to talk with about the place. There will be more to do on the ship and I can use some energy on deck games. Everything is fixed and it is just a matter of getting on board here and getting off at Melbourne. I'm sitting in the van at Muizenburg beach, the sea rolling up the beach a few yards away. The weather has been good since I arrived on Wednesday. I only hope it holds for another week though today has low clouds on the hills around False Bay.

I had quite an unusual day yesterday after meeting a fishing boat skipper at Kalk Bay - a Mr Clark, thirty-seven years a fisherman, and his father fifty years before him in False Bay. I left False Bay with them at 2:00am and we went way beyond Cape Point about ten to fifteen miles south of it. It was a bit rough out there with the boat hopping about. The fishermen (about fifteen of them) started about dawn to fish along the side of the boat each in his own compartment. They pulled in the fish one after the other using two lines. The boat was forty-seven feet long with a powerful eighty-eight horse power diesel engine driving it. The skipper kept the engine turning all the time to keep the boat head on to the sea, the boat rising and falling as the seas passed underneath.

Going out I stayed in the wheelhouse as the boat ploughed through the sea up and down, the spray sweeping from end to end, the crew sleeping down below in their quarters. Coming back about noon was very nice and I got a photo of Cape Point. The sea was behind us, the wind too, the sun shining and I sat on the deck as the fishermen tied their catch up for sale at the quayside. They are all coloured men and out of every pound worth of fish sold they pay the skipper owner six shillings for the use of the boat. We got back at 1:30pm and it was a very enjoyable change for me. I didn't feel like being sick, even with the smell of fish and bait everywhere. I went back to the camp and slept for a few hours then, feeling tired after only half a night's sleep. Well darling it is evening and I will be in town in the morning hoping to find another letter from you waiting there. A big hug and kisses for you from your loving husband Bill. Good night darling.

21 September Tuesday. Well dear here we are again with two letters from you this morning. One dated 14th and another the 18th September which means it has only taken four days for the last one to get here. There must be something wrong between here and Rhodesia because the earliest we ever got a letter was nine days. I notice you have written your last letter and sound pleased about it. I will write again on the weekend and post it just before the ship sails on Monday at 12 noon. Hurray, six days to go.

Answering the first of your two letters I have noted the comment that I am being spoiled for future reference. Jimmy Hall enjoyed his trip alright but didn't want me to leave him. We had to go and have some morning tea first in Fort Victoria and a last cigarette before he saw me off. Will probably see him over our side one day.

I don't think it will be impossible for you to get a few days rest spell, especially if we are going away for two weeks. Andrew and Lorraine will enjoy going out on excursions with me. I guess talking about holidays, it's not been much of a holiday for me. You could call it a rest I suppose but it's mighty lonely by oneself after a few days, just counting the days slowly off.

Glad to hear the balance of the money has arrived. Go ahead and spend £50-£100 on yourself, you've earned it dear. This trip with van and boxes is costing us a few pounds. I'm wondering whether it was worth bringing all that stuff because by the time we take delivery in Melbourne the boxes will have cost over £100. I thought I had plenty of money with me but one way and another I've got through about £150 since I left Lusaka. I'll have a few Rhodesian and South African pennies for the children left though. I did have a look around the shops here for something in the ruby line for your parents but there's nothing decent under about £20-£25 so I've left it. I have quite a selection of African souvenirs picked up along the way though. You can have a good time going through them all. Sorry I forgot to say Avis's baby is a boy. I just forgot its name now - could be a girl. I forget really.

It sounds as though Andrew has settled down now playing with Barrie and the new car and visiting people with an electric train. I bet he wants to go there again. I am sitting in the sun writing. I have the van in getting a little painting done on it so that it will be respectable on arrival and have taken a double-decker bus out here riding on top. It is lovely weather but so cold at night – forty-five degrees this morning.

24 September 1959 Cape Town. Dearest Alice, I have great pleasure in stating that this is my last letter from Africa. Hoping this finds you all as well as when I last heard from you earlier in the week. Just three days left after today and I will be on my way at last. It seems an age of waiting. On Tuesday afternoon I got back to the camp and was talking to the caretaker when he mentioned that a couple had recently arrived from New Zealand in a van similar to ours. I went over and met them later and was invited to supper with them in their VW van. They are from Inglewood in the North Island and have waited twenty-five years they said to do this trip and left New Zealand in June. Having been as far as Livingstone they are seeing the Cape before going by ship to England in five weeks time. They will spend the next few years seeing Europe and getting home for Christmas 1960, by way of America and Canada. We had a pleasant evening talking about this and that. They had sold up a business in New Zealand.

About 8:00pm another car arrived with a caravan and parked nearby. I found out yesterday morning that they are going on the *Dominion Monarch* to New Zealand after thirty years in Southern Rhodesia, from England - man and wife and two boys about eleven and fourteen. He said they are looking for a place where there are no natives and the future looks brighter. So after seven days camped here by myself I now have two interesting lots of neighbours suddenly.

Yesterday afternoon and evening I was out at some people's house at Plumstead not far from Wynberg and had dinner there and a pleasant evening for a change. I met a chap at a hotel in Muizenburg who has had thirty odd years with the Cape Town Fire Brigade. It turned out he knew the proprietor of the old

VanNiekirks Hotel very well, they were schoolmates together etc. He invited me along to his brother-in-law's house on Wednesday (yesterday), making an appointment to meet me at the Plumstead Railway Station at 2:00pm. I turned up on time only half expecting to meet him there but he was there at exactly 2 o'clock and we went along to his sister's house.

We had afternoon tea and talked about this and that, mostly South Africa's troubles until the head of the house came home. His name is Hedges and a very nice chap. Mrs Hedges was saying earlier how he had had a stamp album worth £300 stolen recently, so I asked him if he collected stamps. After a while he showed me some of his collection and it is quite large. Compared to mine, I haven't even started yet. He has offered me stamps and has our address when I offered to get him Australian stamps in exchange. He said he did have a correspondent in Australia but he hadn't heard from him for some time.

One of his albums, beautifully lettered, is going in an exhibition at Pretoria shortly. They are very keen Methodists, non-drinkers and he was saying how he had been offered a job in America by one of his correspondent's, a Methodist minister in Kansas. He would leave South Africa but for his mother who is ninety years old and living with them. She is fit but mentally about five years old poor old thing. They have a lot to put up with I could see. The old lady has a fear of going to bed and all sorts of hallucinations. The other day she said to Hedges, 'Who are those two women staying with you?' He said, 'My wife and daughter mother.' The old lady replied, 'Why didn't you tell me you had got married - trying to hide it from me.' They have been married twenty-five years already. Mrs Hedge's mother also lives with them. She is eighty-two but in possession of her senses still, so there is always somebody with bigger troubles than your own.

Just a little over two weeks now darling and you'll all be at the wharf to meet me. I suppose the children will be getting excited now the days are ticking over. It'll be lovely to see you again after so long, especially to see you and feel you close to me again. We seemed to get along from the time we left the church, remember? I took a photo of that church in Green Market Square the other day, thought it would be nice to have for the future.

The future, let's not talk about that until I've been back a couple of weeks. Live for the day meanwhile and enjoy ourselves before getting down to the serious side of things. There's no future in being too serious about anything so far as I can see, as long as we're all together and I can find something that will allow us to live with the maximum of comfort, that'll do us nicely. I'd like £130 a month without killing myself to get it and liking what I'm doing.

Another day is coming to a close. On Saturday I move to town, Sunday load the van and Monday load myself. Sending all my love to you and wishing the days away. I say goodbye again across the ocean with lots of real kisses not far away now.

26 September 1959 Saturday. Dearest Alice, I'm staying in town now from this morning at the International Hotel, Hof Street. I took my three toolboxes down to the baggage master this morning ready for Monday then packed the van and did some shopping around the city. It is terrible driving here. I should be alright in Melbourne after this practice. I'm all set to be alongside the *Dominion Monarch* tomorrow morning for loading and then another forty-eight hours and I'll be on my way over to you - lovely thought.

I had the unusual experience of meeting somebody with the same name as myself about half an hour ago. He is an ex-Senator Latimer from East London. He sat in the House here in the Cape until the present government abolished the Senate for being opposed to their plans. He is about sixty-five years of age, originally from England, ex-army and well educated by the way he speaks and his knowledge of politics. It's the first time I met anyone outside our family with the same name.

I may have four or five people to see me off on Monday. It's amazing how one meets people, Mr and Mrs Sigley from Inglewood, New Zealand, Charles Hazeldene and his sister, Mrs Hedges with her daughter. I think people take the opportunity of coming on board a ship - it makes an unusual outing anyway.

27 September 1959 Sunday 11:00am. Darling Alice, Here I am at last sitting on the *Dominion Monarch*'s deck. It is a glorious cloudless day and I'm in the shade of a deck house near the stand watching cars being unloaded. The crane about thirty feet away is hoisting them from the hold onto the wharf. The *Dominion Monarch* came in at 6:00am this morning. I heard her hooting from where I am staying in Hof Street.

After breakfast I drove down to the wharf where I handed the van over to the Automobile Association representative. They were there even though I was an hour early. I came on board half an hour ago and from where I am sitting I can see the van waiting with about twelve other vehicles and the Automobile Association chap draining oil and water and fixing up papers. I was first here and so have everything fixed up already. I want to get a photo of the van hanging in mid air but may have to wait several hours yet. Still time is something I have plenty of at the moment.

If nothing else this time tomorrow will see me nearly on my way. It's lovely to think I'll soon be with you all again, another two weeks only which is not much out of four months. I had a look around and found my cabin number, 282 B Deck. It is well forward so should be fairly quiet as far as the diesel throb goes. I didn't investigate too far in case I started off wrong with the steward as they are cleaning out the cabins now that the Cape passengers have got off. Cabin 282 is against the ship side, no long passage to the port hole. We are supposed to come on at 9:00am tomorrow and I'll be aboard bright and early as you can guess. We sail at 12 noon. Farewell Africa!

8 pm. Well dear I waited until 12 noon but the van is not yet being loaded so decided to go back to the hotel for lunch. After talking some time to an elderly Australian from Queensland I had intended returning to the ship but I ate so much at lunch I decided I felt more like a rest for a few hours so I didn't see the van loaded after all. The food is alright here I suppose but it has the usual mass produced hotel brand on it. I'm looking forward to a bit of nice home cooking as you can guess. It is evening now and only a few hours before I get on board. I didn't sleep so well last night on account of the noisy traffic outside. I suppose I won't tonight either but I don't feel very sleepy, probably a little excited at the thought of sailing tomorrow. I'm looking forward to a letter at Fremantle. This will have reached you by the time I get there.

I think I will sign off now. I can go for a short walk down the road and post this at the post office nearby. You will hear by telegram just as soon as I get ashore at Fremantle. I think of you constantly and the time will soon go now. All my love darling Alice. I do need you so always for keeps, your very loving husband Bill. Bye-bye darling, see you at Port Melbourne, yours ever signing off from Africa for the last time. Bill XXX.

29 September1959 Tuesday 7:30am. Dearest Alice, Here I am at last on my way across and happy as a cricket to see the white capped ocean from where I sit in the writing room. The day is fine, not a cloud in the sky but a stiff breeze blowing to annoy the players of deck sports. I am up early being first sitting so thought I would write a little each day before breakfast. My days are likely to be quite full as I'm on the Sports Committee and from today we will be organising the games. We sailed before 1:15pm, leaving the wharf while I was at lunch.

Before we left Cape Town a chap came on board looking for a spare berth. He had only booked two months ago but wanted to go across to New Zealand to see his mother who is eighty or so years and ailing. There happens to be a cabin opposite my berth, a double which only had one occupant an Irishman. I offered him my cabin - a single one of course but better lighted and against the ship side. After hedging for a bit he finally agreed, so we changed over and I am now in this cabin with Mr Ormansby, a New Zealander who is a building contractor in Johannesburg. We went to the company's agent at the purser's office where he paid his fare and showed his passport and filled in the usual papers. I was given a refund of £14, handy for spending, and I'm happier sharing the cabin. He is quite a decent fellow, only a little older than myself and doesn't snore thank goodness. I told him just now I was happy to find out he didn't snore.

There is a chap on board who was on the *Dominion Monarch* when we went across last time and also on the *Southern Cross* when we came back. You may remember him, Dick Isaacs, in the veterinary department in Nyasaland and he is on long leave again. (He is very fresh complexioned and wears thick glasses. We used to play deck quoits with him a lot.) He is in a similar position to us as his wife and child flew ahead to New Zealand because of her mother's health. She has unfortunately passed away. He met his wife on the *Southern Cross* on that trip we made and they got married over here. He is returning to Nyasaland but he agrees the future in Africa looks a little dim all around.

I see there will be elections in England on 8 October. If Labour wins there will be some extra trouble for the Federation. Well dear I supposed today will see us playing the different games. Time goes quicker that way. This evening I have to assist outside the saloon collecting the subscriptions for the sports' prizes. The chimes are just starting for our first sitting breakfast so I will away and strengthen myself for the morning.

1 October 1959 Thursday 7:45am. Hello again dearest Alice, I missed writing my usual half hour yesterday as I intended to do every day. Yesterday was just a little rough with the wind playing strongly but a cloudless sky. When you threw a deck quoit or tennis ring it just about came back at you. We have got the sports underway and today promises better. The wind has gone and it will be fine. Last night was 'song title guessing' and a dance afterwards. The evening went very quickly and the band was a little better than usual. You remember they weren't that good and they are the same fellows as from our last trip.

My deck tennis partner is Lady McKee who I'm told is the best woman player on board so we'll have a chance of getting somewhere in the competition. Her husband is Sir A. McKee, Air Marshall TSO, DFM, KCB etc and a jolly old stick - one of the 'life and soul of the party' types. I'm glad to see the ship moving steadily on to Australia and I'm trying to make the time pass as quickly as possible. I have just been to the gymnasium where the chap in charge rubbed liniment into my legs and punched the muscles all over. I was stiff from the unaccustomed exercise and then wanting to play the tennis. I don't want to come home to you a cripple, or do you think it might be a good idea if I wasn't so agile? Well darling, roll on the *Monarch* and Melbourne, breakfast time again so away to eat - what a life.

6 October 1959 Wednesday. Dearest Alice, We are still on our way across and the weather very nice and the ship just rolling a little. I haven't kept up writing every morning because I can't post anyway so I have fallen behind. There is not much to write about the journey. You know how much alike the days are on the ship. I could say how much I love you of course and long to hold you close. It won't be long now another eight days. What is eight days out of four months?

Last night was the fancy dress evening and we had a great time. A group of us went as a hospital operating team. We had a patient tied down on a stretcher, hacksaw, chisels, hammer etc from my tool box and were a great success, clowning about. We won the group prize anyway - thirty shillings. I have been in all the games but I'm out of the competitions now except for deck tennis. My partner is Lady McKee and I'm fortunate that she is a fairly good player and agile. We are up to the semi-finals and were to play this morning but she is not feeling too good after the party last night. Tomorrow morning at 10:00am we will see how good we are. We had a death on board the other day a very old man. Nobody is supposed to know officially and very few do as we are told to forget it. He was buried very early in the morning without the ship stopping.

9 October 1959 Saturday. Freemantle, Australia. Well darling here I am in Australia at last. I haven't been ashore yet. We got in very early this morning and I have received your very welcome telegram and letter. I just have to be patient a few days longer and you'll all be there waiting on the wharf. The information we have here is that we will be arriving at noon on Wednesday 13th, I hope so dear. There is not a great deal to write about darling. Nothing that can be written will make up for one real hour with you. Myself and partner did win the tennis and I have a prize that I chose for you. I just haven't got any enthusiasm for further writing so will close now for the last time. I just intend to wander about Fremantle like we did last time and will send a telegram from the port office here as well. Cheerio my darling Alice. Looking for Wednesday and signing off for the last time. Yours forever - Bill XXXX. Big cuddles and kisses on Wednesday for Andrew, Lorraine and baby Robert too. (You watch out for this Andrew.) [Hand drawing of the ship].

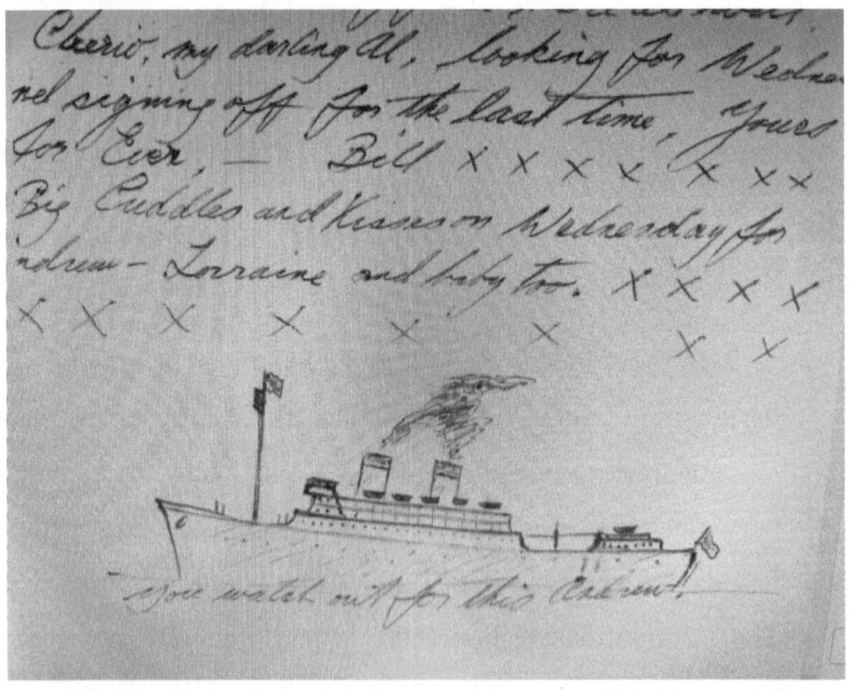
Cheerio, my darling Al, looking for Wedne
nd signing off for the last time, Yours
for Ever, — Bill X X X X X X X
Big Cuddles and Kisses on Wednesday for
ndrew – Lorraine and baby too. X X X X
X X X X X X X X
You watch out for this Andrew!

Bill's last letter from Africa.

EPILOGUE

Alice looks back in 1997[2] Our return to Australia seemed to come at the right time. Apart from wanting to be with my dying mother Rose we could see that change in Africa was inevitable and that the change would not all be good. We always had a good relationship with the native Africans living with us on the farm, despite the rigid class structure, and there was always help available when it was needed. Around thirty natives lived permanently on our land, all supported by Bill's modest wage. We helped our workers buy wives and bicycles and looked after them as best we could and they were good to us too. I set up home surgery hours to treat minor cuts, bites, rashes and so on. Two native babies were born during our time there - one in our car.

Another reason to return to Australia was our children. I was worried they would grow up expecting to always get their

[2] White Family Tree Committee (1999) *Fruits of the Orchard: The Family of Henry White and Elizabeth Raney. 150 Years in Australia 1949 – 1999.* Openbook Publishers. ISBN 0-646-36649-1

own way with the social structure of the time causing the natives to do whatever they asked.

After all our travels I never dreamed I would end up back in Donvale where I started, with Bill and I purchasing my maternal grandparent's house on the hill overlooking the Dandenong Ranges and our children going to the same school and same church that I and my family before me had done.

Once the children had grown up Bill and I travelled extensively, mainly in Australia and New Zealand. In 1975 we went back to Africa and visited many of the places where we had been so happy. Our four children grew up and did well at university and careers. They all married and between them gave us nine beautiful grandchildren. We had our good times and our bad times like everyone else. I thank God for a wonderful life, a husband who has done all that was possible to make us happy and a very supportive family.

Editor's Note: Bill and Alice were married for fifty-one years. They had four children Andrew, Lorraine, Robert and Rae-Ellen and nine grandchildren. Alice died in 2005 and Bill in 2008 both aged in their eighties. They are buried at the Eltham Cemetery, a few miles from Donvale.

The Latimer family in Donvale Australia 1964

INDEX

A

B

C

M

N

www.ingramcontent.com/pod-product-compliance
Lightning Source LLC
LaVergne TN
LVHW041101080826
845145LV00007B/1648

9780975657270